# The Colourful Biography

## of

# Chinese Characters

A picture is indeed worth a thousand words.

## (Volume 1 – the 1$^{st}$ 100)

## S. W. Well

ISBN-978-0-692-28454-4

Publisher: Suntific

*Books by the Intellectual Engagé for Intellectuals*

The complete book of Chinese characters that covers every aspect of, and therefore answers all the questions one might have for, these fascinating ancient language symbols from script evolution to colour-illustrated biographies including proper Stroke sequences and from the complete Compound anatomy to the trinity of Sounds, Semantics, and Synopses. This series of books is the ultimate guide and reference for first-time learners as well as masters of the language. It is for both the teachers and self-motivated students.

This is the 1st volume of the series, covering the 1st 100 most frequently used Chinese characters as presented with their full colour illustrations and arranged in columns from right to left on the front cover.

To:  Claudia B. Sun

The young lady who inspired the
colour coding scheme for the
Chinese characters according to their
etymological classes, which then
allows these characters' stories to be
told most accurately and properly for
learning and memorization.

To: Rocky

My loyal and faithful friend,

the best dog anyone could ask for.

# Contents

# Preface

Almost everyone who has learnt or is learning the Chinese language and therefore its fascinating written characters was told that *there is a story behind each of the Chinese characters* and would like to know these stories for the simple reason to make the learning, memorizing, writing, and using of these beautiful ancient characters the way they were created and intended for, and therefore altogether simple and easy.

Sadly, the answers to this simple question, *"What is the story behind each of the Chinese characters?"*, have only been the privilege of the very few elites of the Chinese language but remained mysteries to almost all native Chinese language users who, like most foreign Chinese language workers, have only extended their attentions to the most straightforward but very limited pictographic characters that amount to less than 5% of the total Chinese characters used today. The majority of Chinese characters are composites of other characters structurally put together with considerations of semantics, phonetics, and certainly aesthetics. It is these characters that require the most attention in learning, memorizing, writing, and using. Unfortunately, it is these characters that are much less known or sometimes conveniently construed with stories that are completely unrelated to their originals. Very often, for structural and aesthetic reasons, the component characters are in quite different forms in the composite characters or only portions of the component characters are present in the composite characters.  This certainly makes correlating the component characters with the composite characters difficult and therefore the story telling challenging. A unique and pioneering 10-colour scheme is devised to conquer this time-honoured challenge as well as to classify all the Chinese characters.

This series of books aims to answer the simple questions *What is the story behind each of the Chinese characters?"* and *"How to properly write and use these Chinese characters?"* from their authentic script forms through history, and to tell the fascinating story of each of the 7,070 frequently used Chinese characters in the most vivid colourful illustrations.  Also included for all the Compound characters are their comprehensive Anatomy diagrams, which trace every Compound character back to the rudimentary Pictographs, to make the learning and understanding of these characters thoroughly exciting and utterly rewarding.

Each volume of the book covers 100 Chinese characters based on their usage frequencies.  And this is Volume 1 of the book *The Colourful Biography of Chinese Characters*.

**S. W. Well**

**March of 2014**

*The Year of the Horse* 甲午

# 1. 的

**Script Evolution**

昒 的 的 的

**The Story**

昒 昒 昀 的 的

/ㄉㄧˋ, di⁴/　　"bright and clear"

**Associative Compound** (會意) of

日 (/ㄖˋ, ri⁴/ "Sun") and

勺 (/ㄕㄠˊ, shao²/ [ㄕㄨㄛˋ, shuo⁴] "ladle"

referring to *the Plough* or *Big Dipper asterism*)

to imply *bright and clear as the Sun and the Plough* (*Big Dipper*),

hence "*bright and clear*".

日 + 勺 ≡ 昀 昀

昀 also carries the semantics of "*target*" as *target* need be *bright and clear*. Later, A Customary Alternate 的 was created for 昀 with 日 changed to 白 and used in place of 昀. Eventually, 的 took the place of Standard Form with more extended semantics, whilst 昀 stepped back as Original (本字).

昀 昀 → 的 的

1

## The Stroke Sequence

的 的 的 的 的 的 的 的
的 的 的 的 的 的 的 的

## The Anatomy

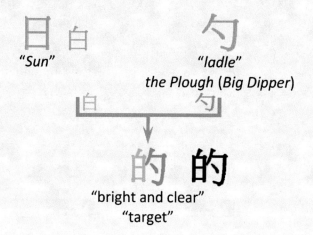

日 白      勺

"Sun"             "ladle"
            the Plough (Big Dipper)

白      勺

的   的

"bright and clear"
"target"

## The Trinity – Sound(s), Semantics, and Synopses

/ㄉㄧˋ, di⁴/

| | |
|---|---|
| target | 目**的**, 標**的**, 眾矢之**的**; |
| *struc. particle at end of sentence* | 偷懶是不會成功**的**; |
| *in classical Chinese,* | |
|     bright and clear | 「**旳旳**者獲，提提者射。」; |
|     target | 「論之應理，猶矢之中**的**。」 |

/ㄉㄧˊ, di²/

| | |
|---|---|
| indeed | **的**確; |
| true | **的**保; |
| exact | **的**款; |

2

*in classical Chinese,*

    indeed                            「掩妝無語，**的**是銷凝處。」

**/・ㄉㄜ, de$^5$/**     Recital Pronunciation //・ㄉㄧ, di$^5$//

*possessive particle*                我**的**[底], 冬天**的**[底];

*struc. particle*

    *to form adj. \**

        *after noun*              美麗**的**, 快樂**的**, 痛苦**的**, 民生**的**,
                                    瞞怨**的**;

        *after phrase*            跨國**的**, 境外**的**, 無言**的**, 說好**的**,
                                      先前**的**, 最後**的**, 吃力不討好**的**;

    *after adj. or adv.*

        *for emphasis*           漫長**的**, 足夠**的**;

        *for affirmation*       可以**的**

\*: To form an *adv.*, the character 地 (Usage Rank #20) should be used.

**Note**: /・ㄉㄜ, de$^5$/ is actually the variation of /ㄉㄧˋ, di$^4$/.

In singing, it is mostly pronounced as //・ㄉㄧ, di$^5$//.

**It is this sound/semantics combination propelling the character 的 to the most frequently used character status.**

**Radical:** 白.

# 2. 一

## Script Evolution

## The Story

/一, yi/    //一ㄧ, yi⁴//    //一ㄧ, yi²//    "one"

**Ideograph** (指事) of *one ubiquitous horizontal line*

    to denote *the number one*,

hence *"one"*.

**Note**: The MPS 『一』 is based on this character's form 『一』 and sound.

The iconic symbols denoting *the number one* as represented through time by the character 一 are shown below.

     Bone          Bronze          Seal         Standard

## The Stroke Sequence

4

# The Trinity – Sound(s), Semantics, and Synopses

/一, yi/　　　//一ヽ, yi$^4$//　　　//一ˊ, yi$^2$//

**Note**: The 1$^{st}$ tone of 一 as used only in counting (as in *1, 2, 3, …*)

is changed to

the 4$^{th}$ tone (//一ヽ, yi$^4$//) when followed by a 1$^{st}$, 2$^{nd}$, or 3$^{rd}$
tone character, or

the 2$^{nd}$ tone (//一ˊ, yi$^2$//) when followed by a 4$^{th}$ tone
character.

| | |
|---|---|
| one * | 一人, 一本書, 一杯水, 一起; |
| first | 一級主管, 一回生，二回熟; |
| single | 一目了然, 一絲不苟; |
| entire | 一路上, 一天到晚, 一覺醒來; |
| focused | 一心求好, 一心一意; |
| always | 一再, 一直; |
| same | 言行不一, 長短不一, 前後不一; |
| every | 一隊十人; |
| one time, once | 一而再，再而三; |
| certain | 一天，他回來了; |
| just | 天一亮, 一聽就懂; |
| always | 一聽到吃餃子，就高興了，<br>天氣一涼，就感冒了; |
| generally | 一般來說; |
| suddenly | 把手一揮, 兩手一攤, 嚇一跳; |

*:『壹』(Usage Rank #4,968) is often used in
writing financial numbers to avoid alteration.

*used in pair to mean*

    on one hand …

        on the other hand …　　　　　　　一則以喜，一則以憂;

*used with* 二

    either (… or …)　　　　　　　　一不做，二不休;

    on one hand

        (… on the other hand …)　　　　一不偷，二不搶,

                                    一不沾親，二不帶故;

*used with* 半 *and two similar quantity words to mean*

    either … or …　　　　　　　　一年半載, 一時半晌, 一時半刻;

another　　　　　　　　　　　　　　蟬，一名知了;

accidentally　　　　　　　　　　　一不小心;

effortlessly or tentatively

    (*in between 2 identical verbs*)　　搖一搖, 拍一拍;

*in classical Chinese,*

    to unite　　　　　　　　　　　「不嗜殺人者能一之。」;

    unexpectedly　　　　　　　　「嗟乎，

                          為[為]法之敝一至此哉！」;

    all　　　　　　　　　　　　　「端而言，蝡而動,

                          一可以為[為]法則。」;

    *used in pair to mean*

        on one hand …

        on the other hand …　　　「泰氏其臥徐徐，其覺于于,

                         一以己為[為]馬,

                         一以己為[為]牛。」;

*often used with* 何 *to mean*
how (why) so much

「上有絃歌聲，
音響一何悲。」；

*surname*

姓氏

**Radical:** 一 (itself).

# 3. 是

## Script Evolution

## The Story

/ㄕˋ, shi$^4$/  “correct”

**Associative Compound** (會意) of

日 (/ㄖˋ, ri$^4$/ “Sun”, *also providing sound*) and

正 (/ㄓㄥˋ, zheng$^4$/ “orthogonal”, “proper”)

to imply *Sun straight on top at correct position*, hence “*correct*”.

日 + 正 ≡ 昰 昰

**<u>Note</u>**: 日 (/ㄖ帀ˋ, ri$^4$/) and 是 (/ㄕ帀ˋ, shi$^4$/) share the same sound, the Virtual Rhyme 帀 that is omitted in their specifications.

For obvious aesthetic reasons, Standard Form changed 2 (last two) of the 5 orthogonal Strokes in 正 to the more artistic slanted Strokes as in 疋. Hence, the Standard Form of this character is the aesthetic and artistically well balanced 是 in lieu of the all too serious 昰 with only orthogonal Strokes.

昰 昰 → 是 是

是　是 → 是　是

It is important to note that at time of the Bronze Script the character told the story of *Sun* (  ) *above being correct time to go* ( ) *places and do* ( ) *things.*  The stories of *Sun at correct position* as told through time by the character are shown below.

Bronze　　　Seal　　　Standard

## The Stroke Sequence

## The Anatomy

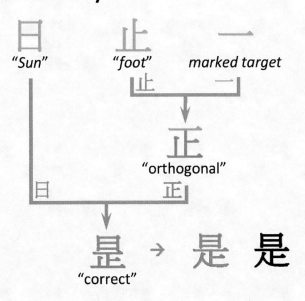

日　　止　　一
*"Sun"*　　*"foot"*　　*marked target*

止　　一

正
*"orthogonal"*

日　　正

是 → 是　是
*"correct"*

9

# The Trinity – Sound(s), Semantics, and Synopses

/ㄕˋ, shi⁴/

| | |
|---|---|
| correct, right, proper, appropriate | 是非, 不是時候; |
| important matter | 國是; |
| existing | 滿手都是油; |
| *verb* to be | 他是學生; |
| to approve | 不是其言; |
| yes | 是，我馬上來; |
| this (*adj.*) | 是日; |
| *used with* 惟 *to emphasize object*<br>    *between* 惟 *and* 是 | 惟利是圖, 惟你是問; |
| *in classical Chinese,* | |
| this (*adj.*) | 「夫子至於是邦也，<br>    必聞其政。」; |
| this (*pron.*) | 「是乃仁術也，<br>    見牛未見羊也。」; |
| therefore | 「心安是國安也；<br>    心治是國治也。」; |
| *surname* | 姓氏 |

**Radical:** 日.

# 4. 在

**Script Evolution**

屮　　𡉻　　𡉻　　在　　在　　在

**The Story**

𡉻　𡉻　在　在

/ㄗㄞˋ, zai⁴/　　"existing"

**Associative Compound** (會意) of

土 (/ㄊㄨˇ, tu³/ "soil", "place") and

才 (/ㄘㄞˊ, cai²/ originally "tree trunk for beam of a house"

referring to *building houses, also providing sound*)

to imply *place to build a house and stay existing*,

hence "*existing*".

土　+　才　≡　在　在

It is important to note that the Semantic-Phonetic Component 才 is the Original (本字) of 在. In other words, 在 is the re-created character from its Original 才, Pictograph (象形) of *a tree trunk used for beam of a house*. Later, 才 (/ㄘㄞˊ, cai²/ Usage Rank #346) was used to carry the semantics of "*talent*", "*ability*". Then Associative Compounds

在在 (/ㄗㄞˋ, zai⁴/ "existing") and

11

材材 (/ㄘㄞˊ, cai[2]/ "useful wood" Usage Rank #548) were created for the original semantics of 才. The pictures of *tree trunk used as beam for building a house* as rendered through time by the character 才 and the stories of *material to build a house and stay existing* as told through time by the character 在 are shown below.

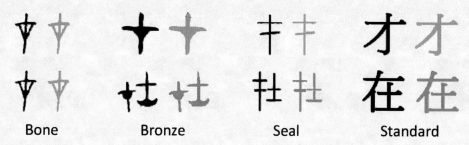

| Bone | Bronze | Seal | Standard |

## The Stroke Sequence

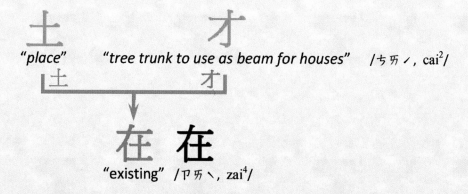

## The Anatomy

土 "place"　　才 "tree trunk to use as beam for houses"　/ㄘㄞˊ, cai[2]/

土　　　才

在 在 "existing" /ㄗㄞˋ, zai[4]/

## The Trinity – Sound(s), Semantics, and Synopses

/ㄗㄞˋ, zai[4]/

existing　　　　　　　　　　青春永在;

| | |
|---|---|
| alive | 父母健在; |
| at (*position*) | 在位十年, 在野; |
| up to, based on | 事在人爲[為]; |
| *before verb to indicate* on-going | 他在看, 我在聽; |
| at (*time, place*) | 在早上, 在家, 在場; |
| having special knowledge (fluent) in | 在行; |
| to be in (to mind, to care) | 在意, 在乎, 不在乎; |
| in (*area*) | 在某方面; |
| place, area | 在在皆是; |
| *used with* 所 *to emphasize* | |
|     *words that follow* | 在所不惜, 在所難免; |
| *in classical Chinese,* | |
|     alive | 「父在，觀其志； |
| |   父沒，觀其行。」; |
|     up to | 「謀事在人，成事在天。」; |
|     place | 「無日不營，無在不衞。」; |
|     to observe | 「在璿璣玉衡，以齊七政。」; |
| *surname* | 姓氏 |

**Radical:** 土.

# 5. 不

## Script Evolution

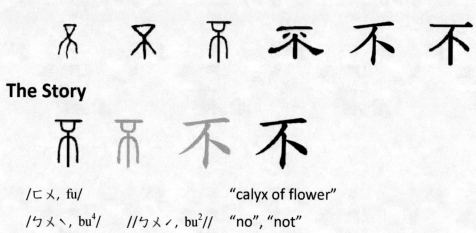

## The Story

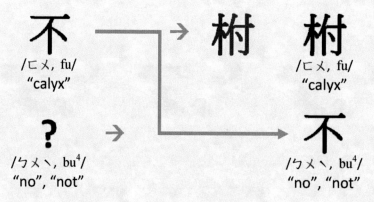

/ㄈㄨ, fu/                            "calyx of flower"

/ㄅㄨˋ, bu$^4$/     //ㄅㄨˊ, bu$^2$//    "no", "not"

**Pictograph** (象形) of *a calyx of flower*,

hence *"calyx"*.

Later, for the same sound (/ㄅㄨˋ, bu$^4$/) the character started to carry the semantics of *"no"*, *"not"* surrendering its original semantics of *"calyx"* to the Semantic-Phonetic Compound 柎 (/ㄈㄨ, fu/) with Radical 木 (/ㄇㄨˋ, mu$^4$/ "tree") and Phonetic Component 付 (/ㄈㄨˋ, fu$^4$/). This process of character creation, or re-creation rather, is called Semantic Bifurcation (假借).

不         →         柎    柎

/ㄈㄨ, fu/                            /ㄈㄨ, fu/

"calyx"                               "calyx"

?     →                         不

/ㄅㄨˋ, bu$^4$/                        /ㄅㄨˋ, bu$^4$/

"no", "not"                          "no", "not"

Most dictionaries list the character 不 (/ㄅㄨˋ, bu⁴/ //ㄅㄨˊ, bu²//) as **Pictograph** (象形) of *a bird soaring into the sky* (the horizontal line on top)

*of no return*,

hence "*no*", "*not*".

It is worth noting that the Pictograph of *a bird diving down to ground* to mean "*to come down to*" as described by most dictionaries is actually an Associative Compound telling the story of *an arrow* (  ) *coming down to ground* ( 一 ) for the character 至 (/ㄓˋ, zhi⁴/ "to come down to" Usage Rank #327).

Bone Bronze Seal Standard

The pictures of *a calyx of flower* as rendered through time by the character 不 are shown below.

Bone Bronze Seal Standard

## The Stroke Sequence

## The Trinity – Sound(s), Semantics, and Synopses

/ㄅㄨˋ, bu⁴/ //ㄅㄨˊ, bu²//

not 不行, 不對, 吃不完, 拿不動;

| | |
|---|---|
| *used after* 好 *to emphasize* 好 | 好不快樂, 好不傷心; |
| *at end of sentence for question* | 好不? [=好不好?], |
| | 冷不? [=冷不冷?]; |

*in classical Chinese,*

    *void character for tone change*    「徒御不驚，大庖不盈。」

**<u>Note</u>**: The 4th tone of 不 is changed to the 2nd tone (//ㄅㄨˊ, bu$^2$//) when followed by a 4th tone character.

/ㄈㄡ, fou/

    *surname*                    姓氏

/ㄈㄡˇ, fou$^3$/

    *in classical Chinese,*

        *same as* 否

        *at end of sentence for question*    「未知從今去，

                                當復如此不？」

/ㄈㄨ, fu/

    *in classical Chinese,*

        calyx                    「常棣之華，鄂不韡韡。」

**Radical:** 一 (/一, yi/ "one"), the 1st Stroke; originally 不 (itself).

# 6. 了

## Script Evolution

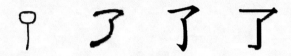

## The Story

/ㄌㄧㄠ∨, liao$^3$/　"to end", "to finish"

**Pictograph** (象形) of *an armless baby*

　　to imply *useless baby to end all hopes,*

hence *"to end", "to finish"*.

## The Stroke Sequence

**Common Fallacy:** Combining the 1$^{st}$ & 2$^{nd}$ Stroke as a single Stroke.

## The Trinity – Sound(s), Semantics, and Synopses

/ㄌㄧㄠ∨, liao$^3$/

　　to end, to finish　　　　　　　　　了斷, 責任未了, 不了了之;

　　readily, without reserve　　　　　直截[接]了當;

| | |
|---|---|
| to understand, to comprehend | 一目了然; |
| *before* 無 *to mean* completely | 了無新意; |
| *after verb and* 得 *to indicate* possibility | 辦得了, 走得了; |
| *after verb and* 不 *to indicate* inability, impossibility | 吃不了, 來不了; |
| *before* 得 *or* 不得 *for* extraordinariness | 了得, 了不得; |
| *after* 得 *or* 不得 *for* seriousness | 還得了, 不得了; |
| smart, keen | 小時了了，大未必佳; |
| *used with* 知 *as name for* cicada | 知了; |
| *in classical Chinese,* to complete | 「今日大案已了，我明日一早 進城銷差去了。」 |

/‧ㄌㄜ, le⁵/

| | |
|---|---|
| *after verb to indicate* completion | 吃了飯就去; |
| *at end of sentence to indicate* completion (*already*) | 他走了一些日子; |
| realization | 說著說著他就來了; |
| affirmation | 這就難了; |
| *used after verb and often with* 吧 *to indicate* objection | 得了(吧); |
| frustration | 算了(吧) |

**Radical:** 亅 (/ㄐㄩㄝˊ, jue² "an upside-down hook"), the 2ⁿᵈ Stroke; originally 了 (itself).

# 7. 有

## Script Evolution

有　有　有　有　有　有

## The Story

有　有　有　有

/ㄧㄡˇ, you$^3$/　"to possess", "to have"

**Associative Compound** (會意) of

又 (/ㄧㄡˋ, you$^4$/ "hand *holding something*") and

肉 (月/ㄖㄡˋ, rou$^4$/ "meat", *also providing sound*)

to imply *hand holding a piece of meat* or

　　　　*hand possessing something valuable*,

hence "*to possess*".

又　+　月　≡　有　有

It is important to note that at time of the Bone Script, the character told the simple story of *hand hodling something* (有) to mean "*to possess*". At time of the Bronze Script the character told the story of *hand holding* (有) *meat* (有) to make the idea of *possession* clearer, thus leading to the Seal Script then Standard Script. The stories of *hand possessing something valuable* as told through time by the character 有 are shown below.

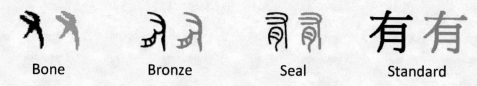

| Bone | Bronze | Seal | Standard |
|------|--------|------|----------|

More importantly, at time of the Seal Script the piece of *meat* (肉月/ㄖㄡˋ, rou⁴/) was shaped almost identical to *Moon* (月 /ㄩㄝˋ, yue⁴/) as shown below.

Bone  Bronze  Seal  "Moon"      "meat"  Seal  Bronze  Bone

In the Standard Script, the two characters (肉 and 月) when used as Radicals or components continued to be indistinguishable except for the trained eyes.

月 月 月 月 ≠ 月 月 肉 月

To make them even more confusing, some typeface and font designs actually have these two share the exact same form, 月 月, which is for *Moon*.

For the character 有, the piece of *meat* had been shaped and then written as the *Moon* more than 2,000 years ago.  And there has never been any exception in all typeface and font designs.  Moreover, all dictionaries list 有 (/ㄧㄡˇ, you³/ "to possess", "to have") under the Radical 月 (/ㄩㄝˋ, yue⁴/ "Moon") and turned its story to

**Semantic-Phonetic Compound** (形聲) of

月 (/ㄩㄝˋ, yue⁴/ "Moon") *for semantics* and

又 (/ㄧㄡˋ, you⁴/ "hand *holding something*") *for sound*

to mean "*to have but not desirable*" referring to *the Moon's constant changing of shape*.  Later, it only meant "*to have*".

月 ＋ 又 ≡ 有 有

"Moon"     /ㄧㄡˋ, you⁴/     /ㄧㄡˇ, you³/   "to have"

And as if to eliminate altogether the confusion caused by the two brown Strokes in 月 and 月, a character was created purposefully with these two Strokes removed as

有　有　→　𠂇

to actually mean *"not to have"* or 沒有 (/ㄇㄟˊ ㄧㄡˇ, mei² you³/) with the Conjoint Pronunciation of

沒 (/ㄇㄟˊ, mei²/ "not") and

有 (/ㄧㄡˇ, you³/ "to have"),

thus /ㄇㄡˇ, mou³/ or /ㄇㄠˇ, mao³/ reflecting a sound and its meaning in the Cantonese dialect. Notwithstanding, we know the character 有 started with a *single hand* and was never involved with the *Moon*.

## The Stroke Sequence

有 有 有 有 有 有
有 有 有 有 有 有

## The Anatomy

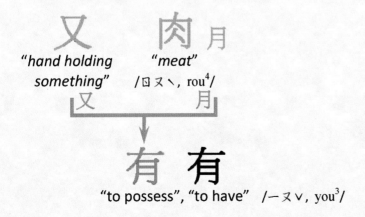

又
*"hand holding something"*

肉 月
*"meat"*
/ㄖㄡˋ, rou⁴/

有 有
"to possess", "to have"　/ㄧㄡˇ, you³/

21

# The Trinity – Sound(s), Semantics, and Synopses

/一ㄡˇ, you³/

| | |
|---|---|
| to possess, to own | 所**有**, 擁**有**; |
| to have (*showing fact or status*) | **有**困難, **有**禮貌, **有**錢, **有**說**有**笑; |
| existing | 還**有**; |
| plentiful, abundant, resourceful | 富**有**; |
| many (*for time or age*) | 經營**有**年, **有**了年紀; |
| *before verb to show* politeness | **有**勞, **有**請; |
| certain | **有**一天早上; |
| some, any | **有**人說, **有**誰見過; |

*in classical Chinese*,

| | |
|---|---|
| abundant, resourceful | 「止基迺理，爰眾爰**有**。」; |
| *void character used before noun for tone change* | 「當舜之時，**有**苗不服，禹將伐之。」; |
| *surname* | 姓氏 |

/一ㄡˋ, you⁴/

| | |
|---|---|
| plus (and) | 六十**有**三; |

*in classical Chinese*,

| | |
|---|---|
| plus (and) | 「吾十**有**五而志於學，三十而立。」 |

**Radical:** 月; originally 又.

# 8. 和

**Script Evolution**

**The Story**

/ㄏㄜˊ, he$^2$/ "harmonious"

**Associative Compound** (會意) of

㤓 (口 /ㄎㄡˇ, kou$^3$/ "mouth" in upside-down image to refer to *mouth blowing air down*),

𠌫 (Pictograph of *a pan pipe flute showing 3 breath holes*), and

禾 (/ㄏㄜˊ, he$^2$/ "grain crop") *for sound*

to imply *mouth blowing air down through breath holes of a pan pipe flute*

or *playing a pan pipe flute to make harmonious music*,

hence "*harmonious*".

㤓 + 𠌫 + 禾 ≡ 龢 龢

It is important to note that at time of the Bone Script no *breath hole* of the *pan pipe flute* was in the picture. To emphasize *mouth blowing air* (⚟) through the *pipes* (▦) *two breath holes* were added (▦) in the depiction by the Bronze Script. The number of *breath holes* increased to *three* (▦ to indicate *many*) at time of the Seal Script. More importantly, at time of the Bronze Script a simple Variant form (稞 稞) without the *pan pipe flute* appeared with the *mouth* (⊌) not *blowing air down* (⚟), that is

　　口 (/丂ㄡˇ, kou$^3$/ "mouth") and

　　禾 (/ㄏㄜˊ, he$^2$/ "grain crop") *for sound*

The simple form 咊 would eventually become the preferred form for the original semantics of "*harmonious*" as well as all the extended semantics with their variation pronunciations, whilst the original character form 龢 remained as a Standard character only for its original semantics of "*harmonious*" and used almost exclusively in persons' names. For writing preference, the Variant form 和 eventually took the place of Standard Form.

咊　咊　＝　和　和

Most dictionaries list the character 咊 and 和 (/ㄏㄜˋ, he$^4$/) as **Semantic-Phonetic Compound** (形聲) of

　　口 (/丂ㄡˇ, kou$^3$/ "mouth") *for semantics* and

　　禾 (/ㄏㄜˊ, he$^2$/ "grain crop") *for sound*

to mean "*to respond accordingly*".

口　＋　禾　≡　咊　咊

"mouth"　　　/ㄏㄜˊ, he$^2$/　　　/ㄏㄜˋ, he$^4$/　"to respond accordingly"

The story of *playing a pan pipe flute to make harmonious music* as told through time by the character 和 (咊, 龢) is shown below.

| Bone | Bronze | Seal | Standard |

## The Stroke Sequence

## The Anatomy

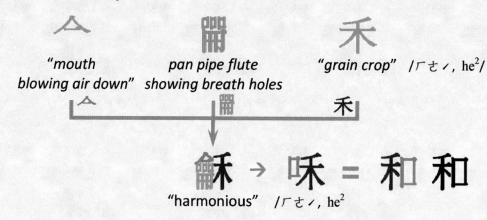

"mouth blowing air down"     pan pipe flute showing breath holes     "grain crop"  /ㄏㄜˊ, he²/

"harmonious"  /ㄏㄜˊ, he²/

## The Trinity – Sound(s), Semantics, and Synopses

/ㄏㄜˊ, he²/     Recital Sound [ㄏㄨㄛˊ, huo²]

| | |
|---|---|
| harmonious, harmonized | 和諧, 和鳴, 和聲; |
| peace, end of competition | 講和, 和平, 和局; |
| balanced | 中和; |
| friendly | 和氣, 和睦, 和好; |
| mild, smooth | 柔和; |
| soft, gentle | 和藹, 溫和, 心平氣和, 和顏悅色; |
| warm | 和暖, 和煦, 風和日麗; |
| mixing of various kinds | 和菜; |
| sum | 總和; |
| not separated from | 和衣而眠, 和盤托出; |
| to | 我和你說話; |
| and, together with | 我和你; |

26

*in classical Chinese,*

| | |
|---|---|
| moderation | 「禮之用，**和**爲[為]貴。」; |
| truce, peace | 「故不若亟割地求**和**，<br>以疑天下慰秦心。」; |
| to keep friendly relation with | 「臣聞以德**和**民，<br>不聞以亂。」; |
| soft, gentle | 「風神雅淡，識量寬**和**。」; |
| warm | 「清**和**好時節，<br>微風吹袂衣。」; |
| from | 「好幾處都有，<br>都稱贊得了不得，<br>還**和**我們尋呢！」; |
| and | 「三十功名塵與土，<br>八千里路雲**和**月。」; |

| | |
|---|---|
| *name of the Japanese race* | **和**服; |
| *surname* | 姓氏 |

//ㄏㄢ丶, han$^4$//    Alternative Pronunciation to /ㄏㄜˊ, he$^2$/ to mean

| | |
|---|---|
| and, together with | 我**和**你 |

/ㄏㄜ丶, he$^4$/

| | |
|---|---|
| to respond accordingly | 應**和**; |
| to match, to go along | 附**和**; |
| to support | 唱**和**; |

*in classical Chinese,*

| | |
|---|---|
| to go along, to echo | 「客有吹洞簫者，<br>倚歌而**和**之。」 |

/ㄏㄨㄛˋ, huo⁴/

    to mix, to combine                        攪和, 攙[摻]和, 和麪[麵]*,

                                                    和稀泥;

/˙ㄏㄨㄛ, huo⁵/

    cosily warm                               暖和

/ㄏㄨˊ, hu²/

    to acquire the card winning

    a card game                               和牌

*: Some dialectal pronunciation would have 『和麪』 pronounced as

    /ㄏㄨㄛˊ ㄇㄧㄢˋ, huo² mian⁴/.

**Note**: The 6 sound/semantics combinations of 和 are second only to

    the 8 sound/semantics combinations of 那 (Usage Rank #121).

**Radical**: 口.

# 9. 人

## Script Evolution

## The Story

/ㄖㄣˊ, ren²/    "person", "human"

**Pictograph** (象形) of *a person extending his arms to do something*, hence "*person*", "*human*".

**Note**: Also in the form 『亻』 as Radical or component, or

『勹』 as in 方 ([ㄈㄤˋ, fang⁴] "to banish"

Usage Rank #53).

The pictures of *a person extending his arms to do something* as rendered through time by the character 人 are shown below.

| Bone | Bronze | Seal | Standard |

## The Stroke Sequence

# The Trinity – Sound(s), Semantics, and Synopses

/ㄖㄣˊ, ren$^2$/

| | |
|---|---|
| person | 一人, 好幾人; |
| person with proper human conduct | 做人, 爲[為]人; |
| man, human | 人類, 人爲[為], 人造, 人文,<br>人聲鼎沸, 人山人海; |
| person with certain identity | 證人, 介紹人, 亞洲人; |
| every person | 人手一冊; |
| other people | 己所不欲，勿施於人; |
| person's character, disposition | 畫如其人; |

*in classical Chinese,*

| | |
|---|---|
| every person | 「若能同心一力，<br>　人自爲[為]戰，<br>　大功可立。」; |
| person's character, disposition | 「頌其詩，讀其書，<br>　不知其人，可乎？」; |
| *surname* | 姓氏 |

**Radical:** 人 (itself).

# 10. 這

## Script Evolution

這 這 這 這

## The Story

這 這 這 這

/ㄧㄢˋ, yan⁴/ "to greet"

/ㄓㄜˋ, zhe⁴/ "this"

**Associative Compound** (會意) of

辵 (辶 /ㄔㄨㄛˋ, chuo⁴/ "to walk and stop") and

言 (/ㄧㄢˊ, yan²/ "to speak", *also providing sound*)

to imply walking up and greeting with words,

hence *"to greet"*.

辶 + 言 = 這 這

A relatively new character and non-existing at time of the Seal Script (thus in grey colour as shown above), 這 was a phonetic variation to the Associative Compound 迎 (/ㄧㄥˊ, ying²/ "to greet") of

辵 (辶 /ㄔㄨㄛˋ, chuo⁴/ "to walk and stop") and

卬 (/ㄧㄤˇ, yang³/ "to look up", *also providing sound*)

to imply *walking with eye looking up to greet*,

31

hence *"to greet"*.

Later, 這 started to replace the character 者 (/ㄓㄜˋ, zhe⁴/ "this") which originally was 者 (/ㄓㄨˇ, zhu³/ "to cook"), whereas 者 would then become 者 (/ㄓㄜˇ, zhe³/ "person", "thing"). This process of character creation, or re-creation rather, is called Semantic Bifurcation (假借). The diagram below shows the identity change of 這 and 者 (ancient sound [ㄓㄨˇ, zhu³]).

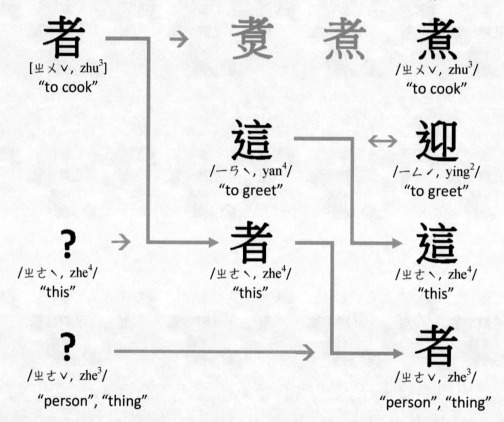

## The Stroke Sequence

這
這

## The Anatomy

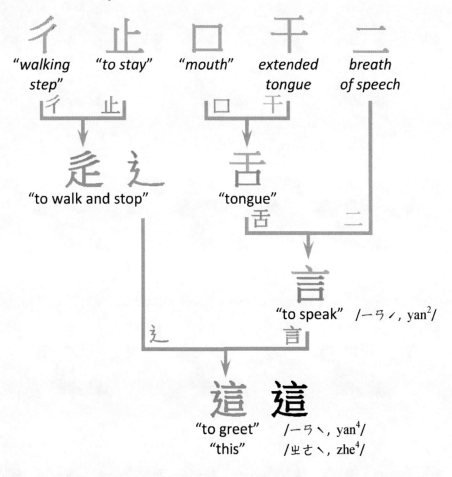

彳 "walking step"  止 "to stay"  口 "mouth"  干 extended tongue  二 breath of speech

辵 辵 "to walk and stop"

舌 "tongue"

言 "to speak"  /一ㄢˊ, yan²/

這 這

"to greet"  /一ㄢˋ, yan⁴/
"this"  /ㄓㄜˋ, zhe⁴/

## The Trinity – Sound(s), Semantics, and Synopses

/ㄓㄜˋ, zhe⁴/

   this (*adj. opposite to* 那 "that")      這些, 這個, 這樣, 這種, 這天, 這時候;

| | |
|---|---|
| this (*pron.*) | **這**就是了； |
| immediately, right away | 他**這**就來； |
| here | 在**這**(兒), **這**裏[裡]； |
| *in classical Chinese,* | |
|   this (*pron.*) | 「**這**就是門生治下 |
| | 一個鄉[鄉]下農民， |
| | 叫做王冕。」； |
|   *void character (middle of clause)* | 「待道是顛[顛]狂睡囈， |
| | 兀的不青天**這**白日。」 |

/ㄓㄟˋ, zhei$^4$/　Conjoint Sound of /ㄓㄜˋ, zhe$^4$/ and /ㄧ, yi/ for『這一』

| | |
|---|---|
| this one | **這**些, **這**個, **這**種, **這**天 |

**Note**: In Mandarin, it is important never to say /ㄓㄟˋ ㄧ, zhei$^4$ yi/
   as that would mean『這一一』("this one one")
   with a redundant『一』(/ㄧ, yi/ "one").

**Radical**: 辵 (辶).

# 11. 中

**Script Evolution**

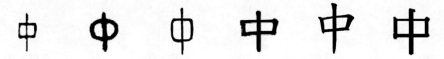

**The Story**

/ㄓㄨㄥ, zhong/    "inside"

**Associative Compound** (會意) of

　　□ (/ㄨㄟˊ, wei[2]/ "perimeter", "surrounding") and

　　| (/ㄍㄨㄣˇ, gun[3]/ "through")

to imply *going through the inside of an area*,

hence *"inside"*.

The story of *going through the inside of an area* as told through time by the character 中 is shown below.

| Bone | Bronze | Seal | Standard |

## The Stroke Sequence

## The Anatomy

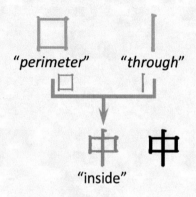

"perimeter"        "through"

中  中
"inside"

## The Trinity – Sound(s), Semantics, and Synopses

/ㄓㄨㄥ, zhong/

inside                           心中, 會中, 夢中, 其中, 途中,
                                 當中, 話中有話;

centre                           中央;

within (*a period of time*)      一年之中;

middle                           中等, 中級;

medium                           中號;

in the middle of                 中途, 中間;

in the midst of                  盡在不言中;

proper                           適中;

36

| | |
|---|---|
| neutral | 中立, 中和; |
| *after verb to show* on-going status | 開會中, 睡眠中, 行進中; |
| *name of China* | 中國*, 中國人; |
| *surname* | 姓氏 |

*:『中國』means *"the nation at the centre of the world"*.
   Hence, by virtue of its name, there is only one China.

/ㄓㄨㄥˋ, zhong⁴/

| | |
|---|---|
| correct | 言中, 說中了; |
| to hit exactly | 命中目標, 百發百中; |
| to match exactly | 中規中矩; |
| to suit, to fit | 中意, 中用; |
| pleasant to | 中聽, 中看; |
| to hit (*by chance or luck*) | 中獎; |
| to gain status passing examination | 中了舉人, 考中研究所; |
| to be affected by | 中邪, 中毒, 中暑; |
| *in classical Chinese*, | |
| to the point | 「朕涉道日寡，舉錯不中。」; |
| to match exactly | 「未嘗不中吾志也。」; |
| to gain status passing examination | 「這王大老爺， |
| | 就是前科新中的。」 |

**Radical:** │ (/ㄍㄨㄣˇ, gun³/ "through"), the last Stroke; originally 口.

# 12. 大

## Script Evolution

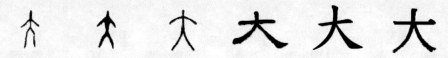

## The Story

/ㄉㄚˋ, da⁴/    "important"

**Pictograph** (象形) of *a man with arms extended and legs apart*

to imply *man as important as heaven and earth*,

hence *"important"*.

It is important to note that when serving as the component of a Compound, 大 may still mean *"a man"*. The pictures of *a man with arms extended and legs apart* as rendered through time by the character 大 are shown below.

| Bone | Bronze | Seal | Standard |

## The Stroke Sequence

# The Trinity – Sound(s), Semantics, and Synopses

/ㄉㄚˋ, da⁴/

| | |
|---|---|
| important, grand | 大志, 大事, 大計, 大年初一; |
| large, big | 大山大海; |
| heavy | 大雨; |
| strong (in degree, volume) | 大風, 大浪, 力氣大, 雷聲大，雨點(兒)小; |
| stronger | 大聲點兒, 大點兒聲, 大點兒力; |
| to exaggerate, to boast | 自大; |
| eldest | 大哥, 大伯, 老大; |
| respectable | 老大爺, 老大娘; |
| adult | 大人, 一家大小; |
| old (*used after* 多 *to mean* how old) | 多大歲數, 多大了; |
| self-reliant | 大姑娘, 大老爺們兒; |
| *before noun to show* respect | 大名, 大作, 大體; |
| quite | 大快人心, 大有來頭, 大費周章; |
| in a grand fashion | 大興土木, 大紅大紫; |
| very | 大清早, 大熱天, 天已大亮; |
| grand, important | 大合唱, 大團圓, 大喜之日; |
| at most | 大不了; |
| extremely | 大方, 大不敬, 大傻瓜; |
| even (*before or after certain time*) | 大後天, 大前天; |
| overall, generally | 大約, 大致, 大概; |

*used with* 不 *to mean*

    not quite, not much                            不**大**高興, 不**大**說話, 不**大**一致;

*math*, larger (quantity, value)          甲**大**於乙;

*in classical Chinese*,

    to boast                                      「是故君子不自**大**其事，
                                                       不自尚[尚]其功。」;

    unusual, important                          「余少有**大**志，夸邁流俗。」，
                                                       「雖**大**旨同歸，所託或乖。」;

    *as in* 大夫, *together to mean*

        ancient bureaucratic title           士，**大**夫, 士**大**夫;

        *surname*                                姓氏;

    surname                                   姓氏

/ㄉㄞˋ, dai⁴/

    *as in* 大夫, *together to mean*

    medical doctor                           李**大**夫;

    *in classical Chinese*,

    *as in* 大王, *together to mean*

        your majesty (highness)             「**大**王聖明。」

/ㄊㄞˋ, tai⁴/

    *in classical Chinese*,

    grand (*same as* 太)                     **大**[太]上皇, **大**[太]后, **大**[太]子

**Radical:** 大 (itself).

# 13. 爲

**Script Evolution**

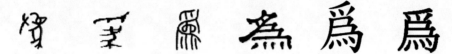

**The Story**

/ㄨㄟˊ, wei² /    "to administrate", "to undertake"

**Associative Compound** (會意) of

爪 (爫 /ㄓㄠˇ, zhao³/ "palm-down hand") and

禹 (/ㄒㄧㄤˋ, xiang⁴/ "tamed elephant")

to imply *handling an elephant to do work* or

*handling a matter of large scale*,

hence *"to administrate"*, *"to undertake"*.

The *tamed elephant* with its trunk hanging down in the Seal ( 爲 ) and Standard ( 爲 ) Script is quite different to 象 (/ㄒㄧㄤˋ, xiang⁴/), the Pictograph character for *elephant* with its trunk and front legs raised as seen below.

Standard   Seal   Bronze   Bone       Bone   Bronze   Seal   Standard

41

At time of the Bone Script, the *elephants* in these two characters were almost identical except that a *hand* was to reach or on the *elephant's trunk* to imply *handling the elephant* for 爲. At time of the Bronze Script the *hand* ( ) was changed to a *palm-down hand* ( ). Coming to the time of the Seal Script the *elephant* ( ) under the *palm-down hand* ( ) was already tamed with its trunk hanging down and front legs on the ground. The stories of *handling a matter of large scale* as told through time by the character 爲 are shown below.

Bone Bronze Seal Standard

The Alternate 為 為, based on the *hand* ( ) in the Bone Script and *tamed elephant* ( ) in the Seal Script, is often used in lieu of 爲. In some places, 為 is used as the Standard Form, whereas 爲 would be treated as Original (本字).

## The Stroke Sequence

為 為 為 為 為 為 為 為 為 為
為 為 為 為 為 為 為 為 為 為

## The Anatomy

爪
*"palm-down hand"*

舄
*"tamed elephant"*

爲 爲
*"to administrate"*

## The Trinity – Sound(s), Semantics, and Synopses

/ㄨㄟˊ, wei[2]/

| | |
|---|---|
| to administrate, to manage | 爲政, 爲事; |
| to undertake, to do | 爲善, 爲所欲爲, 爲非作歹; |
| doing, undertaking | 所作所爲, 毫無作爲; |
| to take on responsibility | 爲人師表; |
| to behave | 爲人, 爲人處世; |
| to make | 別跟我爲難 [=別難爲*我]; |
| to feel | 令我爲難; |
| potential for greatness | 大有可爲, 年輕有爲; |
| to be, as | 以爲, 認爲, 爲荷, 畜牧爲生, 四海爲家, 以此爲準, 指鹿爲馬; |

*: See /˙ㄨㄟ, wei[5]/ below.

43

| | |
|---|---|
| is (are) | 天下**爲**公, 十寸**爲**一尺, |
| | 三十六計，走**爲**上策; |
| to | 化整**爲**零; |
| *after adv. to mean* | |
| level (degree) *for emphasis* | 大**爲**失望, 甚**爲**重要, 廣**爲**流傳; |
| *in classical Chinese,* | |
| to administrate | 「**爲**政以德，譬如北辰， |
| | 居其所，而眾星共之。」; |
| to establish | 「**爲**秦有天下， |
| | 裂都會而**爲**之郡邑， |
| | 廢侯衛而**爲**之守宰。」; |
| to become | 「高岸**爲**谷，深谷**爲**陵。」; |
| to make | 「井渫不食，**爲**我心惻。」; |
| by | 「從來禦魑魅， |
| | 多**爲**才名誤。」; |
| is | 「何鄉[鄉]**爲**樂土， |
| | 安敢尚[尚]盤桓？」; |
| with | 「道不同不相**爲**謀。」; |
| then | 「君子有勇而無義**爲**亂， |
| | 小人有勇而無義**爲**盜。」; |
| if | 「王甚喜人之掩口也， |
| | **爲**近王，必掩口。」; |
| *aux. word at end of sentence* | |
| *for inquisition* | 「君子質而已矣， |
| | 何以文**爲**？」; |

*aux. word at end of sentence*

    *for sigh*　　　　　　　　「歸休乎君，

　　　　　　　　　　　　　予無所用天下爲！」；

    *or*　　　　　　　　　　「豈薪樞之未弘，

　　　　　　　　　　　　　爲網羅之目尙[尚]簡？」；

*surname*　　　　　　　　　姓氏

/ㄨㄟˋ, wei⁴/

    *for*　　　　　　　　　因爲, 爲什麼, 爲人爲己,

　　　　　　　　　　　　　爲生活努力, 爲了見你一面;

    *by*　　　　　　　　　　爲人所敬;

*in classical Chinese*,

    *for reason of*　　　　「天行有常，不爲堯存，

　　　　　　　　　　　　　不爲桀亡。」；

    *for*　　　　　　　　　　「花徑不曾緣客掃，

　　　　　　　　　　　　　蓬門今始爲君開。」，

　　　　　　　　　　　　　「最恨年年壓金線，

　　　　　　　　　　　　　爲他人作嫁衣裳。」；

    *to, towards*　　　　　「此中人語云，

　　　　　　　　　　　　　不足爲外人道也。」；

    *to help*　　　　　　　「公尸燕飲，福祿來爲。」；

    *shall*　　　　　　　　「克告於君，君爲來見也。」

/˙ㄨㄟ, wei⁵/

    *to make*　　　　　　難爲

**Radical:** 爪 (爫 /ㄓㄠˇ, zhao³/ "a palm-down hand") for 爲;

    火 (灬, /ㄏㄨㄛˇ, huo³/ "fire") for 為.

# 14. 上

## Script Evolution

## The Story

/ㄕㄤˋ, shang[4]/     "above"

**Ideograph** (指事) with *an object above a horizontal surface*

    to indicate *above*,

hence *"above"*, *"on top"*.

**<u>Note</u>**: This is the up-down mirrored image of 下 (/ㄒㄧㄚˋ, xia[4]/ "below"

    Usage Rank #45).

The iconic symbols denoting *the concept of above* as represented through time by the character 上 are shown below.

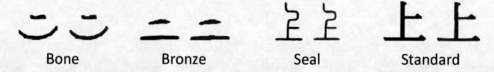

    Bone         Bronze        Seal        Standard

## The Stroke Sequence

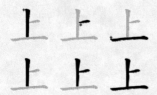

# The Trinity – Sound(s), Semantics, and Synopses

/ㄕㄤˋ, shang⁴/

| | |
|---|---|
| above | 上面, 以上; |
| top, supreme | 上湯, 上好, 上策; |
| people at higher position | 皇上, 太上皇; |
| high | 上級, 上流; |
| up | 上游; |
| upper | 上衣, 上身; |
| near, over (*in number*) | 成千上萬, 上千人; |
| previous, before | 上一篇, 上集, 上一位, 上個月, 上午; |
| *used with* 下 *to mean* more or less | 十天上下 [=十天左右]; |
| on the surface of, on top of | 門上, 山上, 桌上, 地上, 海上, 天上, 船上, 車上, 飛機上; |
| on, in (*for range, area, or domain*) | 路上, 書上, 文學上, 感情上; |
| ideal for, giving good result | 上手, 上眼, 上像, 上鏡頭, 朗朗上口; |
| in the area of, regarding | 資金上, 時間上; |
| to rise, to go up, to get up on (in) | 上去, 上升, 上樓, 上山, 上馬, 上車, 上船, 上牀[床], 上飛機; |
| to get on | 上路, 上網; |
| to go (to / up to) | 上街, 上學, 北上的列車, 上那兒?, 上菜市場, 上京趕考; |
| to move | 上進, 上前; |

| | |
|---|---|
| to bring up | 上菜, 上演; |
| to present to high authority | 上書, 上奏, 上報, 上繳, 上香; |
| to add | 上新貨; |
| to coat | 上漆, 上(顏)色; |
| to put on | 上妝, 上裝; |
| to apply (topical medicine) | 上藥; |
| to give (lecture), to receive (lesson) | 上課; |
| to set up, to engage | 上燈, 上鎖, 上膛, 上緊發條; |
| to lift up to | 上吊; |
| to take on, to fall into | 上癮, 上鈎; |
| to log in, to register | 上帳[賬]; |
| to appear on | 上臺, 上報(紙), 上電視; |
| to be included in | 上榜; |
| *after verb to indicate* up direction | 爬上去, 跳上來, 報上來; |
| *after verb to mean* over | 看上去, 摸上去; |
| *after verb to indicate* results | 考上大學, 關上大門, 記上一筆, 看上了; |
| *after verb to indicate* on-going status | 愛上, 迷上, 盯上; |
| *after* 早 *or* 晚 *to indicate* a period of time | 早上, 晚上; |
| *in classical Chinese,* Emperor | 「上問左右, 左右爭欲擊之。」; |

| | |
|---|---|
| elderly, superior | 「忠順不失，以事其上。」; |
| to step (go) up | 「欲窮千里目， |
| | 　更上一層樓。」; |
| previous, precedent | 「上不及虞夏之時， |
| | 　而下不修湯武。」; |
| near | 「王員外共借了 |
| | 　上千兩的銀子與荀家。」; |
| by side of | 「子在川上，曰： |
| | 『逝者如斯夫， |
| | 　不舍晝夜。』」; |
| *surname* | 姓氏 |

/ㄕㄤˇ, shang$^3$/

the 3$^{rd}$ tone in

Mandarin pronunciation　上聲

**Radical:** 一 (/一, yi/ "one"), the last Stroke; originally 上 (itself).

# 15. 個

## Script Evolution

個　個　個　個

## The Story

箇　箇　箇　個　個

/ㄍㄜ丶, ge⁴/　　"single one"

**Associative Compound** (會意) of

竹 (⺮ /ㄓㄨˊ, zhu²/ "bamboo") and

固 (/ㄍㄨ丶, gu⁴/ "to secure", "to fasten", *also providing sound*)

to imply *a bamboo piece used for fastening*,

hence *"bamboo nail"*, *quantity word for* small objects, *"single one"*.

**Note**: 固 and 箇 have the same ancient sound (still existing in some
　　　dialects today).

It is important to note that 个, Pictograph of *a small bamboo nail*, was
also used like 箇 for the *quantity word for* small objects and semantics of
*"single one"*. And 箇 was often used for *people*. This led to the creation of
Semantic-Phonetic Compound 個 with Radical 人 (亻 /ㄖㄣˊ, ren²/ "person")
and Phonetic Component 固 (/ㄍㄨ丶, gu⁴/ "solid with no leaks"). 個 did not

exist at time of the Seal Script (thus in grey colour as shown above).

亻 + 固 ≡ 個 個

"person"　　　　/ㄍㄨㄟ, shao²/　　　/ㄍㄜˋ, ge⁴/　"single one"

## The Stroke Sequence

個 個 個 個 個 個 個 個 個 個

個 個 個 個 個 個 個 個 個 個

## The Anatomy

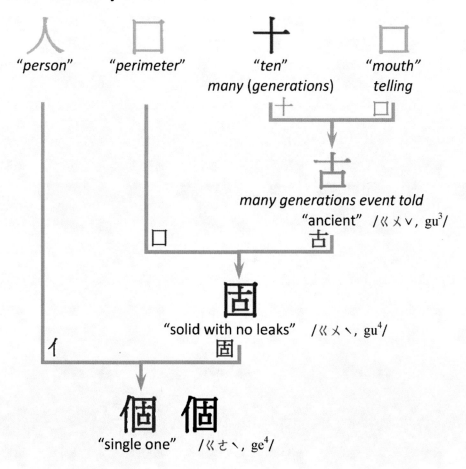

人　　　　口　　　　十　　　　口
"person"　　"perimeter"　　"ten"　　　"mouth"
　　　　　　　　　　many (generations)　telling

十　　口

古
many generations event told
"ancient"　/ㄍㄨˇ, gu³/

口　　　　　　古

固
"solid with no leaks"　/ㄍㄨˋ, gu⁴/

亻　　　固

個 個
"single one"　　/ㄍㄜˋ, ge⁴/

51

# The Trinity – Sound(s), Semantics, and Synopses

/ㄍㄜˋ, ge⁴/

| | |
|---|---|
| single one | 好幾**個**; |
| single | **個**位數; |
| each, every | **個個**爭先恐後; |
| individual | **個**人, **個**性; |
| this | **個**中好手, **個**中滋味; |
| countable number, a few | **個**數, **個**把件(兒); |
| body size or shape | 矮**個**子, 高**個**子; |
| size, volume | **個**頭, 小**個**(兒); |
| match | 你不是他的**個**兒; |
| *quantity word, for* small-size objects | 一**個**包子, 兩**個**饅頭 |

/ˑㄍㄜ, ge⁵/

| | |
|---|---|
| one | 吃**個**梨, 行**個**禮, 來**個**不理不睬; |
| time period (*used after time word*) | 今(兒)**個**, 明(兒)**個**, 昨(兒)**個**; |
| *aux. word at pause of speech* | 這**個**, 那**個**, 一**個**, 來**個**; |
| *aux. word after verb to emphasize* | |
|    *adv. which follows* | 笑**個**不停; |
|    *subject which follows* | 見**個**面(兒), 說**個**話(兒), 握**個**手 |

/ㄍㄜˇ, ge³/

| | |
|---|---|
| *used with* 自 *to mean* | |
|    oneself | 他自**個**兒來了; |
|    one's own | 那是他自**個**兒的事，你別插手 |

**Radical:** 人 (亻).

# 16. 國

## Script Evolution

## The Story

/ㄍㄨㄛˊ, guo$^2$/     "kingdom", "country"

**Associative Compound** (會意) of

口 (/ㄨㄟˊ, wei$^2$/ "perimeter", "area with boundary") and

或 ([ㄩˋ, yu$^4$] "kingdom", "country")

to imply *a kingdom with declared territorial boundary*,

hence "*kingdom*", "*country*".

 +

It is important to note that the Semantic-Phonetic Component 或 is the Original (本字) of 國. In other words, 國 is the re-created character from its Original 或 (Usage Rank #151), an Associative Compound (會意) of

口 (/ㄨㄟˊ, wei$^2$/ "perimeter", "territory"),

戈 (/ㄍㄜ, ge/ "weaponry" referring to *the military*), and

二 (Pictograph of *borderlines*)

to imply *territory requiring the military to defend its borderlines*,

53

hence *"kingdom"*, *"country"*.

$$口 + 戈 + 二 ≡ 或\ 或$$

Later, 或 started to carry the semantics of *"or"* with the sound /ㄏㄨㄛˋ, huo⁴/ surrendering its original semantics of *"kingdom"*, *"country"* to the Associative Compound 國 (/ㄍㄨㄛˊ, guo²/). This process of character creation, or re-creation rather, is called Semantic Bifurcation (假借).

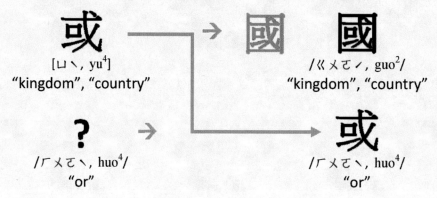

或
[ㄩˋ, yu⁴]
"kingdom", "country"

國 國
/ㄍㄨㄛˊ, guo²/
"kingdom", "country"

?
/ㄏㄨㄛˋ, huo⁴/
"or"

或
/ㄏㄨㄛˋ, huo⁴/
"or"

Of course, the Associative Compound 域 (/ㄩˋ, yu⁴/ Usage Rank #1,024) was formed with the original meaning of 或, that is

土 (/ㄊㄨˇ, tu³/ "soil") and

或 ([ㄩˋ, yu⁴] "kingdom", *also providing the sound*)

to imply *soil of a kingdom,*

hence *"territory"*.

$$土 + 或 ≡ 域\ 域$$

It is important to note that at time of the Bone Script the character 或 (國) told the story of *territory* ( ▢ ) *requiring the military* ( ⟟ ) *to defend*. The stories of *territory requiring the military to defend its borderlines* and *a country with declared territorial boundary* as told through time by the character 或 and 國 are shown below.

| Bone | Bronze | Seal | Standard |

## The Stroke Sequence

**Common Fallacy:** Exchanging the last 2nd & 3rd Stroke.

## The Anatomy

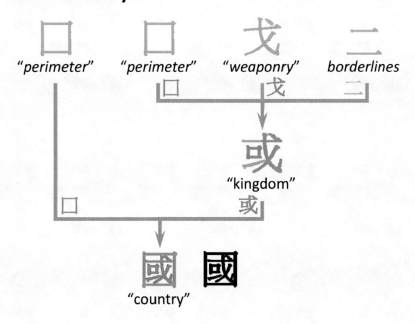

口 "perimeter"  口 "perimeter"  戈 "weaponry"  二 borderlines

或 "kingdom"

國 國 "country"

## The Trinity – Sound(s), Semantics, and Synopses

/ㄍㄨㄛˊ, guo$^2$/

| | |
|---|---|
| country, nation | 中國, 國家, 保家衛國; |
| national | 國旗, 國歌, 國劇; |
| native | 國人, 國土, 國貨; |
| *in classical Chinese*, | |
| kingdom, nation | 「大君有命，開國承家， 小人勿用。」; |
| city | 「遍國中無與立談者。」; |
| *surname* | 姓氏 |

**Radical:** 囗 (/ㄨㄟˊ, wei$^2$/ "perimeter").

# 17. 我

## Script Evolution

玓　我　我　我　我　我

## The Story

我　我　我　我

/ㄨㄛˇ, wo³/　　"heavy powerful axe-like weapon"

"I, me (we, us)"

**Pictograph** (象形) of *a heavy powerful axe-like weapon with long handle.*

Later, holding *the powerful weapon* and calling everyone's attention to oneself justified the character to be used to refer to *oneself* or *the first person "I"*. And 我 started to be used as such. This process of character creation, or re-creation rather, is called Semantic Bifurcation (假借).

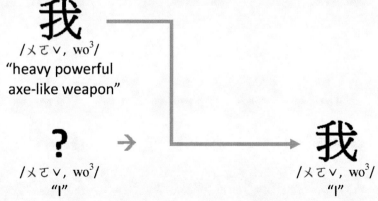

我
/ㄨㄛˇ, wo³/
"heavy powerful
axe-like weapon"

?
/ㄨㄛˇ, wo³/
"I"

我
/ㄨㄛˇ, wo³/
"I"
"heavy powerful axe-like weapon"

The pictures of *a heavy powerful axe-like weapon with long handle* as rendered through time by the character 我 are shown below.

| Bone | Bronze | Seal | Standard |

## The Stroke Sequence

我 我 我 我 我 我 我
我 我 我 我 我 我 我

**Common Fallacy:** Exchanging the last 2 Strokes.

## The Trinity – Sound(s), Semantics, and Synopses

/ㄨㄛˇ, wo³/      Recital Sound [ㄜˇ, e³]

   I, me, (we, us)                      我方, 我們, 我在聽音樂;

   self                                    大公無我;

   *in classical Chinese,*

      heavy powerful weapon        「我伐用張，於湯有光。」;

      *surname*                         姓氏

**Radical:** 戈 (/ㄍㄜ, ge/ "ancient weapon used in war"); originally 我 (itself).

# 18. 以

## Script Evolution

以  以  以  以  以  以

## The Story

目  目  以  以

/ㄧˇ, yi³/   "to base on"

**Associative Compound** (會意) of

人 (/ㄖㄣˊ, ren²/ "person") and

目 (ㄙ /ㄧˇ, yi³/ "tool to use", *also providing sound*)

to imply *the tool to use* or *to base on*,

hence "*to use*", "*to base on*".

人 + ㄙ ≡ 以  以

It is important to note that the Semantic-Phonetic Component 目 is the Original (本字) of 以. In other words, 以 is the re-created character from its Original 目, Pictograph (象形) of *spade-like farming tool for turning soil*, hence "*tool to use*", "*to base on*". At time of the Bone Script of a form of the character actually told the story of *a man* ( ) *using the farming tool* ( ). After 目 was used exclusively for the semantics of "*to base on*", the Associative Compound (會意) 耜 (/ㄙˋ, si⁴/ and ancient sound [ㄙㄧˋ]) with

59

Radical 耒 (/ㄌㄟˇ, $\text{lei}^3$/ “wood handle of farming tool”) and Semantic-Phonetic Component 㠯 (㠯 /ㄧˇ, $\text{yi}^3$/ “spade-like farming tool”) was created for the original *farming tool*.

耒 + 㠯 = 耜 耜

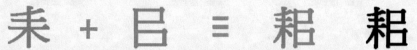

At time of the Seal Script, a form of the character also told the story of *person* ( ) *with his farming tool* ( ), thus leading to the Standard Script with 㠯 written as 厶. The stories of *tool to use* as told through time by the character 以 are shown below.

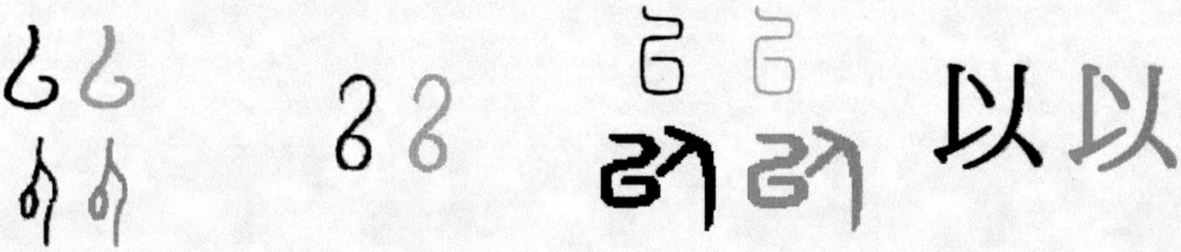

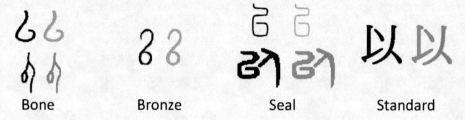

Bone Bronze Seal Standard

## The Stroke Sequence

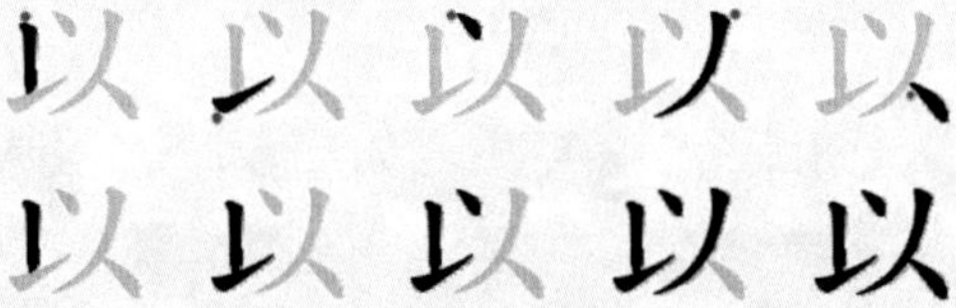

**<u>Note</u>**: Although the Original (本字) 㠯 is not used often, it is still important to know how to write it properly in the Stroke Sequence as shown below.

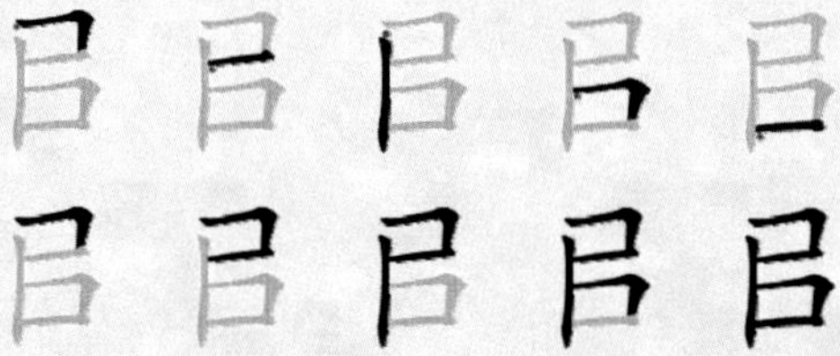

## The Anatomy

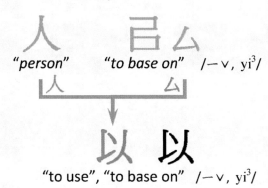

人 "person"　　呂厶 "to base on"　/ㄧˇ, yi³/

人　　厶

以 以

"to use", "to base on"　/ㄧˇ, yi³/

## The Trinity – Sound(s), Semantics, and Synopses

/ㄧˇ, yi³/

| | |
|---|---|
| to use, with | 以身作則, 以卵擊石, 以寡擊眾; |
| to base on | 不以言舉人, 不以人廢言; |
| to regard | 以爲[為]; |
| according to | 物以類聚; |
| for sake of | 以免; |
| thus, resulting | 以致; |
| since, till | 以來, 以往, 以前, 以後; |
| to (*after adj.*) | 難以下嚥, 寬以待人; |
| inclusively (*reference to position*) | 以上, 以下, 以東, 以南, 以西, 以北; |
| *aux. word* (after verb) | (不)可以, 得以, 所以; |
| *in classical Chinese,* | |
| with | 「洗浣泥者以水, 燔腥者用火。」; |
| to rely on | 「富國以農, 距敵恃卒。」; |

| | |
|---|---|
| to believe | 「竊**以**自古中興之主，<br>必有命代之臣。」; |
| can be | 「大則**以**王，小則**以**霸。」; |
| to make | 「向欲**以**齊事王，<br>使攻宋也。」; |
| to base on | 「君子不**以**言舉人，<br>不**以**人廢言。」; |
| according to | 「禮法**以**時而定，<br>制令各順其宜。」; |
| to be at | 「賞**以**春夏而刑**以**秋冬。」; |
| and also | 「亡國之音哀**以**思，<br>其民困。」; |
| to be linked with | 「朕躬有罪，無**以**萬方。」; |
| thus | 「於是關中爲[為]沃野，<br>無凶年，秦**以**富彊。」,<br><br>「不宜妄自菲薄，引喻失義，<br>**以**塞忠諫之路也。」; |
| for sake of | 「郊社不修，宗廟不享。<br>作奇技淫巧**以**悅婦人。」; |
| with | 「各**以**其耦進，反于射位。」; |
| *name for Israel* | **以**阿戰爭; |
| *surname* | 姓氏 |

**Radical:** 人 for 以;

己 (/ㄐㄧˇ, ji³/ "self") for 己.

62

# 19. 要

**Script Evolution**

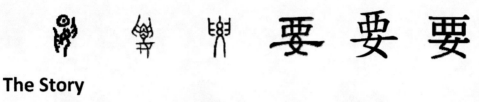

**The Story**

/ㄧㄠ, yao/　　　"to invite", "to set appointment"

**Associative Compound** (會意) of

　　臼 (/ㄐㄩˊ, ju$^2$/ "to join both hands" referring to *politely*),

　　女 (/ㄋㄩˇ, nü$^3$/ "female" referring to *female companions*), and

　　日 (/ㄖˋ, ri$^4$/ "Sun", "day" referring to *certain day*)

to imply *politely inviting to event with female companions on certain day*,

hence *"to invite", "to set appointment"*.

$$ 臼 + 女 + 日 ≡ 𡢃 \quad 𡢃 $$

Standard Form has 𡢃 written as 要, hence 要 in lieu of 𡢃.

$$ 𡢃 \quad 𡢃 \quad → \quad 要 \quad 要 $$

It is important to note that at time of the Bronze Script the character told the story with *food* ( 👹凶) and *female companions* (卉女) for the event. At time of the Seal Script, the scale of the event was drastically reduced to just *fruit* () *on a small table* ( ∩ 几 ).  At time of the Standard Script, the story went back to the original one of *joining both hands* (臼) *politely to present an event with female companions* (女) *on certain day* (日) as told by the Bone Script, thus leading to the Standard Script.  The Variant Form 嫑嬰 was direct descendant from the Bronze Script.  The stories of *presenting an event of importance* as told through time by the character 要 are shown as below.

| Bone | Bronze | Seal | Standard |
|------|--------|------|----------|

## The Stroke Sequence

## The Anatomy

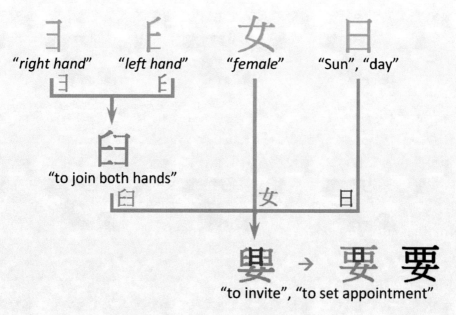

64

# The Trinity – Sound(s), Semantics, and Synopses

/一ㄠ, yao/

| | |
|---|---|
| to invite | 要定; |
| to set appointment or agreement | 要約, 要契; |
| to request, to ask | 要求, 要[邀]功; |
| to compel | 要挾; |
| to intercept | 要擊; |

*in classical Chinese*,

| | |
|---|---|
| to set appointment | 「雖與府吏**要**，<br>渠會永無緣。」; |
| agreement | 「久**要**不忘平生之言，<br>亦可以爲[為]成人矣。」; |
| to invite | 「便**要**還家，<br>設酒殺雞作食。」; |
| to require | 「今之人，<br>修其天爵以**要**人爵。」; |
| to compel | 「以**要**晉國之成。」，<br>「雖曰不**要**君，吾不信也。」; |
| to intercept | 「使數人**要**於路，曰：<br>『請必無歸而造於期。』」; |
| waist [=腰] | 「昔者，楚靈王好士細**要**，<br>故靈王之臣，<br>皆以一飯爲[為]節。」; |
| *surname* | 姓氏 |

/ㄧㄠˋ, yao⁴/

| | |
|---|---|
| key element (point) | 要領, 提要, 綱要, 摘要, 要素; |
| important | 重要, 要事, 要塞, 要文, 要人, 要素, 要道, 要衝; |
| very | 幾個要好的朋友; |
| should (must) | 不要遲到, 上課要專心, 要努力向上; |
| must be | 食材要上好新鮮的; |
| to demand | 要帳[賬], 要錢, 要命*; |
| to want | 不要了, 他要我替他辦件事(兒); |
| to desire | 要好心切; |
| (*of the needy*) to request | 要飯**, 要茶, 要水, 要錢; |
| to need (to be in need of) | 要人幫忙, 我要一枝筆; |
| to want to | 要成功，就得努力, 若要人不知，除非己末爲[為]; |
| to acquire | 這件衣服我要了; |
| to keep | 這本書還要不要; |
| about to | 天要黑了, (快)要下雨了, 他就(快)要回來了; |
| if | 要是我，就沒那麼好說話, 明天要是下雨，我就不去了; |

*: 『要命』can also mean "*life threatening*", "*critically important*", as *in*「這事兒眞[真]要命。」.

**: 『要飯的』means "*pauper*", "*beggar.*
    It is most inappropriate to order food in a restaurant using「要」.

| either … or … | 這件事**要**(麼)就不做， |
| | **要**(麼)就一口氣將它做完; |
| *in classical Chinese,* | |
| in summary | 「**要**言之， |
| | 爲[為]人應以誠字居心。」; |
| to want to | 「若**要**添風月， |
| | 應除數百竿。」, |
| | 「**要**知心腹事， |
| | 但聽口中言。」 |

**Radical:** 西 (覀 /ㄧㄚˋ, ya⁴/ "to cover"), the first 6 Strokes; originally 臼.

# 20. 地

**Script Evolution**

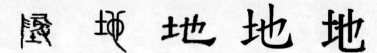

**The Story**

/ㄉㄧˋ, di⁴/　"ground", "land"

**Associative Compound** (會意) of

　土 (/ㄊㄨˇ, tu³/ "soil", "dirt") and

　也 (/ㄧㄝˇ, ye³/ originally Pictograph of *a snake, also providing sound*)

to imply *dirt area or ground where snake lives,*

hence *"ground"*.

<u>**Note**</u>: ㄧㄝ and ㄧ are the same sound.

It is important to note that at time of the Bronze Script of the character told the story of *putting* ( ) *corpse* ( ) *at bottom of cliff* ( ) *to return it to ground* ( ) *for final rest* reflecting the ancient custom of burying the dead. At time of the Seal Script, the character told the story of *ground where snake lives*, thus leading to the Standard Script. The stories of *final resting place for the dead* and *dirt area where snake lives* as told through time by the character 地 are shown below.

| Bronze | Seal | Standard |

## The Stroke Sequence

## The Anatomy

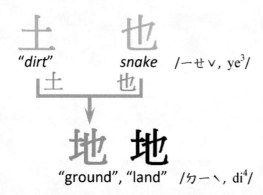

土      也

"dirt"      *snake*   /ㄧㄝˇ, ye³/

地 地

"ground", "land"   /ㄉㄧˋ, di⁴/

## The Trinity – Sound(s), Semantics, and Synopses

/ㄉㄧˋ, di⁴/

| | |
|---|---|
| ground | 地上, 地下, 地層; |
| land | 土地, 高地, 窪地, 山地, 地下水, 地上物; |
| earth | 地球, 地心, 地表; |
| field, piece of land | 田地, 土地, 耕地, 荒地, 種地; |

| | |
|---|---|
| terrain | 地勢; |
| geo-, geographical | 地熱, 地利, 地理; |
| place | 發祥地, 目的地, 根據地; |
| territory, area | 本地, 外地, 腹地, 地方, 殖民地; |
| position | 餘地, 地步, 易地而處, 這步田地; |
| person's mindset | 見地, 心地, 境地; |
| substance | 質地; |
| distance | 三十里地; |
| of ground | 地瓜, 地鼠, 地震; |
| on ground | 地攤; |
| underground | 地道 (/ㄉㄠˋ, dao$^4$/); |
| solid, authentic, original | 地道 (/‧ㄉㄠ, dao$^5$/), |
| | 道 (/ㄉㄠˋ, dao$^4$/) 地; |
| *aux. word after adv.* | 驀地, 忽(然)地, 猛(然)地; |
| *in classical Chinese,* | |
|    ground | 「牀[床]前明月光， |
| | 　疑是地上霜。」; |
|    position | 「自免才地高華， |
| | 　恆有宰輔之望。」; |
|    person's mindset | 「幹告以必有眞[真]實心地、 |
| | 　刻苦工夫而後可， |
| | 　基悚惕受命。」; |
|    base | 「譬王色之錦， |
| | 　各以本采爲[為]地矣。」; |

journey                                      「長門一步**地**，

                                                  不肯暫迴車。」；

*aux. word with* 立, 坐, 臥

    *for emphasis*                             「山門下立**地**，

                                                看有甚麼人來？」

/ • ㄉㄜ, de$^5$/     Recital Pronunciation // • ㄉㄧ, di$^5$//

  *struc. particle*

    *to form adv.* *

        *after noun*                          快樂**地**, 痛苦**地**;

        *after phrase*                      滿心歡喜**地**, 頭也不回**地**;

    *after adv.*

        *for emphasis*                     漸漸**地**, 慢慢**地**, 飛快**地**

    *: To form an *adj.*, the character 的 (Usage Rank #1) should be used.

**Radical:** 土.

# 21. 他

**Script Evolution**

彵 儥 他 他 他

**The Story**

儥 儥 佗 他 他

/ㄊㄚ, ta/　　"the other person", "he", "him"

**Associative Compound** (會意) of

人 (亻 /ㄖㄣˊ, ren[2]/ "person") and

它 (/ㄊㄚ, ta/ "it" originally *a snake-like creature, also providing sound*)

to imply *third person*,

hence "*the other person*", "*he*", "*him*".

亻 + 它 ≡ 佗 佗

Later, for the same sound (/ㄊㄨㄛˊ, tuo[2]/) 佗 started to carry the semantics of "*to carry load*". At time of the Clerical Script, for the semantics of *the third person* the Semantic-Phonetic Component 它 was changed to the other Pictograph for *snake* 也 (/ㄧㄝˇ, ye[3]/ *also providing sound*), hence the new Associative Compound 他 for the semantics of "*the other person*".

佗 佗 → 他 他

72

**Note**: ㄚ, ㄛ, ㄝ are the same sound.

Later, following 他

她 with Radical 女 (/ㄋㄩˇ, nü³/ "female") was created for "*she*", "*her*" and

牠 with Radical 牛 (牛 /ㄋㄧㄡˊ, niu²/ "ox") for *reference to an animal*.

Meanwhile, 它 continued to mean "*it*" (mainly for lifeless objects).

The story of *third person* as told through time by the character 他 (佗) is shown below.

Bronze      Seal      Standard

## The Stroke Sequence

## The Anatomy

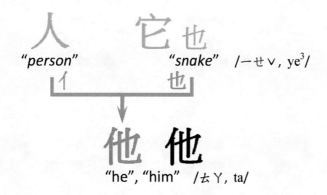

人      它 也

"*person*"      "*snake*" /ㄧㄝˇ, ye³/

亻      也

他 他

"he", "him" /ㄊㄚ, ta/

## The Trinity – Sound(s), Semantics, and Synopses

/ㄊㄚ, ta/

     he, him, (they, them)      他自己, 他們;

| the male companion of a female | 妳的**他**; |
| other | 其**他**, **他**鄉[鄉], **他**國, **他**日, |
| | **他**山之石; |
| by others, of others | **他**殺, **他**力; |
| otherwise | 不疑有**他**; |
| *in classical Chinese,* | |
| other matter | 「人知其一，莫知其**他**。」, |
| | 「王顧左右而言**他**。」 |

/ • ㄊㄚ, ta⁵/

*aux. word after verb to emphasize*
*subject which follows*　　　　說**他**幾句, 唱**他**一段, 喝**他**幾杯

**Radical:** 人 (亻).

# 22. 時

## Script Evolution

薔 坣 時 時 時 時

## The Story

時 時 時 時

/ㄕˊ, shi²/ "the four seasons"

**Associative Compound** (會意) of

日 (/ㄖˋ zhi⁴/ "the Sun"),

之 (ㄓㄓㄗ /ㄓ, zhi/ "ready to go somewhere" referring to *constant change of positions, also providing sound*), and

寸 (/ㄘㄨㄣˋ, cun⁴/ "to handle carefully")

to imply *regular time intervals as result of the Sun's constant change of positions that need be handled carefully*,

hence "*the four seasons*".

日 + 坣 + 寸 = 時 時

**Note**: 之 (ㄓㄓㄗ/ㄓㄢ, zhi/) and 時 (/ㄕㄢˊ, shi²/) share the same sound, the Virtual Rhyme ㄢ that is omitted in their specifications.

It is important to note that at time of the Bone Script and Bronze Script the character told the story of *the Sun's* (▱) (▱) *constant change of positions* () to imply *the four seasons*. The stories of *the four seasons* as told through time by the character 時 are shown below.

| | | | |
|---|---|---|---|
| Bone | Bronze | Seal | Standard |

Most dictionaries list the character 時 (/ㄕ╱, shi$^2$/) as

**Semantic-Phonetic Compound** (形聲) of

日 (/ㄖ╲, ri$^4$/ "Sun") *for semantics* and

寺 (/ㄙ╲, si$^4$/ "to handle appropriately", "court") *for sound*

to mean "*the four seasons*".

$$日 + 寺 = 時 \quad 時$$

"Sun"      /ㄙ帀╲, si$^4$/      /ㄕ帀╱, shi$^2$/    "season"

## The Anatomy

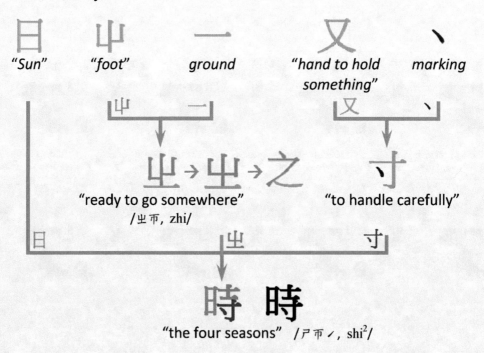

| 日 | 屮 | 一 | 又 | 丶 |
|---|---|---|---|---|
| "Sun" | "foot" | ground | "hand to hold something" | marking |

屮 一 → 屮 → 屮 → 之
"ready to go somewhere"
/屮帀, zhi/

又 丶 → 寸
"to handle carefully"

日 屮 寸 →

時 時
"the four seasons" /ㄕ帀╱, shi$^2$/

## The Stroke Sequence

時 時 時 時 時 時 時 時 時 時
時 時 時 時 時 時 時 時 時 時

## The Trinity – Sound(s), Semantics, and Synopses

/ㄕˊ, shi$^2$/

| | |
|---|---|
| season, seasonal | **時**節, **時**價; |
| time | **時**間, **時**期, 計**時**, 報**時**, **時**鐘, 何**時**何地, 等他多**時**, **時**不我與, 甚[什]麼**時**候; |
| extended period of time | 古**時**, 盛行一**時**; |
| hour | 三小**時**, 幾**時**幾分, 五**時**三刻; |
| moment | 及**時**, 一**時**還想不起來; |
| appointed time | 按**時**, 準**時**; |
| proper time, opportunity | **時**機, 失**時**, 是**時**候了; |
| opportune | 天**時**地利; |
| present time, current | **時**事, **時**局, **時**勢, **時**裝, **時**尚[尚]; |
| certain period in the past | **時**人; |
| frequently, often | **時**常, **時**有所聞, **時時**刻刻; |
| occasion | 有**時**; |
| *in classical Chinese*, | |
| time | 「天不再與，**時**不久留。」; |
| often, frequently | 「學而**時**習之，不亦說乎！」; |

appropriate 「孔子，聖之**時**者也。」；

opportunity 「今不乘**時**報恨，

更待何年！」；

*surname* 姓氏

**Radical:** 日.

# 23. 來

## Script Evolution

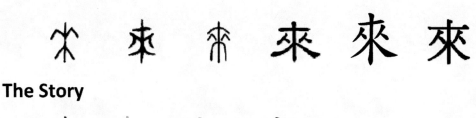

## The Story

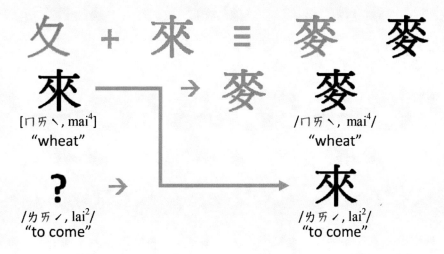

[ㄇㄞˋ, mai⁴]    "wheat"

/ㄌㄞˊ, lai²/    "to come"

**Pictograph** (象形) of *one ripe stem of wheat*, hence "*wheat*".

Later, 來 started to carry the semantics of "*to come*" for the same sound (/ㄌㄞˊ, lai²/). The Associative Compound 麥 (/ㄇㄞˋ, mai⁴/) with Radical 夊 (/ㄙㄨㄟ, sui/ "to walk slowly" referring to *growing slowly*) and Semantic-Phonetic Component 來 ([ㄇㄞˋ, mai⁴] "wheat") was then created for *wheat*.

This process of character creation, or re-creation rather, is called Semantic Bifurcation (假借).

Throughout history, many scholars believed that 來 should still mean "*wheat*" and 麥 should carry the semantics of "*to come*". Those who felt so strongly on this even created the Associative Compounds

徠 (/ㄌㄞˊ, lai$^2$/) with Radical 彳 (/ㄔˋ, chi$^4$/ "small step") and Semantic-Phonetic Component 來 ([ㄇㄞˋ, mai$^4$] "wheat") for "*to come*"

$$彳 + 來 \equiv 徠 \quad 徠$$

and

秣 (/ㄌㄞˊ, lai$^2$/) with Radical 禾 (/ㄏㄜˊ, he$^2$/ "grain crop") and Semantic-Phonetic Component 來 ([ㄇㄞˋ, mai$^4$] "wheat") for "*wheat*".

$$禾 + 來 \equiv 秣 \quad 秣$$

Meanwhile, other Semantic-Phonetic Compounds with 麥 (/ㄇㄞˋ, mai$^4$/ "wheat") as Radical were created, for instance,

$$\underset{\text{"wheat"}}{麥} + \underset{\text{/ㄈㄨ, fu/}}{夫} \equiv \underset{\text{/ㄈㄨ, fu/}}{麩} \quad \underset{\text{"bran"}}{麩}$$

麩 (/ㄈㄨ, fu/ "bran"),

$$\underset{\text{"wheat"}}{麥} + \underset{\text{/ㄇㄧㄢˇ, mian}^3\text{/}}{丏} \equiv \underset{\text{/ㄇㄧㄢˋ, mian}^4\text{/ "flour; noodle"}}{麵} \quad 麵$$

麵 (/ㄇㄧㄢˋ, mian$^4$/ "flour", "noodle"), and

$$\underset{\text{"wheat"}}{麥} + \underset{\text{/ㄐㄩˊ, qu}^2\text{/}}{匊} \equiv \underset{\text{/ㄑㄩˊ, qu}^2\text{/ "fermented grain"}}{麴} \quad 麴$$

麴 (/ㄑㄩˊ, qu$^2$/ "fermented grain", *surname*).

Thus,

麥 (/ㄇㄞˋ, mai⁴/) continues to be "*wheat*" and

來 (/ㄌㄞˊ, lai²/) still carries the semantics of "*to come*".

The pictures of *one ripe stem of wheat* as rendered through time by the character 來 are shown below.

| Bone | Bronze | Seal | Standard |
|------|--------|------|----------|

## The Stroke Sequence

## The Trinity – Sound(s), Semantics, and Synopses

/ㄌㄞˊ, lai²/

| | |
|---|---|
| to come | 來回, 不來, 來過, 來往, 來去自如; |
| moving towards | 過來, 回來, 走來, 上來, 下來; |
| coming, progressing | 來勢, 來頭(兒); |
| originating | 來由, 來源, 來歷, 來路; |
| thoroughgoing, experienced | 過來人; |
| all the way (*from past till now*) | 從來, 由來, 向來, 歷來, 自古以來; |
| future, forthcoming | 來年, 來生, 來世, 來日方長; |
| to move forward | 亂來, 讓我來, 來人哪, 信手拈來; |
| approaching | 來人, 來者不善, 來意不明; |

81

| | |
|---|---|
| arriving, arrived | 來信[函], 人來瘋, 客人來了, 颱風來了, 手到擒來, 與生俱來; |
| to happen, to have | 來不及, 來場大雨, 來了場大病; |
| to make happen | 來點(兒)音樂; |
| to bring * | 來杯水, 來瓶啤酒, 來五個包子, 來客臘味煲仔飯，清蒸活魚, 來碗(兒)炸醬麵[麵]; |
| would like us to bring * | 您來點(兒)什麼？; |
| (speaking, bringing) about | 說來聽聽, 娓娓道來, 拿來看看; |
| shy of (*used after number*) | 三十來歲; |
| in a continuous manner | 說來話長, 一路走來, 看來不錯; |
| *used with 起 after verb to mean ** | |
| as is [=上來] | 吃起來, 喝起來, 聞起來, 看起來; |
| as is | 說起來簡單，聽起來還不錯， 做起來就不知道了; |
| to start | 話還沒說兩句，就吵起來了, 這兩隻狗一見面就打起來了, 這孩子一鬧起來就沒完沒了; |
| in a continuous manner (state) | 買賣雖小，維持起來也不容易, 躲起來, 關起來, 藏起來, 收起來, 走起路來, 說起話來, 做起事來; |
| up | 站起來, 坐起來, 扶起來, 撐起來; |

*: 『來』is the proper word to use for ordering food in a restaurant. It demonstrates one's excellent command of the language.

**: 『起來』by itself means "*to get up*".

*used after* 得 *or* 不 *to indicate*

    capability (to do or appreciate)    做得**來**, 做不**來**, 聽不**來**, 喝不**來**;

*used as in* 不上[下]**來** *after verb, together to mean*

    cannot quite                     說不上**來**, 喘不上(氣)**來**,

                                    停不下**來**, 坐不下**來**;

*used after* 一 and 二 *together to mean*

    first *and* second                  一**來**念他初犯，二**來**念他年輕;

*before verb to show* willingness      我**來**買菜, 你**來**做飯;

*after verb phrase to show* intention    我上課**來**了;

*aux. word at end of opening clause*    不愁吃**來**，不愁穿;

*in classical Chinese*,

    to come                   「有朋自遠方**來**，

                              不亦樂乎？」,

                   「莫放春秋佳日過，

                              最難風雨故人**來**。」;

    since                      「紅豆生南國，

                              秋**來**發故枝？」,

                   「夜**來**風雨聲，

                              花落知多少？」;

    future, next                「今科不中**來**科中。」;

    *after verb to mean*

        at time of *verb*           「去**來**江口守空船，

                            繞船明月江水寒。」;

*surname*                        姓氏

**Radical:** 人 (/ㄖㄣˊ, ren[2]/ "person"), the 3rd & 4th Stroke; originally 來 (itself).

# 24. 用

**Script Evolution**

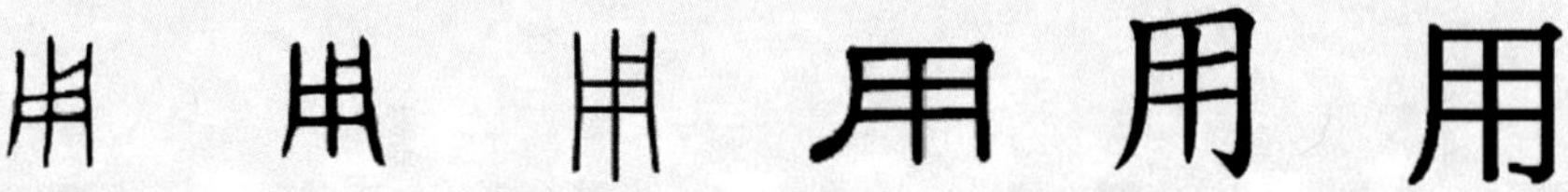

用 用 用 用 用 用

**The Story**

用 用 用 用 用

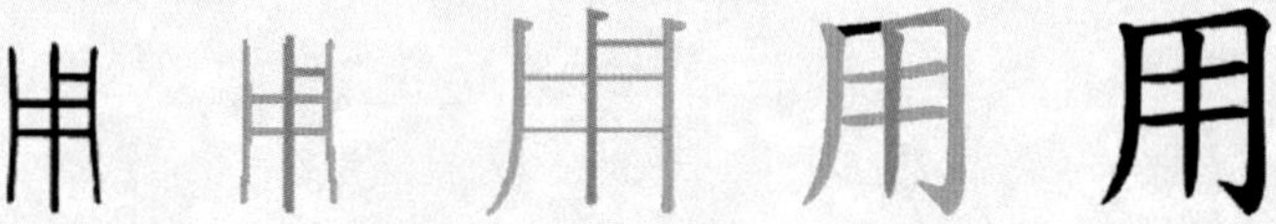

/ㄩㄥˋ, yong⁴/　　"useful", "to use"

**Associative Compound** (會意) of

卜 (卜 /ㄅㄨˇ, bu³/ "to ask for divine guide on future plans") and

冂 (Pictograph of *turtle shell showing cracks* for *results of divine guide*)

to imply *results of divine guide useful* or *using results of divine guide*,

hence *"useful", "to use"*.

卜 ＋ 冂 ≡ 用 用

Standard Form has 用 written as 用, hence 用 in lieu of 用.

用 用 → 用 用

用 用 → 用 用

The story of *results of divine guide useful* as told through time by the character 用 is shown below.

| Bone | Bronze | Seal | Standard |
|---|---|---|---|

It is interesting to note that the Associative Compound 甭 (/ㄅㄥˊ, beng[2]/) of

不 (//ㄅㄨˊ, bu[2]// "not") and

用 (/ㄩㄥˋ, yong[4]/ "to need", *also providing sound*)

with the Conjoint Pronunciation of 不 and 用 means exactly what 不用 suggest, "*not to need*". The Usage Rank of 甭 is #3,723.

不 + 用 ≡ 甭　甭

## The Stroke Sequence

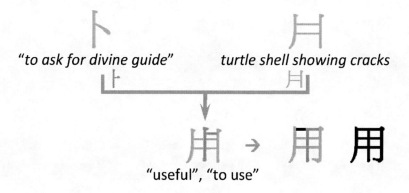

## The Anatomy

卜

"*to ask for divine guide*"

片

*turtle shell showing cracks*

卜　　　片

↓

甯 → 用　用

"useful", "to use"

## The Trinity – Sound(s), Semantics, and Synopses

/ㄩㄥˋ, yong[4]/

useful　　　　　　　　　　　有用, 沒用;

| | |
|---|---|
| to use, to put in use | 使用, 利用, 運用, 應用; |
| using, with | 用手蒙住眼睛, 用腳踩住; |
| use, usage | 沒用, 無用, 用途, 備用; |
| to employ, to commission | 用人不當, 知人善用,<br>用人不疑，疑人不用; |
| to apply | 用心, 用力, 用功, 用料; |
| to have (*food or drink*) | 用餐[饍], 用茶; |
| to need to | 不用急, 不用來了; |
| purpose, effect | 效用, 功用, 作用; |
| expense | 家用, 費用, 省吃儉用; |
| *in classical Chinese*, | |
|     effect | 「禮之用，和爲[為]貴。」; |
|     expense | 「道千乘之國，敬事而信，<br>  節用而愛人，使民以時。」; |
|     implement, tool | 「司空除壇于籍，<br>  命農大夫咸戒農用。」; |
|     to give commission to | 「如有用我者，<br>  吾其爲[為]東周乎！」; |
|     to put in use | 「雖楚有材，晉實用之。」; |
|     to need to | 「生不用封萬戶侯，<br>  但願一識韓荊州。」; |
|     hence | 「吾志所向，一往無前，<br>  愈挫愈勇，再接再厲，<br>  用能鼓勵風潮，<br>  造成時勢。」, |

「又不能備其工，以至敗績，
　　用而無所成也。」；

*surname*　　　　　　　　　　　姓氏

**Radical:** 用 (itself); originally 卜.

# 25. 們

**Script Evolution**

們 伊門 們 們

**The Story**

們 們 們 們

/ㄇㄣˋ, men⁴/                    "plump look of a person"

/˙ㄇㄣ, men⁵/  [ㄇㄣˊ, men²]   *for pluralization* (of pronouns and nouns)

**Associative Compound** (會意) of

人 (亻/ㄖㄣˊ, ren²/ "person") and

門 (/ㄇㄣˊ, men²/ "gate" referring to *unusual large size*,

                 *also providing sound*)

to imply *the large size of a person* or *plump look of a person*,

hence "*plump look of a person*".

亻 + 門 ≡ 們 們

們 is a relatively new character and did not exist at time of the Seal Script (thus in grey colour as shown above).  Later, for the same sound (/˙ㄇㄣ, men⁵/ [ㄇㄣˊ, men²]) the character was used after pronouns and nouns to change them to plural forms.  It is this sound/semantics (usage) combination that easily propelled the character 們 to a top place in the Usage Rank.  It is interesting to note that before settling on 們, others like 懣, 滿, 瞞, 門, and 每 were used to serve this pluralization purpose. This process of character creation, or re-creation rather, is called Semantic Bifurcation (假借).

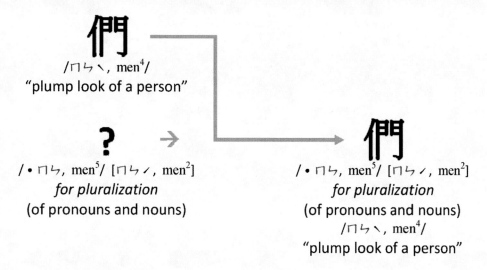

們
/ㄇㄣˋ, men⁴/
"plump look of a person"

? → 們

/‧ㄇㄣ, men⁵/ [ㄇㄣˊ, men²]
*for pluralization*
(of pronouns and nouns)

/‧ㄇㄣ, men⁵/ [ㄇㄣˊ, men²]
*for pluralization*
(of pronouns and nouns)
/ㄇㄣˋ, men⁴/
"plump look of a person"

## The Stroke Sequence

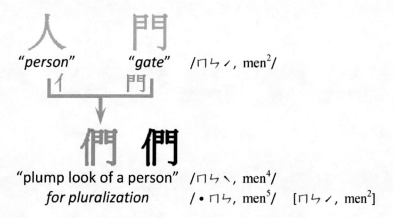

## The Anatomy

人 門
"*person*" "*gate*" /ㄇㄣˊ, men²/
亻 門
↓
們 們

"plump look of a person" /ㄇㄣˋ, men⁴/
*for pluralization* /‧ㄇㄣ, men⁵/ [ㄇㄣˊ, men²]

# The Trinity – Sound(s), Semantics, and Synopses

/ˑㄇㄣ, men[5]/    Recital Sound [ㄇㄣˊ, men[2]]

*pluralization of pronouns*    我**們**, 你[妳]**們**, 他[她]**們**;

*pluralization of nouns*    兄弟**們**, 姊[姐]妹**們**, 父母**們**,

　　　　　　　　　　　　朋友**們**, 哥**們**兒

/ㄇㄣˊ, men[2]/

*part of a river name*    圖**們**江

/ㄇㄣˋ, men[4]/

*in classical Chinese,*

　　*plump look of a person*    **們**渾

**Radical:** 人 (亻).

# 26. 生

## Script Evolution

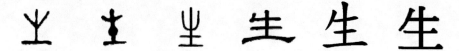

## The Story

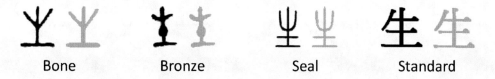

/ㄕㄥ, sheng/ "to grow"

**Pictograph** (象形) of *a plant developing out of soil*,
hence "*to develop*", "*to grow*".

The pictures of *a plant developing out of soil* as rendered through time by
the character 生 are shown below.

| Bone | Bronze | Seal | Standard |
|------|--------|------|----------|

## The Stroke Sequence

# The Trinity – Sound(s), Semantics, and Synopses

/ㄕㄥ, sheng/

| | |
|---|---|
| to develop, to be born, to come out | 出生, 發生, 產生, 面由心生; |
| to grow, to develop into | 生長, 生就, 生成, 生得高大, 生得一副好嗓子; |
| to produce, to generate | 生利, 不事生產, 心生一計, 惹事生非; |
| to give birth to | 生產, 生育, 生殖, 生孩子; |
| birth | 生肖; |
| to become | 生病, 生氣; |
| developed | 生性; |
| to live | 生活, 生存, 求生; |
| living | 生計, 謀生; |
| life | 人生, 殺生, 生命; |
| alive | 生命, 生動, 活生生, 生氣昂然; |
| extremely | 生怕, 生恐; |
| forcefully, brutally | 硬生生, 生拉硬扯; |
| not cooked, raw | 生水, 生肉, 生菜, 魚生, 生魚片(兒); |
| without cooking | 生吞; |
| not processed | 生鐵; |
| unfamiliar, strange | 漠生, 生人, 生硬; |
| novice, inexperienced | 生手; |
| student | 學生, 門生, 師生; |

| | |
|---|---|
| address (title) for educated person | 書生, 儒生; |
| male characters in Chinese Opera | 小生, 老生, 武生, 生旦淨末丑; |
| *in classical Chinese,* | |
| extremely | 「不喜秦淮水, |
| | 生憎江上船。」; |
| *void character for tone change* | 「況我看見你不喜我這 |
| | 煩劇的事，怎生是好？」; |
| surname | 姓氏 |

**Radical:** 生 (itself).

# 27. 到

**Script Evolution**

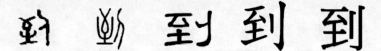

**The Story**

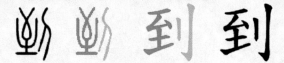

/ㄉㄠˋ, dao[4]/    "to arrive"

**Associative Compound** (會意) of

人 (/ㄖㄣˊ, ren[2]/ "person") and

至 (/ㄓˋ, zhi[4]/ "to come down to")

to imply *a person arriving*,

hence *"to arrive"*.

$$人 + 至 = 到\,\, 到$$

At time of the Seal Script, the Radical 人 was mistakenly written as 刀 (刂) owing to the close resemblance in their forms at the time, thus leading to the character form 到 that had been used since as the Standard.

$$到\,\, 到 \rightarrow 到\,\, 到$$

The story of *a person arriving* as told through time including the horribly embarrassing faux pas by the character 到 (到) is given below.

94

| Bronze | Seal | Standard |
|--------|------|----------|

Most dictionaries list the character 到 (/ㄉㄠˋ, dao⁴/) as

**Semantic-Phonetic Compound** (形聲) of

至 (/ㄓˋ, zhi⁴/ "to come down to") *for semantics* and

刀 (刂 /ㄉㄠ, dao/ "knife") *for sound*

to mean *"to arrive"*.

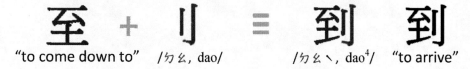

至    +    刂    =    到    到

"to come down to"    /ㄉㄠ, dao/    /ㄉㄠˋ, dao⁴/    "to arrive"

## The Stroke Sequence

## The Anatomy

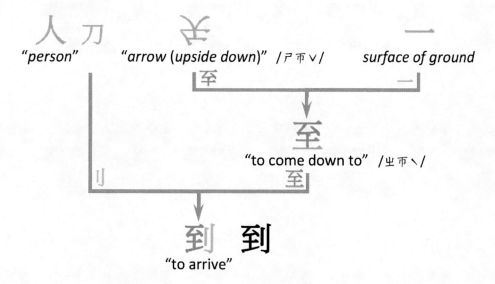

人    刀           一

"person"    "arrow (upside down)" /ㄕㄞˇ/    *surface of ground*

至

一

至

"to come down to" /ㄓㄞˋ/

刂      至

到    到

"to arrive"

# The Trinity – Sound(s), Semantics, and Synopses

/ㄉㄠˋ, dao⁴/

| | |
|---|---|
| to arrive | 遲**到**, 火車**到**站了; |
| to come | 時間**到**了; |
| to reach | **到**期, **到**底, **到**此, <br> **到**頭(兒), **到**頭來; |
| to go to (*place*) [=上] | **到**[上]那(兒)去？, <br> 明(兒)**到**[上]你家拜訪; |
| to have acquired | **到**手; |

*after verb (w/ or w/o 不) to indicate*

| | |
|---|---|
| success, extension | 看**到**, 顧**到**, 說**到**, 聽**到**, 搆不**到**, <br> 做不**到**, 想不**到**; |
| thorough, complete | 周**到**, **到**家, **到**處, <br> 若有不**到**之處， <br>   尚[尚]請多多包涵; |

*in classical Chinese,*

| | |
|---|---|
| to come to | 「人生**到**此，天道寧論。」; |
| covering all, complete | 「所奏懇**到**，形于翰墨， <br>   執省未究，以悲以懼。」, <br> 「君親自然，匪由名敎[教]， <br>   敬授既同，情禮兼**到**。」; |
| *surname* | 姓氏 |

**Radical:** 刀 ( 刂 ); originally 人.

# 28. 作

## Script Evolution

巨　么　爬　作　作　作

## The Story

爬　爬　作　作

/ㄗㄨㄛˋ, zuo⁴/　"to make (garment)", "to give rise to"

**Associative Compound** (會意) of

人 (亻 /ㄖㄣˊ, ren²/ "person") and

乍 ([ㄗㄨㄛˋ, zuo⁴] originally "to make garment", *also providing sound*)

to imply *person making garment*,

hence "*to make (garment)*", "*to give rise to*".

亻　+　乍　=　作　作

It is important to note that the Semantic-Phonetic Component 乍 is the Original (本字) of 作. In other words, 作 is the re-created character from its Original 乍, Pictograph (象形) of *edge of a garment's lapel being worked on*, hence "*to make (garment)*". Later, for the same sound (/ㄓㄚˋ, zha⁴/) 乍 started to carry the semantics of "*suddenly*" surrendering its original semantics to the character 作. This process of character creation, or re-creation rather, is called Semantic Bifurcation (假借).

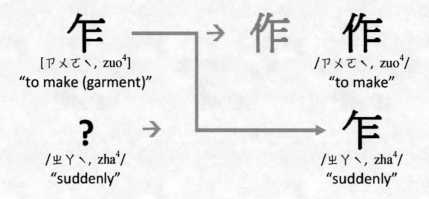

乍 [ㄗㄨㄛˋ, zuo⁴] "to make (garment)"

作 /ㄗㄨㄛˋ, zuo⁴/ "to make"

? /ㄓㄚˋ, zha⁴/ "suddenly"

乍 /ㄓㄚˋ, zha⁴/ "suddenly"

It is interesting to note that at time of the Bone Script and Bronze Script depiction of *edge of garment's lapel* was quite realistic. The story of *garment being made* as told through time by the character 作 is shown below.

Bone          Bronze          Seal          Standard

## The Stroke Sequence

作作作作作作作
作作作作作作作

## The Anatomy

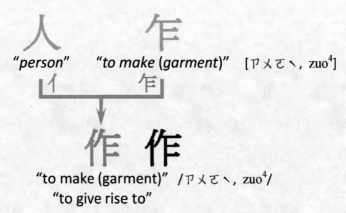

人 "person"   乍 "to make (garment)"   [ㄗㄨㄛˋ, zuo⁴]

亻   乍

作 作
"to make (garment)"   /ㄗㄨㄛˋ, zuo⁴/
"to give rise to"

98

# The Trinity – Sound(s), Semantics, and Synopses

/ㄗㄨㄛˋ, zuo⁴/

| | |
|---|---|
| to make | 作亂, 作惡, 作怪, 作樂, 作假, 作對, 作梗, 作(甚麼)用; |
| to create | 寫作, 作畫, 作文, 天作之合, 小題大作; |
| to give rise to, to excite | 興風作浪, 一鼓作氣; |
| to have | 作嘔, 作夢; |
| to conduct | 作戰, 作弊, 作簡報; |
| to pretend | 裝腔作勢, 裝模作樣; |
| to take on (*work*) | 作媒, 作證, 作業; |
| to be | 作人, 作官, 作客, 作古; |
| to set, to render | 作價, 作廢; |
| as | 當作, 看作, 認賊作父; |
| work, craft, accomplishment | 工作, 傑作, 佳作, 名作, 大作, 作業, 作品, 作物, 作家; |

*in classical Chinese*,

| | |
|---|---|
| to arise | 「雲從龍，風從虎，聖人作而萬物睹。」; |
| to cultivate | 「亦惟助王宅天命，作新民。」; |
| to create | 「述而不作，信而好古。」; |
| to make | 「苦恨年年壓金線，爲[為]他人作嫁衣裳。」; |

deed, enterprise

「毋以小謀敗大作，

毋以嬖御人疾莊后。」；

/ㄗㄨㄛ, zuo/

to form 作揖；

to inflict, to provoke 作弄, 自作自受；

craftsman 木作, 石作, 瓦作；

crafts workshop 作坊；

*in classical Chinese,*

crafts workshop 「禮徑至作所。不復重奏，

稱詔罷民，

帝奇其意而不責也。」

/ㄗㄨㄛˋ, zuo$^2$/

to do (ponder) carefully 作摩 (/‧ㄇㄛ, mo$^5$/)；

to make better, to enhance 作料

**Radical:** 人 (亻).

100

# 29. 出

## Script Evolution

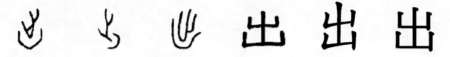

## The Story

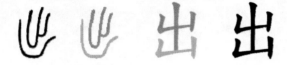

/彳ㄨ, chu/    "to come out"

**Associative Compound** (會意) of

止 (屮 屮 /ㄓ∨, zhi[3]/ "foot") and

凵 (Pictograph of *a den*)

to imply *foot leaving the den*,

hence *"to come out"*.

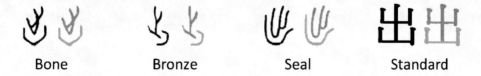

The story of *foot leaving the den* as told through time by the character 出 is shown below.

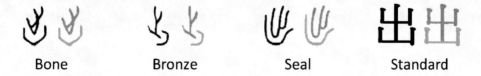

| Bone | Bronze | Seal | Standard |

101

## The Stroke Sequence

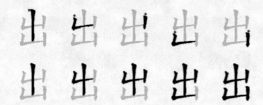

## The Anatomy

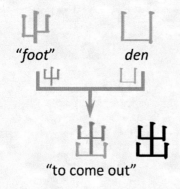

"foot"　　den

出　出
"to come out"

## The Trinity – Sound(s), Semantics, and Synopses

/ㄔㄨ, chu/

| | |
|---|---|
| to come out | 出生, 出世, 出土, 水落石出, 出水芙蓉; |
| to go out, to exit, to get out | 出門, 出口, 出關, 出國, 出差, 出勤, 出去, 出來, 進出, 出入*; |
| source, origin | 出處, 出身; |
| to give out, to send out | 出錢, 出力, 出兵, 出張嘴; |
| to emit, to result (in) | 出汗, 出水, (看得)出神, 出錯, 出疹子, 出亂子; |
| to leave, to depart | 出走, 出發, 出家, 出嫁; |

*: 『出入』 also means "different", "not the same".

| | |
|---|---|
| to flee | 出奔, 出逃; |
| to use, to start | 出口(傷人), 出手(傷人); |
| to utter | 出言不遜; |
| to generate | 出題(目), 出個主意; |
| to pay, to spend | 出納, 支出, 出手大方; |
| to let out | 出氣; |
| to show, to appear | 出席, 出場, 出沒; |
| to bring out | 出示, 出產, 出品; |
| to publish, to release | 出書, 出片; |
| to stand out | 出眾, 出色, 出挑, 出人頭地, 出類拔萃; |
| to exceed | 出人意料, 出神入化; |
| exceedingly | 出奇; |
| *after verb indicating result to mean* out | 看出, 點出, 指出, 釋出, 放出, 拿出, 給出, 說出, 擠出, 做出; |
| *after verb in* 不出(來) *to mean* cannot *verb* out | 看不出(來), 指不出(來), 放不出(來), 說不出(話)(來); |
| *with* 息 *to mean* potential *or* hope for greatness | (沒)有出息 (/•ㄒㄧ, xi⁵/); |
| *used with* 入 *to mean* different | 他前後的話有出入; |
| *in classical Chinese,* to come out | 「出其東門，有女如雲。」; |

| | |
|---|---|
| to leave | 「既醉而**出**，並受其福； 醉而不**出**，是謂伐德。」； |
| to take commission of office | 「君子之道，或**出**或處。」； |
| to be noticeable | 「至言不**出**，俗言勝也。」； |
| to stand out and exceed | 「古之聖人， 其**出**人也遠矣。」； |
| outside | 「入則無法家拂士， **出**則無敵國外患者， 國恆亡。」 |

**Radical:** 凵 (/ㄎㄢˇ, kan[3]/ "open mouth"), the last 2 Strokes; originally 止.

# 30. 就

## Script Evolution

## The Story

/ㄐㄧㄡˋ, jiu⁴/    "to accommodate"

**Associative Compound** (會意) of

京 (帛 /ㄐㄧㄥ, jing/ "man-made high place") and

尤 (/ㄧㄡˊ, you²/ "exception" referring to adapting,

*also providing sound*)

to imply *adapting to high place*,

hence *"to accommodate"*.

京 + 尤 ≡ 就 就

It is important to note that at time of the Bronze Script the character told the story of *tall structure* (帛) *finished by hand* (⺈) for the semantics of "to accomplish". At time of the Seal Script the character told the story of *adapting* (⻊) *to high place* (帛) for the semantics of "to accommodate", thus leading to the Standard Script. The stories of *tall structure finished by hand* and *adapting to high place* as told through time by the character 就 are shown below.

| Bronze | Seal | Standard |
|--------|------|----------|

## The Stroke Sequence

就 就 就 就 就 就 就 就 就
就 就 就 就 就 就 就 就 就 就
就 就

就 就

## The Anatomy

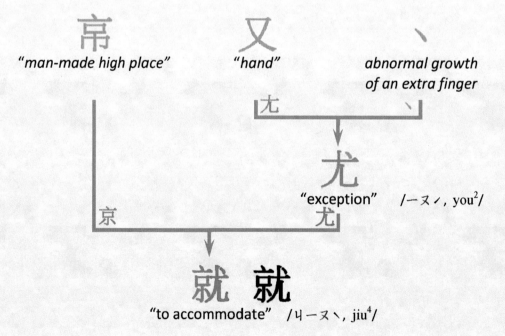

帝
"man-made high place"

又
"hand"

、
abnormal growth of an extra finger

尤

尤
"exception"  /一ㄡˊ, you²/

京

尤

就 就
"to accommodate"  /ㄐㄧㄡˋ, jiu⁴/

106

# The Trinity – Sound(s), Semantics, and Synopses

/ㄐㄧㄡˋ, jiu⁴/

to accommodate, to go along      遷**就**, 將**就**, 半推半**就**,
高不成低不**就**;

to adopt, to accept      避重**就**輕, 因陋**就**簡;

to submit (oneself) to      **就**範, 慷慨**就**義;

to adjust      身子請往前**就**一**就**;

to assume, to undertake      **就**位, **就**職, **就**業;

to attend      **就**學, **就**讀;

accomplished, accomplishment      成**就**, 功成名**就**, 造**就**人才;

to eat (one food) together with
    (another food);      這菜最好是**就**著饅頭吃;

close to      不明**就**裏[裡];

soon      去去**就**來, 他**就**要到了,
待會(兒)**就**知道了;

already      會議早**就**結束了,
一個鐘頭前，我**就**來了;

subsequently      遇到紅燈，**就**得停下來,
一上車，**就**睡著了,
你不同意，那**就**算了;

even (if)      **就**算如此，也得從長計議,
你**就**(是)不說，我也知道,
**就**(是)再多幾天，我也做不完;

just, simply      你**就**直說吧, 我**就**不明白了,
我**就**不信我做不來;

| | |
|---|---|
| only | 就值這些錢, 就剩下這一個了; |
| exactly | 這就對了, 就這樣吧, 就今天吧, |
| | 就這幾天了, 那(兒)就是他家, |
| | 你就這麼傻去相信他; |
| based on, according to | 就事論事, 就商言商, 就[=依]我看; |
| from, by, via | 就近照顧, 就此打住, 駕輕就熟*; |

\*:『駕輕就熟』 *driving a light carriage on (via) a familiar route*
　　　　to mean *"experience makes tasks easy"*.

*in classical Chinese,*

| | |
|---|---|
| to accomplish | 「縱橫計不就, |
| | 　慷慨志猶存。」; |
| to undertake | 「科舉不第,棄文就武。」; |
| to near | 「待到重陽日, |
| | 　還來就菊花。」; |
| to follow | 「是以一皆因就, |
| | 　不敢有所改易。」; |
| using to one's advantage | 「武松把半截棒丟在一邊, |
| | 　兩隻手就勢把大蟲 |
| | 　頂花皮肐瘩地揪住。」; |
| amongst | 「千歌百舞不可數, |
| | 　就中最愛霓裳舞。」; |
| even | 「若是不進學,就到八十歲, |
| | 　也還稱小友。」 |

**Radical:** 尤 (/ㄨㄤ, wang/ "lame foot, crippled leg"), the first 3 Strokes of 尤;
　　originally 京.

# 31. 分

## Script Evolution

## The Story

/ㄈㄣ, feng/    "to divide", "to separate apart"

**Associative Compound** (會意) of

八 (/ㄅㄚ, ba/ "eight", "to divide") and

刀 (/ㄉㄠ, dao/ "knife")

to imply *dividing with a knife*,

hence *"to divide"*, *"to separate apart"*.

八 + 刀 ≡ 分 分

<u>**Note**</u>: 八 ("eight") always carries the notion of dividing, as 8 is the largest
initial number (1 ~ 10) to evenly divide continuously, that is
$8/2 = 4$, $4/2 = 2$, $2/2 = 1$.

The story of *dividing with a knife* as told through time by the character 分
is shown below.

| Bone | Bronze | Seal | Standard |
|------|--------|------|----------|

## The Stroke Sequence

## The Anatomy

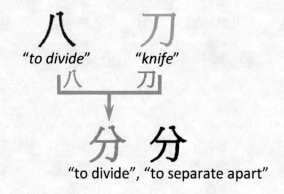

八      刀

*"to divide"*      *"knife"*

分 分

"to divide", "to separate apart"

## The Trinity – Sound(s), Semantics, and Synopses

/ㄈㄣ, feng/

| | |
|---|---|
| to divide, to separate apart | 分家, 劃分, 分手, 分離, 分身乏術; |
| separated | 分久必合; |
| to give portion of | 分給他人; |
| to share | 分享, 分擔, 分憂解勞; |
| to distinguish | 分別, 分辨, 不分男女, 不分青紅皂白; |
| branch, division | 分枝, 分局, 分隊; |
| distinction | 人獸之分; |
| points, score | 分數, 滿分; |

110

| | |
|---|---|
| difference | 是非分明; |
| degree | 一分努力，一分收穫; |
| *math*, fraction | 二分之一, 分子, 分母; |
| *physics*, molecule | 分子; |
| *time unit* minute (1/60 hour) | 時間一分一秒地過去; |
| *weight unit* ( = 0.3125 grammes) | 幾兩幾分; |
| *land unit* 1/10 acre | 一畝三分地; |
| *monetary unit* cent | 一角五分; |
| *angle unit*, minute (1/60 degree) | 三十六度二十分; |
| *in classical Chinese*, | |
| to separate | 「逝者如流水， 哀此遂離分。」; |
| to give portion of | 「衣食所安，弗敢專也， 必以分人。」; |
| to share | 「起與士卒分勞苦。」; |
| to differentiate | 「是非之經，不可不分。」; |
| clear | 「妾身未分明， 何以拜姑嫜？」; |
| difference | 「是君子、小人之分也。」 |

/ㄈㄣˋ, feng[4]/

| | |
|---|---|
| capacity of one's duty, power, and responsibilities | 身分, 本分, 過分; |
| friendship, relationship | 緣分, 情分; |
| ingredient, part | 成分, 糖分, 養分, 分量; |

111

| | |
|---|---|
| share | 部分[份], 等分[份]; |
| individual in a group, member | 一分子, 知識分子, 恐怖分子; |
| *in classical Chinese,* | |
|     capacity of one's duty, power, | |
|     and responsibilities | 「男有分，女有歸。」; |
|     relationship | 「恩愛苟不虧， |
| |    在遠分日親。」 |

**Radical:** 刀; originally 八.

# 32. 於

## Script Evolution

## The Story

/ㄨ, wu/　　　*onomatopoeia for sighs*

/ㄩˊ, yu²/　　*void character, conj., prep.*

**Pictograph** (象形) of *a flying crow*.

This is the soaring version of 烏 (/ㄨ, wu/ "crow"). Both 烏 and 於 were used as onomatopoeia for sighs, like 烏乎 [嗚呼] and 於戲. Later, 於 started to be used as a *void character* (in classical Chinese), then extended its use as *conjunctive* as well as *preposition*.

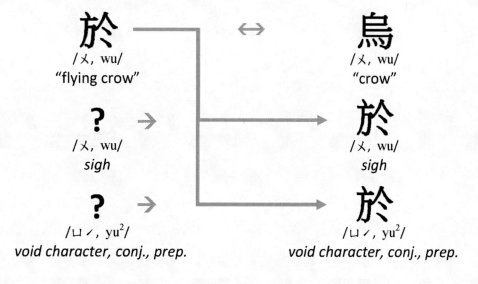

113

This process of character creation, or re-creation rather, is called Semantic Bifurcation (假借).

The pictures of *a flying crow* as rendered through time by the character 於 are shown below.

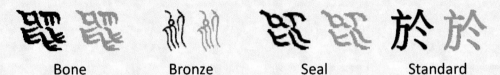

Bone          Bronze          Seal          Standard

## The Stroke Sequence

於 於 於 於 於 於 於 於
於 於 於 於 於 於 於 於

## The Trinity – Sound(s), Semantics, and Synopses

/ㄩˊ, yu$^2$/

| | |
|---|---|
| at, in (*time*) | 生於某年, 於此同時, 於此關頭; |
| at, in (*place*) | 行走於地, 將收藏安置於地窖, 生於斯，長於斯; |
| in (*work, endeavour, enterprise*) | 勤於學業, 工於心計, 忙於國政, 長於醫術, 善於烹飪; |
| with | 於你無關; |
| for | 於事無補, 無濟於事, 於心不忍, 於公於私, 於情於理; |
| to (*place*) | 流落於此, 奔走於此; |
| to, by (*after verb*) | 敗於敵手; |

| | |
|---|---|
| from | 有別**於**此, 異**於**常人, 取之**於**民; |
| on | 用之**於**民; |
| as such | 至**於***, 不至**於**; |
| *used with* 是 *to mean* then | **於**是; |
| *used with* 是乎 *to mean* whereupon | **於**是乎; |
| *after adj. to emphasize* | |
|    *words that follow* | 過**於**保守, 敢**於**承擔, 勇**於**認錯; |
|    *result of comparison* | 一加一等**於**二, 五加一大**於**五, 身高低**於**標準, 事實勝**於**雄辯, 齊心協力勝**於**單打獨鬥; |

*: 『至**於**』 *followed by* <u>phrase</u> *means* "as far as <u>phrase</u> goes".
    For instance,「至**於**工程進度，一切按照原定計畫。」.

*in classical Chinese,*

| | |
|---|---|
| to, onto | 「己所不欲，勿施**於**人。」; |
| from | 「子禽問**於**子貢。」; |
| for | 「始吾**於**人也，<br>    聽其言而觀其行。」; |
| till | 「自吾氏三世居是鄉[鄉]，<br>    積**於**今六十歲矣。」; |
| at | 「千里之行，始**於**足下。」; |
| by | 「郤克傷**於**矢，流血及屨。」; |
| to rely on | 「廣情故，心相**於**。」，<br>「便欲去隨爲[為]弟子，<br>    片雲孤鶴可相**於**。」; |

| | |
|---|---|
| for sake of | 「齊使管仲平戎**於**周。」; |
| than (*after adj. for comparative*) | 「苛政猛**於**虎也。」, |
| | 「噫吁戲危乎高哉, |
| | 　蜀道之難、難**於**上青天。」; |
| as compared with | 「今趙之與秦, |
| | 　猶齊之**於**魯也。」, |
| | 「況將軍之**於**主上, |
| | 　主上之與將軍哉!」; |
| from | 「吾黨之直者異**於**是, |
| | 　父爲[為]子隱, |
| | 　子爲[為]父隱, |
| | 　直在其中矣。」, |
| | 「而人之未達也, |
| | 　無以異**於**眇。」; |
| *void character (start of sentence)* | 「**於**惟餘眈,飢傷喘呼。」; |
| *surname* | 姓氏 |

/ㄨ, wu/

*in classical Chinese,*

| | |
|---|---|
| crow [=烏] | 「徂彼西土,爰居其野。 |
| | 　虎豹爲[為]羣[群], |
| | 　**於**鵲與處。」; |
| *aux. word for sigh or applause* | 「**於**穆清廟,肅雝顯相。」; |
| *used with* 戲 *to mean* alas | **於**戲 [=烏乎, 嗚呼] |

**Radical:** 方 (/ㄈㄤ, fang/ "square"); originally 於 (itself).

# 33. 對

**Script Evolution**

**The Story**

/ㄉㄨㄟˋ, duì⁴/    "to face towards", "to treat"

**Associative Compound** (會意) of

寸 (/ㄘㄨㄣˋ, cun⁴/ "to handle carefully") and

丵 (Pictograph of *a ceremonial implement*)

to imply *carefully holding a ceremonial implement to face towards divinity*, hence *"to face towards", "to treat"*.

寸 + 丵 ≡ 對   對

It is important to note that at time of the Bone Script the character told the story of *hand* ( 彐 ) *holding a ceremonial implement* ( 丵 ) because the character 寸 was not created then.   The story of *carefully holding a ceremonial implement to face towards divinity* as told through time by the character 對 is shown below.

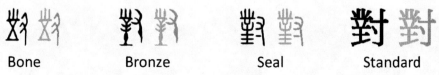

Bone       Bronze       Seal       Standard

Most dictionaries list the character 對 as

**Associative Compound** (會意) of

業 (/ㄓㄨㄛˊ, zhuo² / "scrubby tuft of grass" alluding to *mess, situation*),

士 (/ㄕˋ, shi⁴ / "responsible man") to hint phonetically

事 (/ㄕˋ, shi⁴ / "fact"), and

寸 (/ㄘㄨㄣˋ, cun⁴ / "small measurement", "to handle")

to imply *handling situations by facts responsibly and methodically*,

hence "*to respond properly*".

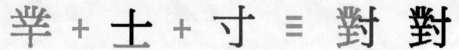

**Note**: At time of the Clerical Script, 士 was reduced to just a single

horizontal Stroke 一, thus leading to the Standard Script.

At time of the Seal Script, the Variant form 對 that renders the base of the

*ceremonial implement* with a rectangle resembling 囗, the character for

"*mouth*", thus resulting the Variant form 對 in the Standard Script.

| Bone | Bronze | Seal | Standard |

The nonchalant rendition had fooled even the editors of the benchmark 康熙

(/ㄎㄤ ㄒㄧ, kang xi/) Dictionary to classify 對 as a 3-component Compound.

**Associative Compound** (會意) of

業 (/ㄓㄨㄛˊ, zhuo² / "scrubby tuft of grass" alluding to *mess*),

囗 (/ㄎㄡˇ, kou³ / "mouth" referring to *spoken words*), and

寸 (/ㄘㄨㄣˋ, cun⁴ / "small measurement", "to handle")

to imply *using spoken words to deal with situations as the method*, hence *"to respond without real interest"*.

This exemplifies the importance of analysing all the scripts of a character.

## The Stroke Sequence

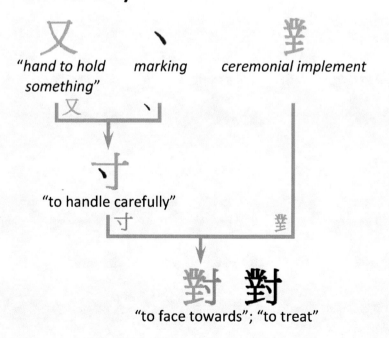

## The Anatomy

又
*"hand to hold something"*

、
*marking*

丵
*ceremonial implement*

寸
*"to handle carefully"*

對 對
*"to face towards"; "to treat"*

119

# The Trinity – Sound(s), Semantics, and Synopses

/ㄉㄨㄟˋ, dui⁴/

| | |
|---|---|
| to face towards | 面**對**面; |
| to treat | **對**人誠懇, **對**不住[起]; |
| to confront | **對**峙, **對**壘, **對**陣; |
| to respond | 應**對**; 無言以**對**; |
| responding (*with spoken words*) | **對**話, **對**答; |
| to correspond | **對**應; |
| corresponding | **對**策; |
| to deal with focus | **對**付; |
| to focus on | **對**症下藥, **對**事不**對**人; |
| to aim at | **對**準目標, **對**空鳴槍; |
| to match | **對**獎, **對**勁(兒), **對對**子; |
| to mix one thing into a nother | 太燙，可**對**[兌]些冷水; |
| to join two objects together | **對對**子, 請把門**對**上; |
| matching pair of people or things | **對**筆, **對**錶, **對**聯, **對**象, **對對**子, 雙雙**對對**, 成雙成**對**; |
| pair | 一**對**兒女, 兩**對**夫妻; |
| proper, correct | **對**不**對**？, 答**對**了, 人數不**對**, 門當戶**對**; |
| opposite (of direction) | **對**面, **對**岸, **對**門, **對**街; |
| opposing | **對**方, **對**手; |
| to check and correct | 校**對**, 核**對**; |
| to calibrate, to adjust | **對**好焦距，按下快門; |

| | |
|---|---|
| to synchronize | 對錶; |
| *used with* 作 *to mean* | |
|     to make metching poems | 吟詩作對; |
|     to be an opponent | 別跟我作對; |
| *used with* 做 *to mean* | |
|     to be in pair | 成雙做對, 參賽者做對廝殺; |
|     to answer correctly | 這道題祇有他做對了; |
|     to handle correctly | 這事要做對了，其他才有希望; |
| one to one | 對談, 對打, 對練, 對飲; |
| together in unison | 對唱; |
| in exchange | 對流; |
| mutually | 對等; |
| towards | 不知對他該說什麼; |
| to | 面對面, 一對一; |
| with | 他對飲食非常講究; |
| *in classical Chinese,* | |
|     facing, towards | 「對酒當歌，人生幾何？」; |
|     to reply to higher authority | 「公問之。對曰： |
| | 『小人有母， |
| | 皆嘗小人之食矣， |
| | 未嘗君之羹。』」 |

**Radical:** 寸.

# 34. 成

**Script Evolution**

成 成 成 成 成 成

**The Story**

成 成 成 成

/彳ㄥˊ, cheng² / "accomplished"

**Associative Compound** (會意) of

戌 (戌 /ㄒㄩ, xu/ Pictograph of *a big hammer*) and

丁 (/ㄉㄧㄥ, ding/ "nail", *also providing sound*)

to imply *hammer on the nail for something done*,

hence "*accomplished*".

戌 + 丁 ≡ 成 成

It is worth noting that the *hammer* ( 成 ) ( 成 ) and *nail* ( I ) ( I ) are obvious in the Bone Script and Bronze Script. At time of the Seal Script, the *hammer* ( 成 ) was written without the short horizontal Stroke ( 成 ) to leave room for the *nail* ( ↑ ), leading to the Standard Script. The story of *hammer on the nail for something done* as told through time by the character 成 is shown below.

| Bone | Bronze | Seal | Standard |

122

It is important to note that the character 戌 without its short horizontal Stroke looks identical to the Standard character 戊 (/ㄨㄟˋ, e wu⁴/ *a long-handled weapon*, "5ᵗʰ of the 10 heavenly symbols for recording time", "good day to start outdoor activities") as shown below.

| Bone | Bronze | Seal | Standard |

Of course, this confusion would result a complete change of the character's story if the *hammer* (戌) was replaced by the *long-handled weapon* (戊) thus removing the theatricals of the *hammer* and *nail*. Could this be the intention of 李斯 (/ㄌㄧˇ ㄙ, li³ si/ 280–208 BCE), the man crafting the Seal Script to unify all Chinese characters' writing scripts and forms as decreed by China's first Emperor 秦始皇 (/ㄑㄧㄣˊ ㄕˇ ㄏㄨㄤˊ, qin² shi³ huang²/ 259–210 BCE) of the Chin (秦 221–206 BCE) Dynasty? Unfortunately, no one knew exactly what the man really had in his mind. After some 300 years, a devoted scholar 許慎 (/ㄒㄩˇ ㄕㄣˋ, xu³ shen⁴/ c. 58 – c. 147 CE) of the East Han (東漢 25–220 CE) Dynasty would come along with the unprecedented scientific analyses and classifications of the Chinese characters in his monumental work 說文解字 (/ㄕㄨㄛ ㄨㄣˊ ㄐㄧㄝˇ ㄗˋ, shuo wen² jie³ zi⁴/ *"Explaining Pictographs and Analysing Compound Characters"*), the first Chinese dictionary and also the first dictionary of mankind. This first dictionary, which took 22 years to complete and used 133,441 characters to list a colossal 9,353 uniquely different characters arranged in 540 groups known as Radicals, and all those that followed for almost 2,000 years classified the character 成 (/ㄔㄥˊ, cheng²/) as

**Semantic-Phonetic Compound** (形聲) of

戌 (/ㄨㄟ, wu⁴/ "good day to start outdoor activities") *for semantics* and

丁 (/ㄉㄧㄥ, ding/ "nail") *for sound*

to mean *"accomplished"*.

戌 ＋ 丁 ≡ 成 成

"good day to start"  /ㄉㄧㄥ, ding/     /ㄔㄥˊ, cheng²/ "accomplished"

## The Stroke Sequence

成 成 成 成 成 成

成 成 成 成 成 成

**Note**: Calligraphists write the first 2 Strokes of 成 in a different sequence like

for all characters with the component 戌 or 戉 as shown below.

成 成 成 成 成 成

成 成 成 成 成 成

## The Anatomy

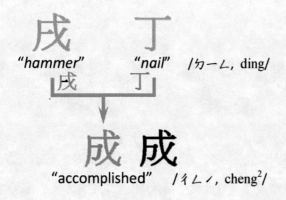

戉　　　丁

"hammer"　　　"nail"   /ㄉㄧㄥ, ding/

戉　　丁

↓

成 成

"accomplished"   /ㄔㄥˊ, cheng²/

124

# The Trinity – Sound(s), Semantics, and Synopses

/ㄔㄥˊ, cheng[2]/

| | |
|---|---|
| accomplished | 完成, 功成名就, 大功告成; |
| to accomplish, to succeed | 成交, 成功, 成事不足，敗事有餘; |
| full grown, fully developed | 成人, 成犬; |
| finished | 成品, 成果, 成藥; |
| allowed, acceptable | 成不成？; |
| to establish | 成就, 成家; |
| existing, established | 成規, 成語, 現成; |
| to become | 點石成金, 鐵杵磨成繡花針; |
| to reach, to be | 成千上萬, 成雙成對; |
| to aid, to facilitate | 成全, 玉成其事, 成人之美; |
| existing establishment | 守成; |
| one tenth | 九成把握; |
| entire, complete | 成天到晚; |
| forming an integral entity or body | 成分, 成員; |

*in classical Chinese*,

| | |
|---|---|
| existing establishment | 「帝王之業，<br>草創與守成孰難？」; |
| complete | 「不以字害其成句，<br>不以句累其全篇。」; |
| ancient land unit | 「有田一成，有眾一旅。」; |
| *surname* | 姓氏 |

**Radical:** 戈; originally 戍.

# 35. 會

**Script Evolution**

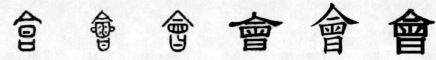

**The Story**

/ㄏㄨㄟˋ, hui⁴/   "to gather"

**Pictograph** (象形) of *a three-piece Chinese steamer for cooking* with

 *lid,*

⊞ *tray with holes at bottom to let steam in to steam food it holds*

*(the 3 vertical lines to indicate steam coming from bottom), and*

ㅂ *pot holding boiling water generating steam*

*that must be stacked together to work properly*

to imply *coming (putting) together for a single well-defined purpose,*

hence *"to gather (for a common goal)".*

In actual culinary practices, multiple trays are often stacked together at once of course. The pictures of *a three-piece steamer* as rendered through time by the character 會 are shown below.

Bone         Bronze         Seal         Standard

126

It is worth noting that the character 曾 (Usage Rank #634) is actually a Pictograph of *a hot steamer with lid removed* showing

><  *cloud of steam,*

⬤ *tray with holes at bottom to let steam in to steam food it holds*

      *(the 3 vertical lines to indicate steam coming from bottom),* and

⊌ *pot holding boiling water generating steam,*

referring to *the tray with holes used for steaming,*

hence *"steamer tray"* ([ㄗㄥˋ, zeng⁴]),

  *"tier"* (/ㄘㄥˊ, ceng²/) as a steamer usually has multiple *tiers* of trays,

   *"already"* (/ㄘㄥˊ, ceng²/) as the picture shows *steaming already done.*

It is important to note that at time of the Bone Script, the *steamer tray* was rendered with *steam* ( ) ( ) and *two tiered trays* ( ⊞ ). At time of the Bronze Script, the *steamer tray* was rendered with *steam* (⎪ ⎪), *two tiered trays* (⊕), together with *pot holding boiling water generating steam* ( ⌣ ) to make the idea of *steaming* clearer, thus leading to the Seal Script then Standard Script. The pictures of *a hot steamer with lid removed* as rendered through time by the character 曾 are shown below.

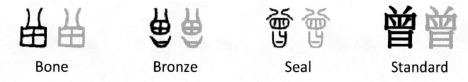

| Bone | Bronze | Seal | Standard |

Later, for the same sound (/ㄗㄥ, zeng/) and referring to the *hierarchy of steamer trays* the character 曾 started to carry the semantics of *"great (for ancestors of grandparents in family trees)"*, surrendering its original semantics of "tier", "layer" to the Associative Compound 層 (/ㄘㄥˊ, ceng²/ Usage Rank #467) with Radical 尸 (/ㄕ, shi/ "layout") and Semantic-Phonetic Component 曾 (/ㄘㄥˊ, ceng²/ "tier", "layer"),

尸 ＋ 曾 ＝ 層 **層**

and the semantics of *"steamer tray"* to the Associative Compound 甑 (/ㄗㄥˋ, zeng[4]/) with Radical 瓦 (ㄨㄚˇ, wa[3]/ "pottery") and Semantic-Phonetic Component 曾 ([ㄗㄥˋ, zeng[4]] "steamer tray").

瓦 ＋ 曾 ＝ 甑 **甑**

Today, the character 屜 (/ㄊㄧˋ, ti[4]/ "drawer") is used for *steamer trays*.

The diagram below shows how the Pictograph of *a hot steamer with lid removed* 曾 to carry the semantics of *"steamer tray"*, *"tier"*, *"already"* originally helped the creation of the Compound characters 甑 and 層.

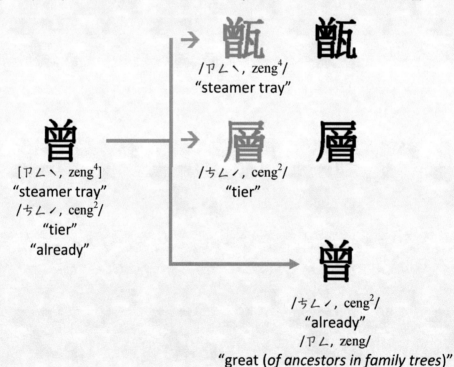

曾

[ㄗㄥˋ, zeng[4]]
"steamer tray"
/ㄘㄥˊ, ceng[2]/
"tier"
"already"

→ 甑 **甑**

/ㄗㄥˋ, zeng[4]/
"steamer tray"

→ 層 **層**

/ㄘㄥˊ, ceng[2]/
"tier"

曾

/ㄘㄥˊ, ceng[2]/
"already"
/ㄗㄥ, zeng/
"great (*of ancestors in family trees*)"

## The Stroke Sequence

## The Trinity – Sound(s), Semantics, and Synopses

/ㄏㄨㄟˋ, hui[4]/

| | |
|---|---|
| to gather | 會合; |
| gathering | 宴會, 晚會; |
| combined together to give | 會意字; |
| to meet | 會面, 會晤, 相會, 會一會; |
| meeting | 會議, 會商, 開會; |
| to understand, to comprehend | 意會, 體會, 心領神會; |
| to pay fund | 會帳, 會款; |
| professional society | 工程師協會, 教[教]師協會; |
| purpose-oriented organization | 工會, 農會, 同鄉[鄉]會; |
| metropolitan, municipal centre | 都會, 省會; |
| opportunity | 機會, 適逢其會, 風雲際會; |
| able, capable | 我會游泳, 會不會寫字？; |
| to be good at | 你眞[真]不會說話; |

| | |
|---|---|
| can | 他很**會**巴結奉承; |
| will | 他**會**來, 他不**會**這麼快來,<br>他**會**不**會**親自下廚?; |
| could it be | **會**是他嗎?, 怎麼**會**是他?,<br>**會**不**會**他還沒醒?; |
| private loan club | 標**會**, 合**會**, 互助**會**; |
| in classical Chinese, | |
| to join together | 「雷、夏既澤,<br>　　灘、沮**會**同。」; |
| to meet | 「宣言曰:<br>　『我見相如, 必辱之!』<br>　　相如聞, 不肯與**會**。」; |
| opportunity | 「是天賜我以報秦之**會**也。」; |
| to understand | 「危樓還望,<br>　　嘆此意、今古幾人曾**會**。」; |
| so happen to be at time of | 「**會**其怒, 不敢獻,<br>　　公爲[為]我獻之。」; |
| to pay bill | 「二人又吃了一回,<br>　　起身**會**鈔而別。」 |

/ㄏㄨㄟˇ, hui³/

| | |
|---|---|
| short moment | 一**會**(兒), 等**會**(兒); |
| in classical Chinese, | |
| particular moment | 「適來公子尚[尚]在懷中啼哭,<br>　　此一**會**不見動靜,<br>　　多是不能保也。」; |

130

tribulation, misfortune 「鄙猥小吏，原來上應星魁，
眾多弟兄；
也原來都是一**會**之人。
今者上天顯應，
合當聚義。」；

group 「今日夏德有采，
遭際這一**會**員外。」

/ㄎㄨㄞˋ, hui⁴/

accounting **會**計;

*surname* 姓氏

/ㄍㄨㄟˋ, gui⁴/

*place name* **會**稽

**Radical:** 曰 (/ㄩㄝ, yue/ "to utter"), the last 4 Strokes; originally 會 (itself).

# 36. 可

## Script Evolution

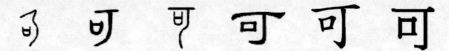

## The Story

[《さ, ge]     "to sing (with music)", "song"

/丂さˇ, ke³/   "to approve"

**Associative Compound** (會意) of

    口 (/丂ㄡˇ, kou³/ "mouth") and

    己 (/ㄏさ, he/ "type of wind instrument", *also providing sound*)

to imply *singing with music*,

hence *"to sing (with music)"*.

$$口 \ + \ 己 \ \equiv \ 可 \quad 可$$

**Note**: The MPS 『ㄜ』 and 『さ』 are based on the form and sound of 『己』.

Later, 可 started to carry the semantics of *"to approve"* for the same sound (/丂さˇ, ke³/) and the Associative Compound 哥 (/《さ, ge/) with two *singing mouths* (可可) was created for duet *"singing"*.

$$可 \ + \ 可 \ \equiv \ 哥 \quad 哥$$

Soon thereafter, 哥 started to carry the semantics of *"older brother"* for the same sound (/ㄍㄜ, ge/).   And *singing* was finally given to the Associative Compound 歌 (/ㄍㄜ, ge/) with Radical 欠 (/ㄑㄧㄢˋ, qian⁴/ "to blow air from mouth") and Semantic-Phonetic Component 哥 (/ㄍㄜ, ge/ "to sing").

欠 ＋ 哥 ≡ 歌　歌

The diagram below shows how 可 changed its identity whilst supporting the creation of two new characters 哥 and 歌. This process of character creation, or re-creation rather, is called Semantic Bifurcation (假借).

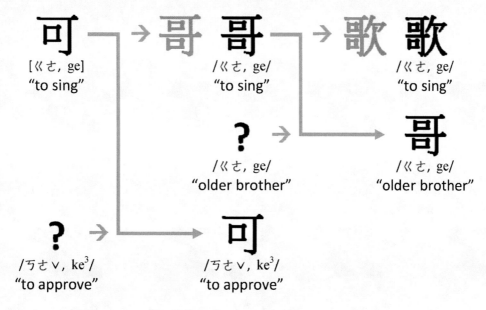

**Note**: For the semantics of "may not", and "cannot be",

The character form 可 (/ㄎㄜˇ, ke³/ "may", "can be") is flipped

to its L-R mirrored image (negated) as 叵 and given the Conjoint

Pronunciation (合音) of

不 (/ㄅㄨˋ, bu⁴/ "not", "no") and

可 (/ㄎㄜˇ, ke³/ "may", "can be")

as illustrated below.

133

/�541ㄜˇ, ke³/
"may", "can be"
"able"

/ㄆㄜˇ, po³/
"may not", "cannot be"
"unable"

It is interesting to see how the vertical curly Stroke (in brown colour) in the Seal Script became two totally different styles of Stroke in the Standard Script. This was done obviously for the convenience of right-handed handwriting as well as aesthetics. The Usage Rank of 叵 is #5,031.

The story of *singing with music* as told through time by the character 可 is shown below.

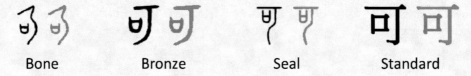

| Bone | Bronze | Seal | Standard |

## The Stroke Sequence

## The Anatomy

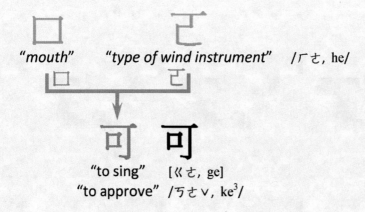

□                    己
"mouth"    "type of wind instrument"    /ㄏㄜ, he/

可
"to sing"    [《ㄜ, ge]
"to approve"    /ㄎㄜˇ, ke³/

134

# The Trinity – Sound(s), Semantics, and Synopses

/ㄎㄜˇ, ke³/

| | |
|---|---|
| to approve | 許可; |
| may | 可以, 可能, 不可以, 可不可以; |
| can be | 可靠, 事情可大可小; |
| to delight, to suit | 可口, 可人, 可身; |
| delightful, lovely | 可人兒; |
| deserving | 可貴, 可敬, 可愛, 可惜, 可憐, 可惡, 可恨; |
| rather | 我可不這麼想; |
| truly, indeed | 他本事可大了, 你興趣可不小, 我可不知道他有自己的打算, 這麼棘手的問題可把他難住了; |
| but | 可是, 他雖然笨，可很用功; |
| how could it | 可不是嗎？; |
| *used before words that need to be emphasized* | 你可回來了, 這可好了, 可有得你操心了; |
| *used to make sentence inquisitive to mean* ever | 你可知道？, 你可想過？; |
| *in classical Chinese,* | |
| to approve of | 「吾子好道而可吾文， 或者其於道不遠矣。」; |
| to fit | 「凜凜威顏多雅秀， 佛衣可體如裁就。」; |

135

to face towards

「高坐寂寥塵漠漠，
　一方明月**可**中庭。」；

to be able to, may

「彼蒼者天，殲我良人。
　如**可**贖兮，人百其身。」；

to recover (*from illness*)

「待軍師病**可**，行之未遲。」；

deserving

「町畽鹿場，熠燿宵行，
　不**可**畏也，伊**可**懷也。」，

「**可**憐無定河邊骨，
　猶是深閨夢裏[裡]人。」；

approximately

「年**可**十六七。」；

roughly

「奪彎代之御，**可**數百步。」，

「洛陽女兒對門居，
　纔**可**容顏十五餘。」；

yet

「相見情已深，
　未語**可**知心。」；

how

「蚤是傷春夢雨天，
　**可**堪芳草更芊芊。」；

indeed

「穀雨初晴，
　**可**是麗人天氣。」；

*surname*　　　　　　　　姓氏

/ㄎㄜˋ, ke⁴/

Khan　　　　　　　　　　可汗 [=克汗];

Khan's wife　　　　　　　可敦 [=賀敦]

**Radical:** 口.

# 37. 主

## Script Evolution

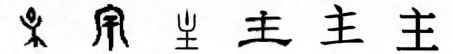

## The Story

[ㄓㄨㄟ, zhu⁴]    "column (of a building)"

/ㄓㄨ∨, zhu³/    "main", "core"

**Pictograph** (象形) of

　　*column* supporting

　　*a beam* (shown as *cross section*),

hence "*column (of a building)*".

It is interesting to note that at time of the Bronze Script the character depicts *a column* (  ) *supporting building's roof* (  ). The pictures of *column of a building* as rendered through time by the character 主 are shown below.

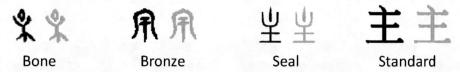

Bone        Bronze        Seal        Standard

Later, for the same sound (/ㄓㄨ∨, zhu³/) 主 started to carry the semantics of "*main*", "*core*" surrendering its original semantics of "*column*" to the Associative Compound 柱 (/ㄓㄨㄟ, zhu⁴/) with Radical 木 (/ㄇㄨㄟ, mu⁴/ "*wood*") and Semantic-Phonetic Component 主 ([ㄓㄨㄟ, zhu⁴] "*column*").

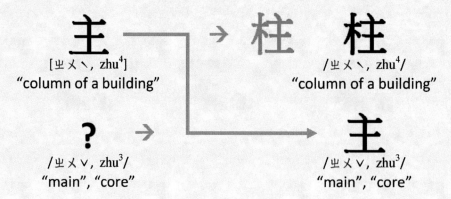

[ㄓㄨㄟ, zhu⁴]
"column of a building"

/ㄓㄨㄟ, zhu⁴/
"column of a building"

?

/ㄓㄨˇ, zhu³/
"main", "core"

/ㄓㄨˇ, zhu³/
"main", "core"

This process of character creation, or re-creation rather, is called Semantic Bifurcation (假借).

Most dictionaries, focusing on the character's Seal Script only, tell quite a different story, *i.e.* **Pictograph** (象形) of *a lit lamp accented with its core flame*, hence "*core*".

## The Stroke Sequence

## The Trinity – Sound(s), Semantics, and Synopses

/ㄓㄨˇ, zhu³/

| | |
|---|---|
| main, core, key | 主角, 主將, 主帥, 主嫌, 主要; |
| emperor, king | 君主; |
| master | 主僕; |
| host | 賓主; |
| leader, person in charge | 一家之主, 做主, 敎[教]主; |
| to play the lead or key role | 主講, 主辦, 主持, 主事, 主使, 主動, 主宰, 主掌; |

| | |
|---|---|
| to hold strong opinion of | 主戰, 主和, 主張; |
| owner | 失主, 債主, 地主, 入主; |
| one's own | 主觀, 主見; |
| person (people) on one side of dispute | 苦主; |
| symbolic plaque for worship or memorial, spiritual god | 木主, 神主; |

*in classical Chinese*,

| | |
|---|---|
| Emperor | 「報主身已老, 入朝病見妨。」; |
| leader | 「侯主侯伯，侯亞侯旅。」; |
| symbolic plaque for worship or memorial, spiritual god | 「祭祀則共匰主。」; |
| to be in charge of, to control | 「使之主事而事治， 百姓安之。」; |
| to hold strong opinion of | 「是以不主寬惠， 亦不主猛毅， 主德義而已。」; |
| to uphold | 「主忠信，無友不如己者。」; |
| | 「主此盛德兮， 牽於俗而蕪穢。」; |
| to presage | 「又觀乾象， 太白臨于雒城之分， 主將帥身上多凶少吉。」 |

**Radical:** 丶 (/ㄓㄨˇ, zhu[3]/ "determinedly"), the 1st Stroke; originally 主 (itself).

# 38. 發

**Script Evolution**

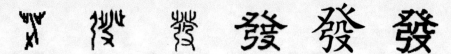

**The Story**

/ㄈㄚ, fa/    "to launch"

**Associative Compound** (會意) of

> 癶 (/ㄅㄛ, bo/ "left and right steps" referring to *marching steps,*
> > *also providing sound*),

> 殳 (/ㄕㄨ, shu/ "to use long-poled weapon"), and

> 弓 (/ㄍㄨㄥ, gong/ "bow (for archery)")

to imply *carrying long-poled weapons and bows in marching steps* or
> *launching a military offence,*

hence *"to launch"*, *"to deploy"*.

**<u>Note</u>**: ㄛ and ㄚ are the same sound.

It is important to note that at time of the Bone Script the character told a simpler story of *carrying long-poled weapons* ( ) in *marching steps* ( ). The stories of *launching military offence* as told through time by the

140

character 發 is shown below.

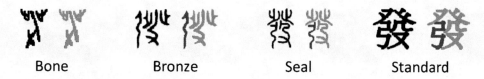

| Bone | Bronze | Seal | Standard |

## The Stroke Sequence

## The Anatomy

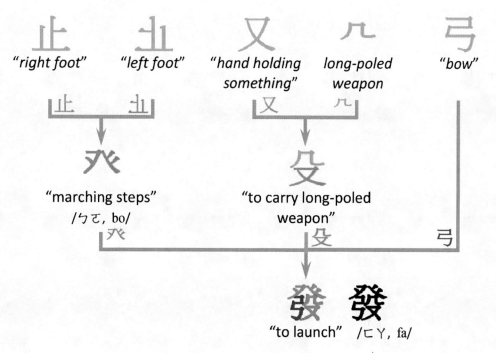

止 "right foot"  屮 "left foot"  又 "hand holding something"  殳 long-poled weapon  弓 "bow"

癶 "marching steps" /ㄅㄛ, bo/

殳 "to carry long-poled weapon"

發 發 "to launch" /ㄈㄚ, fa/

141

# The Trinity – Sound(s), Semantics, and Synopses

/ㄈㄚ, fa/

| | |
|---|---|
| to launch | 發兵, 百發百中, 彈無虛發; |
| to make move, to campaign | 發動, 發難, 先發制人; |
| to emit | 發光; |
| to develop<br>(*biologically or chemically*) | 發育, 發芽, 發炎, 發酵, 發麵[麵]; |
| to generate | 發音, 發聲, 發電; |
| to start out | 發跡, 發財, 發生, 發現; |
| to give rise to | 啟發, 發展, 一觸即發; |
| to be in (*physical or mental state*) | 發情, 發瘋, 發愣, 全身發癢; |
| to show colour change | 臉色發白, 菜葉發黃; |
| to start journey, expedition | 出發; |
| to give out, to send out | 發放, 發餉, 散發, 發壓歲錢; |
| rounds of ammunition | 三發子彈, 十發炮彈; |

*in classical Chinese*,

| | |
|---|---|
| to grow | 「紅豆生南國，<br>　春來發故枝。」; |
| to start journey | 「一家皆移什物赴新居，<br>　而妾留守，明日即發。」; |
| to inspire | 「振聾發聵。」; |
| to reveal | 「喜怒哀樂之未發，<br>　謂之中。」 |

**Radical:** 癶.

# 39. 年

## Script Evolution

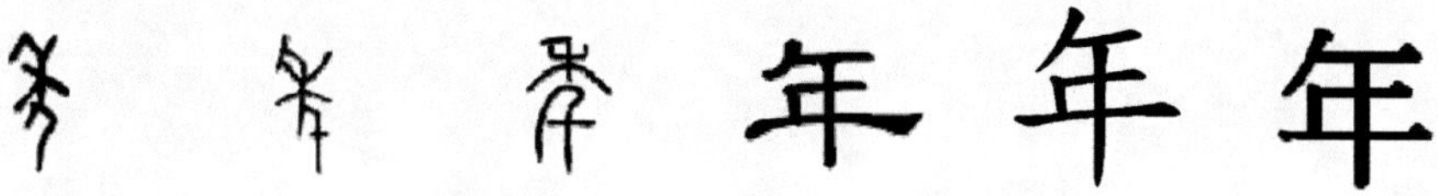

秊 秊 秊 年 年 年

## The Story

秊 秊 季 年 年

/ㄋㄧㄢˊ, nian² /     "agricultural harvest"

**Associative Compound** (會意) of

禾 (/ㄏㄜˊ, he²/ "grain crop") and

千 (/ㄑㄧㄢ, qian/ "thousand" referring to *ripe and plentiful*,

*also providing sound*)

to imply *plentiful ripe grain crop*,

hence *"agricultural harvest"*.

禾 + 千 = 秊 秊

At time of the Clerical Script, 4 Strokes (brown colour) in 秊 were written

as 3 Strokes (brown colour) leading to the Standard Form 年 as shown below.

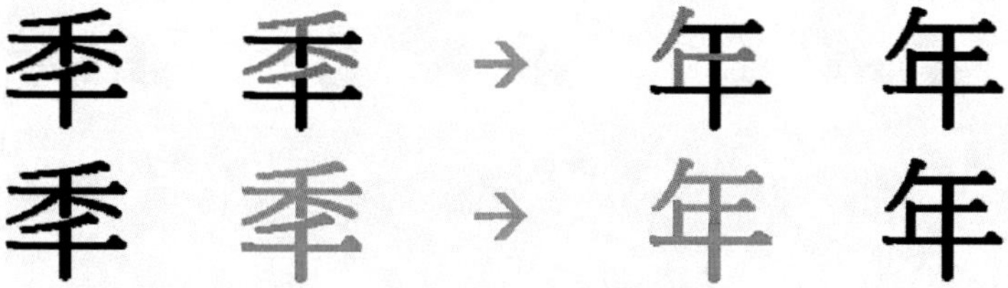

秊 秊 → 年 年

秊 秊 → 年 年

Ancient agricultural practice would give only one harvest per year. Hence, 年 (秊) also carries the semantics of "*year*". It is important to note that the character 千 (/ㄑㄧㄢ, qian/ "thousand" Usage Rank #403) was originally in the form of 人 (亻 /ㄖㄣˊ, ren$^{2}$/ "adult person") at time of the Bone Script. Later, the way to write *one* (一) *thousand* ( ), *i.e.* or 千, became the character on its own to carry the semantics of "*thousand*". Hence, the Semantic-Phonetic Component 千 ( at time of the Bone Script) of 秊 秊 carries the notion of *ripe* (from *adult person*) and *plentiful* (from *thousand*). The story of *plentiful ripe grain crop* as told though time by the character 年 (秊) is shown below.

Bone Bronze Seal Standard

It is interesting to note that contrary to pairing the *grain crop* (禾) with an *adult person* (人 亻), the character 季 季 (/ㄐㄧˋ, ji$^{4}$/ "season" Usage Rank #968) pairs the *grain crop* (禾) with a *child* (子). Hence, 季 is an Associative Compound of

禾 (/ㄏㄜˊ, he$^{2}$/ "grain crop") and

子 (/ㄗˇ, zi$^{3}$/ [ㄗㄧˇ] "child" referring to *young and not ripe,*

*also providing sound*)

to imply *young crop* or

*time for grain crop to grow to be young* (*and not ripe*) *crop*,

hence "*season*".

禾 + 子 ≡ 季 季

This *young crop* notion later gave the semantics of "*youngest of siblings*" for the character 季 to carry.

Almost all dictionaries classify 季 as an Associative Compound (季) of

子 (/ㄗˇ, zi³/ "child" referring to *young and not ripe*) and

稚 (稺 /ㄓˋ, zhi⁴/ [ㄓㄧˋ] "crop seedling", *also providing sound*)

in Reduced Form 稚 稺)

to imply *youngest child*,

hence *"youngest of siblings"*.

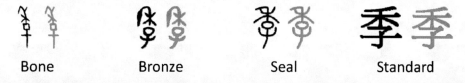

This linguistic faux pas is most obvious, because, like the character 年 (秊), the character 季 was created at time of the Bone Script, some two thousand years before the arrival of the characters 稚 and 稺 at time of the Seal Script. The story of *time for grain crop to grow to be young crop* as told though time by the character 季 is shown below.

| Bone | Bronze | Seal | Standard |
|------|--------|------|----------|

## The Stroke Sequence

## The Anatomy

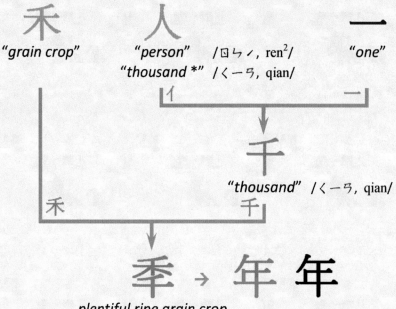

禾
"grain crop"

人
"person"  /ㄖㄣˊ, ren$^2$/
"thousand *"  /ㄑㄧㄢ, qian/

一
"one"

千
"thousand"  /ㄑㄧㄢ, qian/

秊 → 年 年

plentiful ripe grain crop
"agricultural harvest"  /ㄋㄧㄢˊ, nian$^2$/

*: Semantic Bifurcation

## The Trinity – Sound(s), Semantics, and Synopses

/ㄋㄧㄢˊ, nian$^2$/

| | |
|---|---|
| agricultural harvest | 豐年, 歉年, 荒年, 年荒; |
| year | 年頭*, 年中, 年尾, 年終, 年底, |
| | 年前, 今年, 明年, 後年, 去年, |
| | 前年, 全年, 終年, 長年, 經年, |
| | 整年, 多年, 每年, 三年, 潤年, |
| | 民國元年, 年年有餘, 年復一年; |
| long time period (*usually eventful*) | 年頭**, |

*: 『年頭 (/ㄊㄡˊ, tou$^2$/』 means "*beginning of a year*".

**: 『年頭 (/・ㄊㄡ, tou$^5$』 is used to refer to "*unusual times*".

146

| | |
|---|---|
| annual(ly), yearly | 年鑑, 年表, 年刊, 年薪, 年會, 年度, 年利(率), 年產(量); |
| yearly festival, *in particular* | |
| the Chinese New Year | 過年, 新年, 年三十(兒), 年夜飯; |
| of the Chinese New Year | 年節, 年糕, 年畫, 年貨; |
| person's age | 年事, 年齡, 年紀, 年歲, 年幼, 年少, 年長, 年輕力壯, 延年益壽; |
| person of certain young age | 少年, 青年, 青少年; |
| adulthood | 成年; |
| time period of person's life | 童年, 少年, 青年, 中年, 盛年, 壯年, 老年, 晚年; |
| era, time period | 九十年代, 康熙年間; |
| *in classical Chinese*, | |
| agricultural harvest | 「七月以來，霖潦未止，濱河南北，田正洿下，年之有亡未可知。」; |
| New Year | 「度臘不成雪，迎年遽得春。」; |
| person's age | 「年過半百不稱意，明日看雲還杖藜。」; |
| time period | 「經營上元始，斷手寶應年。」; |
| *surname* | 姓氏 |

**Radical:** 干 (/ㄍㄢ, gan/ "to interfere"), the 2nd, 3rd, and 6th Stroke; originally 禾.

# 40. 動

**Script Evolution**

動 動 動 動 動 動

**The Story**

動 動 動 動

/ㄉㄨㄥˋ, dong⁴/　"to move", "to start"

**Associative Compound** (會意) of

力 (/ㄌㄧˋ, li⁴/ "effort") and

重 (/ㄓㄨㄥˋ, zhong⁴/ "heavy", *also providing sound*)

to imply *exerting efforts to move a heavy object*,

hence *"to move"*.

力 ＋ 重 ＝ 動　動

It is important to note that at time of the Bone Script the character told the story of *walking and stopping* ( ） *with a large parcel* ( ). At time of the Bronze Script, the character told the story of *walking and stopping* ( ) *with a heavy object* ( ). At time of the Seal Script, the character told the story of *exerting efforts* ( ) *to move a heavy object* ( ), thus leading to the Standard Script. The stories of *moving a large heavy object* as told through time by the character 動 are shown below.

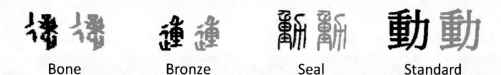

| Bone | Bronze | Seal | Standard |
|------|--------|------|----------|

## The Stroke Sequence

動 動 動 動 動 動 動 動 動 動

動 動 動 動 動 動 動 動 動 動

動

動

## The Anatomy

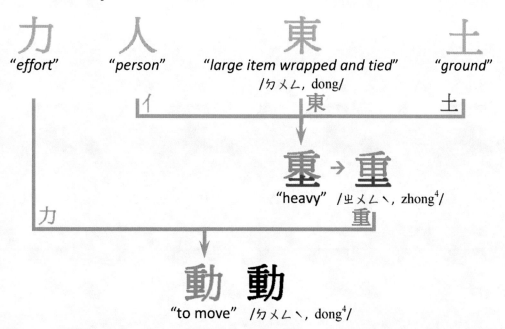

力 "effort"　　人 "person"　　東 "large item wrapped and tied" /ㄉㄨㄥ, dong/　　土 "ground"

亻　東　土

埀 → 重 "heavy" /ㄓㄨㄥˋ, zhong⁴/

力　　重

動 動 "to move" /ㄉㄨㄥˋ, dong⁴/

# The Trinity – Sound(s), Semantics, and Synopses

/ㄉㄨㄥˋ, dong⁴/

| | |
|---|---|
| to move | 別**動**, 機**動**, 啟**動**, 開**動**, 發**動**, 牽**動**, 風吹草**動**; |
| motion, movement | **動**作; |
| *used with* 靜 *to mean* | |
|     motion *or* movement | 毫無**動**靜; |
| to start | **動**工, **動**身; |
| to use | **動**筆, **動**手, **動**腦筋, **動**筷子; |
| to touch | 不**動**葷腥, 別**動**我的東西; |
| to agitate | **動**怒; |
| to arouse | **動**容, **動**人, **動**心; |
| aroused | 感**動**, 心**動**; |
| to exercise | 活**動**, 運**動**, **動**一**動**，比較不冷; |
| often, always | **動**輒得咎; |
| *used as a pair with* 不 *in between* | |
|     *to mean* almost as a habit | **動**不**動**就生病; |
| *used after verb to mean* effect | 移**動**, 說**動**, 提不**動**; |
| *in classical Chinese,* | |
|     often, always | 「每一獨往，**動**彌旬日。」, |
| | 「人生不相見， |
| |   **動**如參與商。」 |

**Radical:** 力.

150

# 41. 同

## Script Evolution

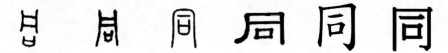

## The Story

/ㄊㄨㄥˊ, tong[2]/    "to converge", "in agreement"

**Associative Compound** (會意) of

凡 (/ㄈㄢˊ, fan[2]/ "all") and

口 (/ㄎㄡˇ, kou[3]/ "mouth" referring to *spoken words*)

to imply *all saying the same words*,

hence *"to converge"*, *"in agreement"*.

凡 + 口 ≡ 同   同

It is important to note that Radical 凡 is a Pictograph of *a mould* to imply *results all the same*, hence *"all"*. At time of the Seal Script of the Radical 凡 ( 𦱳 ) was written as ⺆ (⺆ /ㄇㄠˇ, mao[3]/ "to repeat", "to duplicate") to give the Semantic Component 口 ( ⼐ ) proper space. The pictures of *a mould* as rendered through time by the character 凡 and the story of *all saying the same words* as told through time by the character 同 are shown below.

151

| Bone | Bronze | Seal | Standard |

## The Stroke Sequence

## The Anatomy

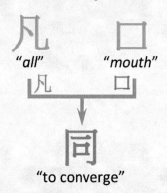

凡　　　　口
"all"　　　"mouth"

凡　　　　口

↓

同

"to converge"

## The Trinity – Sound(s), Semantics, and Synopses

/ㄊㄨㄥˊ, tong[2]/

| | |
|---|---|
| to converge, to join | 會同, 夥同; |
| to unify, to make alike | 同化; |
| to feel the same | 同情; |
| together | 同居, 同甘共苦, |
| | 有福同享，有難同當; |

| | |
|---|---|
| in agreement | 贊同, 同意, 同心協力; |
| common, alike | 同類, 同學, 同事, 同胞, 相同; |
| same | 共同, 同心圓, 同父異母, 大同小異; |
| with | 有事同你商量, 我同他一起去; |
| peace, harmony | 世界大同; |
| contract, agreement | 合同; |

*in classical Chinese*,

| | |
|---|---|
| to meet together | 「勸君稍盡離筵酒, 　千里佳期難再同。」; |
| to unify | 「協時月正日, 　同律度量衡。」; |
| to participate in | 「不知三軍之事, 　而同三軍之政者, 　則軍士惑矣。」; |
| in common, the same | 「同居長干里, 　兩小無嫌猜。」; |
| peace, harmony | 「是故謀閉而不興, 　盜竊亂賊而不作, 　故外戶而不閉, 　是謂大同。」; |
| *surname* | 姓氏 |

/ㄊㄨㄥˋ, tong⁴/

| | |
|---|---|
| lane, alley | 胡同 [=衚衕] |

**Radical:** 口; originally 冃 (凡).

# 42. 工

## Script Evolution

## The Story

/《ㄨㄥ, gong/　　"craft"

**Pictograph** (象形) of *a wood crafting tool*,

hence "*craft*".

The pictures of *a wood crafting tool* as rendered through time by the character 工 are shown below.

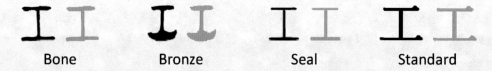

Bone　　　　Bronze　　　　Seal　　　　Standard

## The Stroke Sequence

工　工　工
工　工　工

## The Trinity – Sound(s), Semantics, and Synopses

/《ㄨㄥ, gong/

craft, technique, skill　　　　　　　　雕工, 唱工, 巧奪天工;

154

| | |
|---|---|
| craftsmanship | 工藝; |
| craftsman, technician | 木工, 礦工, 水電工; |
| productive work | 上工, 加工, 怠工, 工酬, 工資; |
| construction | 施工, 竣工; |
| (related to) engineering | 化工, 工程, 工業; |
| to emphasize, to favour | 工於心計; |
| to specialize in | 專工太空科學; |
| cleverly and delicately finished | 工整; |
| time and dedication (*oft. with* 夫) | 這得花多大的工啊？, |
| | 一盞茶的工夫, 毫不費工夫, |
| | 他花了好些年的工夫研究漢字; |

*in classical Chinese*,

| | |
|---|---|
| skill, technique | 「爲[為]我草眞[真]籙, |
| | 天人慚妙工。」; |
| craftsman | 「工欲善其事, |
| | 必先利其器。」; |
| to specialize in | 「工文學者非所用, |
| | 用之則亂法。」; |
| cleverly and delicately finished | 「怪道我常弄本舊詩, |
| | 偷空兒看一兩首, |
| | 又有對的極工的, |
| | 又有不對的。」; |
| time and dedication (*oft. with* 夫) | 「藝文不貴, 徒消工夫。」; |
| *a traditional Chinese music note* | 工尺 |

**Radical:** 工 (itself).

# 43. 也

## Script Evolution

## The Story

[ㄕㄜˊ, she[2]]    "snake"

/一ㄝˇ, ye[3]/    "alike", "also"

**Pictograph** (象形) of *a snake*,

hence "*snake*".

**Note**: ㄜ and ㄝ are the same sound.

The MPS 『ㄝ』 is based on this character's form 『也』 and sound.

Later, for the same sound (/一ㄝˇ, ye[3]/) 也 started to carry the semantics of "*alike*", "*also*" as *snakes* are all *alike*. And the Associative Compound 蛇 (/ㄕㄜˊ, she[2]/ Usage Rank #2,551) with Radical 虫 (/ㄏㄨㄟˇ, hui[3]/ "reptile") and Semantic-Phonetic Component 它 ([ㄊㄨㄛ, tuo] originally "snake", a variation Pictograph form of *snake*) was then created for the original semantics of "*snake*". This process of character creation, or re-creation rather, is called Semantic Bifurcation (假借).

**Note**: ㄨㄛ and ㄜ are the same sound.

156

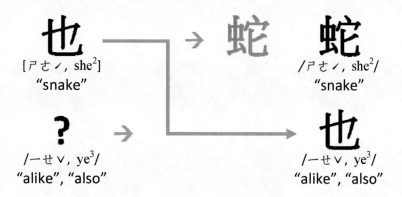

The pictures of *a snake* as rendered through time by the character 也 are shown below.

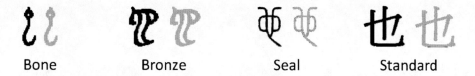

Bone　　　　Bronze　　　　Seal　　　　Standard

## The Stroke Sequence

## The Trinity – Sound(s), Semantics, and Synopses

/ㄧㄝˇ, ye³/

| | |
|---|---|
| alike, likewise | 也該, 也須, 也許, 也是, 也有, 也行, 也成; |
| also, as well | 我懂，你也懂, 這個問題我也碰過; |
| at all | 一點也不, 再也不敢; |
| even | 頭也不回就走了, 進來也不打聲招呼; |

| | |
|---|---|
| indeed | 好在問題也不是很大; |
| or | 不知道對也(是)不對; |
| consequently | 時間久了，他也把事兒給忘了; |
| still | 天氣再冷，也得出門; |

*used with 好 or 只好 to mean*

| might as well | 這樣也好, 也只好如此了; |
|---|---|

*used in a pair to emphasize*

| *one as well as the other* | 飯也不吃，湯也不喝, |
|---|---|
| | 茶也不思，飯也不想; |

*in classical Chinese,*

*at end of sentence to indicate*

| determination | 「孺子可敎[教]也。」, |
|---|---|
| | 「是不爲[為]也， |
| | 　非不能也。」; |
| advisory | 「不可不愼[慎]也。」; |
| inquiry | 「此爲[為]誰也。」; |
| lament | 「難也。」; |

*in the middle of sentence to indicate*

| pause of tone | 「大道之行也， |
|---|---|
| | 　天下爲[為]公。」; |

*used in a pair to emphasize*

| *one as well as the other* | 「也不至於太冷落， |
|---|---|
| | 也不至於太熱鬧了。」 |

**Radical:** 乙 (/一ˇ, yi³/ "2nd of the 10 heavenly symbols for recording time"), the 1st Stroke; originally 也 (itself).

# 44. 能

**Script Evolution**

**The Story**

能能能能

[ㄒㄩㄥˊ, xiong²]    "bear"

/ㄋㄥˊ, neng²/    "able"

**Pictograph** (象形) of *a bear* ( 𰀁 ),

hence *"bear"*.

It is important to note that at time of the Bronze Script rendering of the *bear* was focused on

*head with open mouth* ( 𰀁 ),

*body* ( 𰀁 ), and

*legs with claws* ( 𰀁 ).

At time of the Seal Script, the *legs* ( 𰀁 ) were moved to the right side of the *head and body* ( 𰀁 ) to emphasize the *bear's* ability to climb.  The pictures of *a bear* as rendered through time by the character 能 are shown below.

Bone          Bronze          Seal          Standard

159

Later, for the same sound (/ㄋㄥˊ, neng$^2$/) and referring to bear's great *abilities,* 能 started to carry the semantics of *"able"*, surrendering the original semantics of *"bear"* to the Associative Compound 熊 (/ㄒㄩㄥˊ, xiong$^2$/ "fierce (*of fire*)" Usage Rank #2,023) with Radical 火 (灬 /ㄏㄨㄛˇ, huo$^3$/ "fire") and Semantic-Phonetic Component 能 ([ㄒㄩㄥˊ, xiong$^2$] "bear"). This process of character creation, or re-creation rather, is called Semantic Bifurcation (假借).

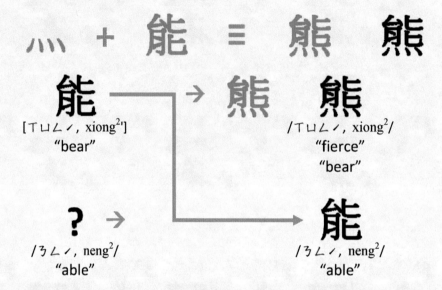

灬 + 能 ≡ 熊 熊

能
[ㄒㄩㄥˊ, xiong$^2$]
"bear"

→ 熊 熊
/ㄒㄩㄥˊ, xiong$^2$/
"fierce"
"bear"

? →
/ㄋㄥˊ, neng$^2$/
"able"

能
/ㄋㄥˊ, neng$^2$/
"able"

## The Stroke Sequence

能 能 能 能 能 能 能 能 能 能
能 能 能 能 能 能 能 能 能 能

## The Trinity – Sound(s), Semantics, and Synopses

/ㄋㄥˊ, neng$^2$/

able

能人, 能者多勞;

| | |
|---|---|
| ability, talent | 能力, 逞能, 智能, 才能, 無能; |
| specialty, expertise | 各盡其能; |
| able to | 能否, 你能不能去？; |
| capable of | 能夠, 這包子他一次能吃二十個, 狗能看家, 無所不能, 盡己所能; |
| energy | 能量, 能源; |

*in classical Chinese*,

| | |
|---|---|
| able | 「賢者在位，能者在職。」; |
| capable | 「非曰能之，願學焉。」; |
| ability, talent | 「夫子聖者與？<br>　何其多能也。」; |
| function, purpose | 「可以染也，名之以其能，<br>　故謂之染溪。」; |
| able person | 「選賢與能，講信脩睦。」,<br>「招賢進能，顯巖穴之士。」; |
| may be | 「少壯能幾時？<br>　鬢髮各已蒼。」; |
| may possibly | 「春花秋月何時了？<br>　往事知多少。<br>　小樓昨夜又東風，<br>　故國不堪回首月明中。<br>　雕欄玉砌應猶在，<br>　只是朱顏改。<br>　問君能有幾多愁？<br>　恰似一江春水向東流！」; |

to reach, to extend 「韓與秦接境壤界，
其地不**能**千里。」；

friendly 「積不相**能**。」；

to be compatible and friendly 「柔遠**能**邇，以定我王。」，

「何素不與曹參相**能**。」；

only 「只益丹心苦，
**能**添白髮明。」；

would rather 「出山定被江潮浼，
**能**爲[為]山僧更少留。」

**Radical:** 肉 (月); originally 能 (itself).

# 45. 下

## Script Evolution

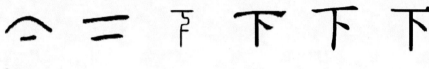

## The Story

/ㄒㄧㄚˋ, xia³/  "under"

**Ideograph** (指事) with *an object below a horizontal surface*

  to indicate *below*,

hence *"below"*, *"under"*.

**Note**: This is the up-down mirrored image of 上 (/ㄕㄤˋ, shang⁴/ "above"

  Usage Rank #14).

  The MPS 『ㄒ』 is based on the archaic form (丅) and sound of 下.

The iconic symbols denoting *the concept of below* as represented through
time by the character 下 are shown below.

| Bone | Bronze | Seal | Standard |

## The Stroke Sequence

下 下 下

## The Trinity – Sound(s), Semantics, and Synopses

/ㄒㄧㄚˋ, xia$^4$/

| | |
|---|---|
| under | 名下, 門下; |
| down | 下游; |
| bottom or under portion * | 底下; |
| subordinate * | 部下, 手下, 屬下; |
| low class (*for people*) | 下人, 下吏, 下流; |
| low-level, low quality | 下策, 下等; |
| humble way to call oneself | 在下, 下官; |
| less than | 不下萬人; |
| next | 下次, 下回, 下文, 下週, 下月; |
| within, inside | 言下之意, 意下如何, 不在話下; |
| *adv.* off, down * | 脫下, 躺下, 坐下, 放下, 寫下, 收下, 立下志願; |
| (down) securely | 設下陷井, 打下基礎, 部下天羅地網; |
| side | 私(底)下, 四下無人; |
| situation, circumstance | 時下, 年下, 眼下; |
| to come or fall down | 下雨, 下山, 順流而下; |
| to take possession of | 奪下, 拿下, 攻下, 連下三城; |
| to send down | 下放; |

*: 『下』 has the tone variation of /‧ㄒㄧㄚ, xia$^5$/.

| | |
|---|---|
| to put, lay, or drop down | 下毒, 下麵[麵], 下餃子, 下網捕魚; |
| to get in, to enter | 下水, 下場比賽; |
| to lower down | 下貨; |
| to exit | 下臺, 你去換他下來; |
| to finish | 下課, 下班; |
| to issue | 下詔, 下命令; |
| to send | 下帖, 下戰書; |
| to set down | 下棋, 下決心; |
| to start (action) | 下刀, 下筆, 下手; |
| to lay (eggs) | 母雞下蛋; |
| to go down (to) | 下江南, 下地獄, 南下列車; |
| to stay (to settle down) | 下榻; |
| to give after consideration | 下定義, 下結論; |
| to lower oneself to | 下嫁, 不恥下問; |
| helping (to swallow down) | 下飯, 下酒; |
| ending, concluding | 下場悽慘, 作奸犯科沒好下場; |
| with capacity to hold | 吃不下, 喝得下, 裝不下, 人太多，坐不下; |
| *quantity word, for* | |
| repetitions | 五十下伏地挺身; |
| *in classical Chinese,* | |
| subordinate | 「建置不久，則輕下慢上。」; |
| to humbly yield way to | 「禮賢下士。」; |

| | |
|---|---|
| to take down, to conquer | 「齊城不下者，兩城耳。」， |
| | 「可引得勝之兵攻之， |
| | 　一鼓可下。」； |
| to travel down to | 「故人西辭黃鶴樓， |
| | 　煙花三月下揚州。」； |
| to feel contempt for | 「此范氏之所以賢鴻 |
| | 　而下愷也。」； |
| to issue | 「吾詔書數下， |
| | 　歲勸民種樹。」； |
| side | 「兩下相思不相見， |
| | 　知他相會是何年。」 |

**Radical:** 一 (/一, ʏi/ "one"), the 1st Stroke; originally 下 (itself).

166

# 46. 過

**Script Evolution**

過 調 過 過 過

**The Story**

調 調 過 過

/ㄍㄨㄛˋ, guo⁴/    "to go through"

**Semantic-Phonetic Compound** (形聲) of

辵 (辶 /ㄔㄨㄛˋ, chuo⁴/ "to walk and stop") *for semantics* and

咼 (/ㄎㄨㄚ, kua/ "droopy mouth") *for sound*

to mean *"to go through"*.

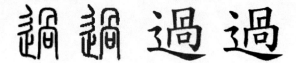

"to walk and stop"   /ㄎㄨㄚ, kua/        /ㄍㄨㄛˋ, guo⁴/   "to go through"

<u>**Note**</u>: ㄨㄚ and ㄨㄛ are the same sound.

It is important to note that at time of the Bronze Script this character was an Associative Compound of

辵 (辶 /ㄔㄨㄛˋ, chuo⁴/ "to walk and stop", *also providing sound*) and

(Pictograph of *a thick thread* 𡿨 *sewn through 4 small plates* ) to imply *going through*,

hence *"to go through"*.

167

The stories of *going through* as told through time by the character 過 are shown below.

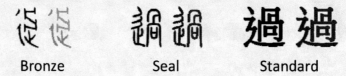

| Bronze | Seal | Standard |

## The Stroke Sequence

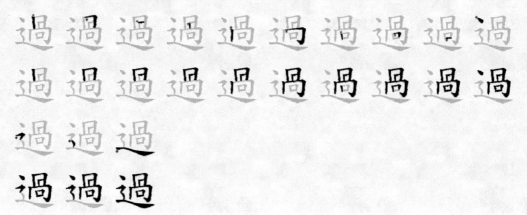

## The Anatomy

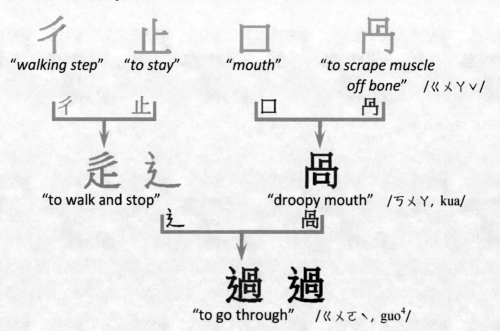

# The Trinity – Sound(s), Semantics, and Synopses

/ㄍㄨㄛˋ, guo⁴/

| | |
|---|---|
| to go through | 經**過**, 路**過**, 情關難**過**; |
| to pass by | 錯**過**班機; |
| passing by | **過**往雲煙, **過**往行人; |
| passed, behind | **過**時, **過**氣; |
| to enter into | 女方尚[尚]未**過**門(兒); |
| to exchange | **過**招, **過**手, **過**從*甚密; |
| entire (going through) | **過**程; |
| transitional | **過**渡期; |
| to transfer, to pass over | **過**戶, **過**帳, **過**手, **過**水; |
| to spend (*time*), to live | **過**年, **過**節**, **過**生日; |
| to pass away, to decease | **過**世, 老太太已**過**了; |
| to endure, sustained | 難**過**, 心裏[裡]不好**過**, |
| | 他倆(兒)有**過**節***; |
| repeated time | 千百**過**; |
| already | 聽**過**, 看**過**, 說**過**, 來**過**, 去**過**, |
| | 吃**過**晚餐, 付**過**帳; |
| to exceed | **過**分, **過**期, 事不**過**三, **過**人之處; |
| exceeding(ly), over | **過**度, **過**獎, **過**激, 超**過**, 睡**過**頭; |
| fault, mistake | **過**錯, **過**失, 改**過**向善, 知**過**能改; |

*:　『**過**從』means "*to interact, communicate, usually for a purpose*".

**:　『**過**節 (/ㄐㄧㄝˊ, jie²/)』means "*to celebrate festival or holiday*".

***:『**過**節 (/‧ㄐㄧㄝ, jie⁵/)』*sustained protuberance* to mean "*conflict*".

169

*used with* 去 *or* 來 *to indicate*

    continuation of motion　　　　走**過**去, 讓我**過**去看看,
　　　　　　　　　　　　　　　　　游**過**來, 有空**過**來坐坐;

*used with* 去 *to mean* in the past　　**過**去他常愛聽莫札特的音樂;

*used with* 來 *to mean* experienced　　我們都是**過**來人;

*in classical Chinese*,

    to pass by　　　　　　　　　「沈舟側畔千帆**過**,
　　　　　　　　　　　　　　　　　病樹前頭萬木春。」;

    to have passed　　　　　　　「三伏適已**過**,
　　　　　　　　　　　　　　　　　驕陽化爲[為]霖。」,

　　　　　　　　　　　　　　　　「朝辭白帝彩雲間,
　　　　　　　　　　　　　　　　　千里江陵一日還。
　　　　　　　　　　　　　　　　　兩岸猿聲啼不盡,
　　　　　　　　　　　　　　　　　輕舟已**過**萬重山。」;

    to spend (*time*), to live　　　「男兒仗劍酬恩在,
　　　　　　　　　　　　　　　　　未肯徒然**過**一生。」;

    to exceed　　　　　　　　　「由也好勇**過**我,
　　　　　　　　　　　　　　　　　無所取材。」;

    exceedingly　　　　　　　　「然吾有饑焉,
　　　　　　　　　　　　　　　　　謂其自爲[為]也**過**多,
　　　　　　　　　　　　　　　　　其爲[為]人也**過**少。」;

    to decease　　　　　　　　「存者忽復**過**,
　　　　　　　　　　　　　　　　　亡沒身自衰。」;

    to go to pay a visit　　　　「臣有客在市屠中,
　　　　　　　　　　　　　　　　　願枉車騎**過**之。」;

fault, mistake

「夫**過**有厚薄，
　則刑有輕重。」

/ㄍㄨㄛ, guo/

*surname*　　　　　　　　　　姓氏

**Radical:** 辵 (辶).

# 47. 子

## Script Evolution

## The Story

/ㄗˇ, zi³/　"offspring"

**Pictograph** (象形) of *a swaddled baby* to imply *offspring*,
hence *"offspring"*.

**Note**: Also in the form 『子』 as Radical or component.

The pictures of *a swaddled baby* as rendered through time by the character 子 are shown below.

| Bone | Bronze | Seal | Standard |
|------|--------|------|----------|

## The Stroke Sequence

**Common Fallacy:** Combining the 1st & 2nd Stroke as a single Stroke.

# The Trinity – Sound(s), Semantics, and Synopses

/ㄗ ∨, zi$^3$/

| | |
|---|---|
| offspring | 子孫, 子嗣, 天子; |
| son | 犬子, 父子, 獨生子, 一子一女; |
| youngster | 子弟; |
| person | 女子, 男子, 內子, 外子, 孩子, 弟子; |
| young, tender (*for animal or plant*) | 子雞, 子薑, 子豬; |
| animal cub | 不入虎穴，焉得虎子; |
| egg, seed | 魚子, 瓜子, 蓮子; |
| *used in contrast to* 母 | 子金, 子音; |
| sub-, derived | 子句, 子目; |

*used with* 兒 *to mean*

| | |
|---|---|
| small change, coin | 他小氣得很，一個子兒也不給,<br>他輸到一個蹦子兒也不剩了,<br>給兩兒蹦子兒，打發他走了; |

*in classical Chinese,*

| | |
|---|---|
| descendant | 「我本漢家子,<br>　將適單于庭。」; |
| you | 「以子之矛陷子之楯何如？」; |
| to care for | 「子庶民，來百工也。」,<br>「私其土，子其人。」; |
| *after a surname to show great*<br>*respect to person so named* | 孔子, 孟子, 老子, 莊子; |

first of the 12 earthly symbols

    often used with the

    10 heavenly symbols

    to record time 一甲子;

first of the 12 hours of day in

    ancient Chinese time scale

    (*i.e.* 11 pm to 1 am) 子時三刻;

one of the 4 categories

    in Chinese classics 經、史、子、集;

one of 5 ancient lord titles 公、侯、伯、子、男

/ • ㄗ, zi$^5$/

*ending character of a noun word*

*as placed after noun* 兒子, 孫子, 鍊子, 筷子, 鍋子,

蝦子, 扇子, 桶子, 盒子, 蓋子,

簾子, 窗子, 桌子, 椅子, 鏡子,

個子, 架子, 棍子, 桃子, 李子,

果子, 餃子, 包子, 韭菜合子;

*verb* 起子, 拍子, 鏟子, 刷子, 梳子,

骰子;

*adj.* 聾子, 瞎子, 傻子, 愣子, 呆子,

色子, 亂子, 老子, 小子;

*quantity word* 兩下子, 這陣子, 這檔子, 這下子

**Radical:** 子 (itself).

# 48. 說

## Script Evolution

說 說 說 說

## The Story

說 說 說 說

/ㄕㄨㄛ, shuo/    "to elucidate", "to explain"

**Associative Compound** (會意) of

言 (/ㄧㄢˊ, yan[2]/ "to speak frankly") and

兌 (/ㄩㄝˋ, yue[4]/ "delighted", *also providing sound*)

to imply *speaking frankly to bring delight*,

hence *"to elucidate"*, *"to explain"*.

言 + 兌 ＝ 說 說

**Note**: ㄩㄝ and ㄨㄛ are the same sound.

## The Stroke Sequence

說 說 說 說 說 說 說 說 說 說
說 說 說 說 說 說 說 說 說 說
說 說 說 說

說 說 說 說

## The Anatomy

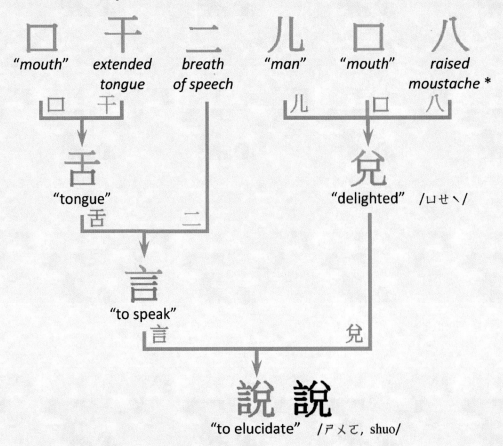

口 干 二 儿 口 八

"mouth"　extended　breath　"man"　"mouth"　raised
　　　　　tongue　of speech　　　　　　　moustache *

口 干　　　　　儿 口 八

舌

"tongue"

舌　　　二

言

"to speak"

言　　　　　　　　　　兌

兌

"delighted"　/ㄩㄝ丶/

說 說

"to elucidate"　/ㄕㄨㄛ, shuo/

\*: The moustache on a smiling face is always raised.

## The Trinity – Sound(s), Semantics, and Synopses

/ㄕㄨㄛ, shuo/

| | |
|---|---|
| to elucidate, to explain | 說明; |
| to give a discourse | 說理, 細說, 說戲; |
| to tell | 說故事, 說書; |
| to talk | 光說不練; |

| to speak | 訴**說**, 演**說**, **說**來聽聽, 有話好**說**; |
|---|---|
| to criticize | **說**三道四; |
| to scold | 讓我來**說說**他, 被他**說**了一頓; |
| to introduce, to propose | **說**媒, **說**和; |
| theory, postulation, argument | 學**說**, 有此一**說**; |

*in classical Chinese*,

| to speak | 「暗相思，無處**說**。」; |
|---|---|
| to explain | 「儒者**說**五經，多失其實。」; |
| to discuss | 「楚人陸鴻漸爲[為]茶論，<br>  **說**茶之功效<br>  并煎茶炙茶之法。」; |
| theory | 「原始反終，<br>  故知死生之**說**。」 |

/ㄕㄨㄟˋ, shui⁴/

| to convince, to persuade | **說**服, 遊**說**, **說**客; |
|---|---|

*in classical Chinese*,

| to convince, to persuade | 「其自任以天下之重如此，<br>  故就湯而**說**之以伐夏救民。」 |
|---|---|

/ㄩㄝˋ, yue⁴/

*in classical Chinese*,

| delighted [=悅] | 「學而時習之，不亦**說**乎！」 |
|---|---|

**Radical:** 言.

# 49. 產

**Script Evolution**

**The Story**

/ㄔㄢˇ, chan³/    "to produce in repeatable fashion"

**Associative Compound** (會意) of

生 (/ㄕㄥ, sheng/ "to produce") and

彥 (/ㄧㄢˋ, yan³ "cave inscription recording life experience",

*also providing sound*) in Reduced Form 彥

to imply *producing something based on recorded experience* or

*producing in repeatable fashion*,

hence "*to produce in repeatable fashion*".

The story of *producing something based on recorded experience* as told

through time by the character 產 is shown below.

| Bronze | Seal | Standard |

178

## The Stroke Sequence

產 產 產 產 產 產 產 產 產 產

產 產 產 產 產 產 產 產 產 產

產

產

## The Anatomy

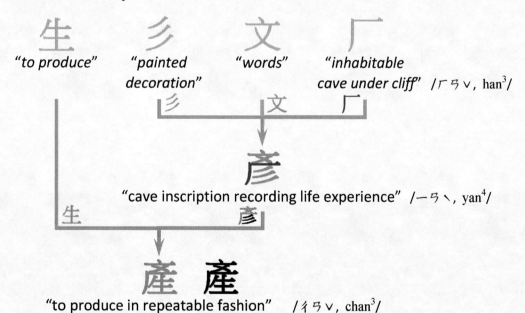

生 彡 文 厂

"to produce"    "painted decoration"    "words"    "inhabitable cave under cliff" /ㄏㄢˇ, han³/

彡 文 厂

彦

"cave inscription recording life experience" /一ㄢˋ, yan⁴/

生 彦

產 産

"to produce in repeatable fashion"    /ㄔㄢˇ, chan³/

## The Trinity – Sound(s), Semantics, and Synopses

/ㄔㄢˇ, chan³/

to produce in repeatable fashion        盛產, 出產, 產卵;

to give birth to                        產子;

179

| | |
|---|---|
| related with birth giving | 產婦, 產科, 產房; |
| produce | 農產; |
| product | 礦產, 海產, 特產, 名產, 產品, 產量, 產能, 產地; |
| industry | 產、官、學; |
| property | 財產, 家產, 不動產; |
| *in classical Chinese,* | |
| to give birth to | 「且父母之於子也， 產男則相賀， 產女則相殺。」; |
| produce | 「德上及飛鳥，下至水蟲， 草木諸產，皆被其澤。」; |
| property | 「居無幾何，致產數十萬。」; |
| *surname* | 姓氏 |

**Radical:** 生.

# 50. 種

**Script Evolution**

種 種 種 種

**The Story**

種 種 種 種

/ㄓㄨㄥˋ, zhong[4]/    "to plant"

**Semantic-Phonetic Compound** (形聲) of

禾 (/ㄏㄜˊ, he[2]/ "grain crop") *for semantics* and

重 (/ㄓㄨㄥˋ, zhong[4]/ "heavy") *for sound*

to mean *"to plant"*.

禾 + 重 ≡ 種 種

"grain crop"    /ㄓㄨㄥˋ, zhong[4]/    /ㄓㄨㄥˋ, zhong[4]/ "to plant"

**The Stroke Sequence**

種 種 種 種 種 種 種 種 種 種

種 種 種 種 種 種 種 種 種 種

種 種 種 種

# 種種種種

## The Anatomy

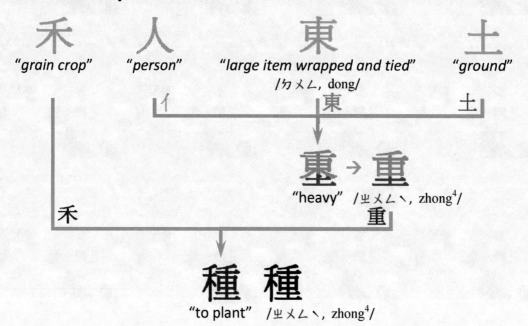

禾     人     東     土

*"grain crop"*    *"person"*    *"large item wrapped and tied"*    *"ground"*

/ㄉㄨㄥ, dong/

亻 東 土

重 → 重

*"heavy"* /ㄓㄨㄥˋ, zhong⁴/

禾 重

種 種

*"to plant"* /ㄓㄨㄥˋ, zhong⁴/

## The Trinity – Sound(s), Semantics, and Synopses

/ㄓㄨㄥˋ, zhong⁴/

to plant, to sow seed       種花, 種菜, 種樹,

種瓜得瓜，種豆得豆,

種禍得禍，種福得福;

to inoculate       種牛痘;

*in classical Chinese,*

to sow seed       「愼[慎]其**種**，勿使數，

亦無使疏。」,

「皋陶邁**種**德，德乃降，

黎民懷之。」;

| to plant | 「東西植松柏， |
| | 　左右**種**梧桐。」; |
| to breed, to rear | 「以肥其身， |
| | 　以**種**其子孫。」; |
| to inoculate | 「**種**痘而愈，遂傳於世。」 |

/ㄓㄨㄥˇ, zhong³/

| seed | 菜**種**, **種**籽; |
| (human) race | 黃**種**人, 白**種**人; |
| breed, species | 雜**種**, 混**種**, 純**種**德國牧羊犬; |
| bloodline | 絕**種**; |
| classification (kind, variety) | 品**種**, 兵**種**, **種**類, 這**種**, 那**種**; |
| courage, grit, guts | 有**種**, 帶**種**; |

*quantity word, for*

| kinds, types | 兩**種**食物, 各**種**情況; |

*in classical Chinese,*

| seed | 「家有好李，常出貨之， |
| | 　恐人得**種**，恆鑽其核。」; |
| human race | 「詔拜前校尉馬賢爲[為]謁者， |
| | 　鎮[鎮]撫諸**種**。」; |
| classification | 「歆乃集六藝羣[群]書， |
| | 　**種**別爲[為]七略。」 |

**Radical:** 禾.

# 51. 行

## Script Evolution

扑　北　竍　行　行　行

## The Story

竍　竍　行　行

/ㄒ一ㄥˊ, xing² / "to walk"

**Pictograph** (象形) of *an intersection of two roads, i.e. crossroads,*

to imply *place where people walk,*

hence *"to walk"*.

It is important to note that when used as a component 行 often appeared in Reduced Form of only its left ( 彳 ) side.  Later, the *left* ( 彳 ) and *right* ( 亍 ) *side* of the *crossroads* were given their own Semantics and Pronunciations, *i.e.* 彳 (/ㄔˋ, chi⁴/ "left step") and

亍 (/ㄔㄨˋ, chu⁴/ "right step")

such that 行 appears to be the combination of *left step* and *right step*.

Most dictionaries list the character 行 as **Associative Compound** (會意) of

彳 (/ㄔˋ, chi⁴/ "left step") and

亍 (/ㄔㄨˋ, chu⁴/ "right step")

to imply *walking,*

hence *"to walk"*.

彳 + 亍 = 行　行

**Note**: The MPS 『彳』 is based on the form and sound of 『彳』.

The pictures of *a crossroads* as rendered through time by the character 行 are shown below.

Bone　　　　Bronze　　　　Seal　　　　Standard

## The Stroke Sequence

行 行 行 行 行 行

行 行 行 行 行 行

## The Trinity – Sound(s), Semantics, and Synopses

/ㄒㄧㄥˊ, xin$^2$/

| | |
|---|---|
| to walk, (to go) on foot, to travel | 行走, 步行, 行人, 行軍, 人行道, 行腳僧人, 行百里路，半九十; |
| going away, travelling | 送行, 遠行, 行前, 行終; |
| group travelling together | 一行人; |
| for (of) travelling | 行李, 行囊, 行裝, 行程, 行期, 行轅, 行館; |
| to move smoothly (unimpededly) | 流行, 風行, 通行, 發行, 運行, 行動, 行車, 行不通*, 行雲流水; |
| Cursive Script of Chinese characters | 行書; |

*: 『行不通』 *moving impeded* to mean "*not working*".

185

| | |
|---|---|
| to practise, to be in practice | 行醫, 行之有年; |
| to carry out | 行刑, 行賄, 行善, 身體力行; |
| to do | 行行好, 多行不義, 例行公事, 行事做風; |
| to administer | 行政; |
| to provide | 行方便; |
| to make effective | 執行, 實行, 推行, 施行; |
| to go (have gone) through | 行大運, 行年五十; |
| act, doing | 行爲[為], 善行, 惡行, 罪行; |
| acceptable, okay | 行不行？, 還不行; |
| capable | 你眞[真]行, 開車騎馬她都行; |
| *used with* 將 *to mean* soon will | 行將就位; |
| round of wine toasting | 酒過三行; |
| *in classical Chinese*, | |
|     to walk | 「三人行，必有我師焉？」, 「行到水窮處, 坐看雲起時。」; |
|     to go | 「幾時杯重把, 昨夜月同行。」; |
|     to move smoothly (unimpededly) | 「天行健, 君子以自強不息。」, 「浮雲終日行, 游子久不至。」, 「言之無文，行而不遠。」; |

| | |
|---|---|
| to undertake, to do | 「多行不義必自斃。」; |
| to make effective | 「推而行之謂之通。」; |
| to have gone through | 「行年二十有五,<br>伉儷猶虛。」; |
| passageway | 「行有死人,尚[尚]或墐之。」; |
| soon (will) | 「衣裳已施行看盡,<br>針線猶存未忍開。」; |
| and also | 「乃使良還,行燒絕棧道。」; |
| element of the Universe | 五行*; |
| *poetry style name* | 短歌行, 琵琶行, 飲馬長城窟行; |
| *surname* | 姓氏 |

*: 『五行』 refers to *metal* (金), *wood* (木), *water* (水), *fire* (火), and *earth* (土).

/ㄒㄧㄥˋ, xin⁴/

| | |
|---|---|
| conduct, behaviour, demeanour | 品行, 操行, 德行, 獸行; |
| *in classical Chinese*, | |
| conduct, behaviour | 「聽其言而觀其行。」 |

/ㄏㄤˊ, hang²/

| | |
|---|---|
| column | 行列, 淚兩行; |
| vertical line of Chinese characters | 一目十行, 字裏[裡]行間; |
| sibling order | 排行老三; |
| business entity | 銀行, 總行, 分行, 商行; |
| trade | 道行, 行當, 各行各業; |
| *used with* 伍 *to mean* army | 行伍出身; |

*in classical Chinese,*

    column

「兩個黃鸝鳴翠柳，
　　一**行**白鷺上青天。」；

    (person's) place

「最苦夢魂，
　　今宵不到伊**行**。」

/ㄏㄤˋ, hang⁴/

things arranged in strictly neat order　樹**行**子;

*in classical Chinese,*

    *in pair to mean* firm, unyielding　「閔子侍側誾誾如也，
　　子路**行行**如也。」

**Radical:** 行 (itself).

# 52. 而

## Script Evolution

## The Story

/ㄦˊ, er²/ "beard"

used for *connecting two actions* or *changing of tones*

**Pictograph** (象形) of *a man's hanging beard*,

hence "*beard*".

Later, for the same sound (/ㄦˊ, er²/) 而 started to be used for *changing of tones* or *connecting two actions*, whilst the Associative Compound 須 (/ㄒㄩ, xu/ "beard") with Radical 頁 (/一ㄝˋ, ye⁴/ "head") and Semantic Component 彡 (/ㄕㄢ, shan/ "hanging hair") was then created for "*beard*".

$$頁 + 彡 = 須 \quad 須$$

Eventually, 須 (/ㄒㄩ, xu/) would carry the semantics of "*must*" surrendering its original semantics of "*beard*" to the Associative Compound 鬚 (/ㄒㄩ, xu/ "beard") with Radical 髟 (/ㄅ一ㄠ, biao/ "hanging hair") and Semantic-Phonetic Component 須 (/ㄒㄩ, xu/ "beard").

$$髟 + 須 = 鬚 \quad 鬚$$

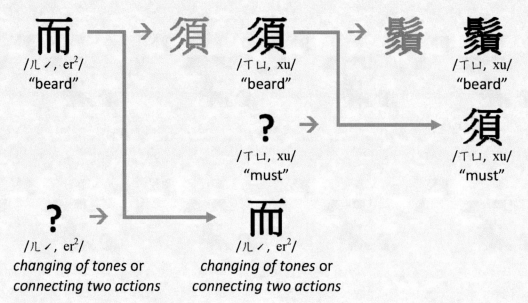

This process of character creation, or re-creation rather, is called Semantic Bifurcation (假借).

The pictures of *a man's hanging beard* as rendered through time by the character 而 are shown below.

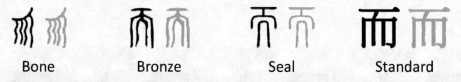

| Bone | Bronze | Seal | Standard |

## The Stroke Sequence

## The Trinity – Sound(s), Semantics, and Synopses

/ㄦˊ, er²/

> *used for changing of tones to mean*
>> but, yet

殘而不瘵, 視而不見, 大而不當;

*used for connecting two actions to mean*

    and also 　　　　　　　　　　　　學而時習之;

    result of first action 　　　　　破門而入, 席地而坐, 從一而終;

    opposite to first action 　　　　不勞而獲;

*used to emphasize the word before and connect the word after*

    as such 　　　　　　　　　　　　然而, 反而, 進而;

but rather 　　　　　　　　　　　　不是悲傷，而是快樂;

and also 　　　　　　　　　　　　　價廉而物美, 而且;

consequently 　　　　　　　　　　應運而生, 喜極而泣, 輕而易舉;

    　　　　　　　　　　　　　　　　唇亡而齒寒, 因此而傷心;

only 　　　　　　　　　　　　　　　而已;

*used with* 爲[為] *to mean* hence 　　爲[為]求學而離家;

to *for time* (*same as* 以) 　　　　從今而後;

excluding (*same as* 以) 　　　　　除此而外;

*used with* 自 *to mean* from … to … 　自南而北, 自壯而老;

*used to connect adv. and verb* 　　欣然而同意;

*used before time word*

    *to emphasize the time* 　　　　而今, 而後;

*in classical Chinese,*

    beard, sideburn 　　　　　　　　「必深其爪，出其目，

    　　　　　　　　　　　　　　　　　作其鱗之而。」;

    if 　　　　　　　　　　　　　　　「人而無信，不知其可也。」;

    as if 　　　　　　　　　　　　　「雖死而生。」;

    capable of 　　　　　　　　　　「行柔而剛，用弱而強。」;

    I 　　　　　　　　　　　　　　　「而可以報知伯矣。」;

| | |
|---|---|
| you [=爾] | 「夫差！<br>而忘越王之殺而父乎？」； |
| from this time on (*same as* 以) | 「由孔子而來，<br>至於今百有餘歲。」； |
| and | 「哀樂而樂哀，皆喪心也。」； |
| and also | 「學而時習之，不亦說乎？」； |
| therefore | 「情動於中，而形於聲。」； |
| just | 「嘻！甚矣憊！雖然，<br>吾今取此然後而歸爾。」； |
| still | 「舜其至孝矣，五十而慕。」，<br>「年四十而見惡焉，<br>其終也已。」； |
| then | 「君子見幾而作，<br>不俟終日。」； |
| yet | 「其爲[為]人也孝弟，<br>而好犯上者鮮矣。」； |
| even | 「夫一麑而不忍，<br>又何況於人乎？」； |
| thus | 「鋌而走險，何能擇？」； |
| *at end of clause/sentence*<br>　*aux. word for emphasis* | 「已而，已而，<br>今之從政者殆而。」； |
| *at start of clause* how could it be | 「爲[為]仁由己，<br>而由人乎哉？」 |

**Radical:** 而 (itself).

# 53. 方

**Script Evolution**

屮　才　方　方　方　方

**The Story**

方　方　方　方

[ㄈㄤˋ, fang⁴]　"to banish"

/ㄈㄤ, fang/　　"square"せ"", "parallel"

**Associative Compound** (會意) of

人 (勺 /ㄖㄣˊ, ren² / "person") and

一 (Pictograph, side view, of *restraining wooden collar*)

to imply *a person (criminal) with restraining wooden collar*

*to be sent away for banishment,*

hence *"to banish"*.

勺　+　一　≡　方　方

Note that the Standard Script has *head* (丶) of *the person* (*criminal*) separated by the *restraining wooden collar* (一) from *his body* (勺), thus adding one Stroke to the character 人 (勺).

Later, for the same sound (/ㄈㄤ, fang/) and referring to the *square* shape of the *wooden collar* and the two *parallel* pieces that make up the *wooden collar*, 方 started to carry the semantics of *"square"*, *"parallel"*, surrendering its original semantics of *"to banish"* to the Associative Compound 放 (/ㄈㄤㄟ, fang⁴/ Usage Rank #242) with Radical 攴 (攵 /ㄆㄨ, pu/ "to hit lightly") and Semantic-Phonetic Component 方 ([ㄈㄤㄟ, fang⁴] "to banish"). This process of character creation, or re-creation rather, is called Semantic Bifurcation (假借).

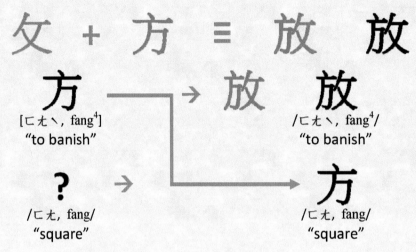

The story of *a person (criminal) with restraining wooden collar to be sent away for banishment* as told through time by the character 方 is shown below.

| Bone | Bronze | Seal | Standard |
|------|--------|------|----------|

## The Stroke Sequence

**Common Fallacy:** Exchanging the 3<sup>rd</sup> & 4<sup>th</sup> Stroke.

## The Anatomy

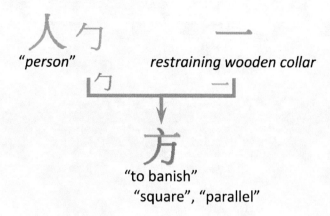

"person"　　restraining wooden collar

"to banish"
"square", "parallel"

## The Trinity – Sound(s), Semantics, and Synopses

/ㄈ尢, fāng/

| | |
|---|---|
| square | 方桌, 方塊, 方巾, 方寸*; |
| square-angled shape | 正方, 長方; |
| righteous (cutting no corners) | 爲[為]人方正, 品行方正; |
| parallel | 方軌, 方軒; |
| in parallel, side by side | 比方; |
| matching, equal | 相方; |
| proper | 大方; |
| direction | 東方, 方向, 方面, 坍方, 右前方, 四面八方; |
| *used with 圓 to mean* area | 方圓百里; |
| place, region | 地方, 遠方, 何方; |
| local, dialectal | 方言, 方音; |

*: 『方寸』 *a square inch of the heart* or *centre of heart* to refer to
"*what's in one's heart or mind*".

| | |
|---|---|
| side, party | 對方, 我方, 雙方, 多方, 各方; |
| method, methodology | 方法, 方式, 方便, 百方迴避, |
| | 千方百計, 教[教]導有方; |
| recipe | 配方, 祕方; |
| medicine prescription | 藥方, 偏方, 處方, 方子; |
| still | 來日方長, 方興未艾; |
| only just (to come to) | 方才, 方知; |
| *math, science* | |
|     power, root | 平方, 立方, 開平方, 開立方; |
|     *to use as for* formula | 方程式; |
| *quantity word, for* | |
|     square objects (pieces) [=塊] | 一方匾額, 一方手帕; |
| *in classical Chinese,* | |
|     in parallel | 「車不得方軌, |
| |    騎不得比行。」; |
|     righteous (cutting no corners) | 「是以聖人方而不割, |
| |    廉而不劌。」; |
|     ground | 「圓, 天也; 方, 地也。」, |
| | 「戴圓履方, 抱表懷繩。」; |
|     just | 「如夢方醒。」; |
|     only just to come to | 「書到用時方恨少。」; |
|     at (*time*) | 「方今之時, 僅免刑焉。」, |
| | 「憚家方隆盛時, |
| |    乘朱輪者十人。」; |

| about to | 「今治水軍八十萬眾，<br>方與將軍會獵於吳。」; |
|---|---|
| *used with* 圓 *to mean* | |
| shape, form | 「方圓大小隨人，<br>腹裏[裡]文章儒雅。<br>有時滿臉桃紅，<br>常在風前月下。」; |
| guideline, principle | 「奇文高論，大或出於繩檢；<br>比聲協句，小亦合於方圓。」; |
| in between sky and ground | 「羅方圓而綺錯，<br>窮海陸而兼薦。」; |
| boundary, range | 「建安二十四年秋七月，<br>築壇於沔陽，方圓九里。」; |
| to arrange | 「至於綾紗等物，<br>猶是本州所出，<br>易於方圓。」; |
| to scheme | 「有事擁遏教化，<br>不得者，無不相問。<br>僕嘗與方圓，<br>行下皆得通暢。」; |
| to be flexible, to adapt | 「非僕之不可苟合，<br>道義之人，皆不合也。<br>而受性介僻，不能方圓。」; |
| *surname* | 姓氏 |

**Radical:** 方 (itself); originally 人 (勹).

# 54. 面

## Script Evolution

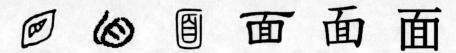

## The Story

/ㄇㄧㄢˋ, mian⁴/    "face"

**Associative Compound** (會意) of

首 (百 /ㄕㄡˇ, shou³/ "person's head"

　　　　　　emphasizing *its front with the nose*) and

囗 (/ㄨㄟˊ, wei²/ "circumference", "to enclose")

to imply *what is enclosed by the boundary of the front of a person's head*, hence "*face*".

**Note**: 百 is the archaic form of 首 (/ㄕㄡˇ, shou³/ "head").

Standard Form has 圓 written as 面, which seems to emphasize the part of a person's face from below the nose bridge, hence 面 in lieu of 圓.

It is interesting to note that at time of the Bone Script and the Bronze

Script the centre detail of *a person's face* was the *eye* (  ). The stories of *a person's face* as told through time by the character 面 are shown below.

Bone          Bronze          Seal          Standard

## The Stroke Sequence

## The Anatomy

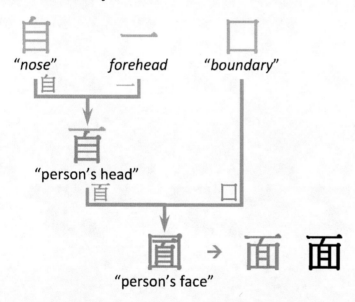

自
"nose"

一
forehead

口
"boundary"

自 一

百
"person's head"

百 口

圓 → 面 面
"person's face"

## The Trinity – Sound(s), Semantics, and Synopses

/ㄇㄧㄢˋ, mian⁴/

face

面部, 面貌, 面色, 面容, 面相,
相面, 青面獠牙, 白面書生,
面有難色, 面如枯槁, 以淚洗面;

199

| | |
|---|---|
| facing | 背山**面**水, **面**壁思過; |
| presence (to appear, to show face) | 出**面**, 見**面**, 會**面**; |
| how one is regarded | 顏**面**, 臉**面**, 情**面**, **面**子*; |
| identity | 雙**面**間諜; |
| in person (face-to-face) | 當**面**, **面**談, **面**商, **面**議, **面**斥, **面**辭, 耳提**面**命, **面**授機宜; |
| surface | 路**面**, 水**面**, 地**面**, 湖**面**, 海**面**, 封**面**, 表**面**, 平**面**, **面**積, **面**額**; |
| referenced (implied) level or surface | 上**面*****, 下**面*****; |
| outer fabric of a garment or quilt | 鵝黃緞**面**(兒)做工講究的旗袍, 被**面**(兒)是山水湘繡的水藍軟緞; |
| direction | 正**面**, 背**面**, 前**面**, 後**面**, 四**面**八方; |
| aspect, angle | 片**面**, 全**面**, 多方**面**; |
| collective layout (of matter) | 場**面**, 局**面**, 世**面**; |
| percentage | 贏**面**, 勝**面**, 輸**面**; |
| *used with* 體 *to mean* | |
| presentable | 出席典禮得穿得體**面***, |
| appropriacy | 小小年紀言談舉止卻不失體**面**, |
| honourable | 年輕時做了些不體**面**的事; |

*:　『**面**子』means "*what one is positively regarded or recognized as*" or "*surface of an article, e.g. garment, quilt*".

**:　『**面**額』means "*value shown on surface of banknote*".

***:『**面**』should be pronounced in the 5th tone, *i.e.* /‧ㄇㄧㄢ, mian[5]/.

*math geometry,*

    plane                                  點、線[綫]、**面**、體;

*quantity word, for*

    flat objects                     一**面**牆, 兩**面**鏡子, 三**面**國旗;

*in classical Chinese,*

    face                              「人心之不同，如其**面**焉。」;

    to face                         「次日**面**聖，諸事完畢，
                                     才回家來。」;

    to see one's face             「年月不**面**，思企深劇。」;

    to show presence (face)     「夫爲[為]人子者，
                                  出必告，反必**面**。」;

    facing towards              「北山愚公者，
                                  年且九十，**面**山而居。」;

    in person (face-to-face)     「**面**刺王過，
                                  王至掩耳起走。」;

    (*of man*) beautiful face     「帝乃為公主置**面**首*，
                                  左右三十人。」

\*: 『面首』 *man with beautiful face and hair* to mean
           *"pretty man for woman's sexual indulgence"* or
           *"male concubine"*.

**Radical:** 面 (itself); originally 首 (百).

# 55. 後

**Script Evolution**

後 後 後 後 後 後

**The Story**

後 後 後 後

/ㄏㄡㄟ, hou⁴/     "behind", "late"

**Associative Compound** (會意) of

彳 (/ㄔㄟ, chi⁴/ "left step", "small path"),

幺 (/一ㄠ, yao/ "the youngest", *also providing sound*), and

夊 (/ㄙㄨㄟ, sui/ "to walk slowly")

to imply *on small path the youngest walking slowly and trailing behind*,

hence "*behind*", "*late*".

彳 + 幺 + 夊 ≡ 後 後

**<u>Note</u>**: 幺 and ㄡ are the same sound.

The MPS『彳』is based on the form and sound of『彳』.

The story of *on small path the youngest walking slowly and trailing behind*
as told through time by the character 後 is shown below.

後後 後後 後後 後後

Bone          Bronze          Seal          Standard

## The Stroke Sequence

後後後後後後後後後
後後後後後後後後後

## The Anatomy

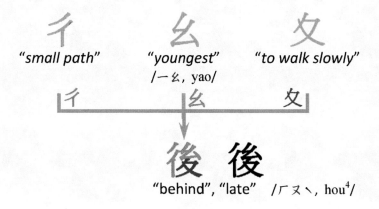

彳      幺      夊

*"small path"*    *"youngest"*    *"to walk slowly"*

/一ㄠ, yao/

後 後

"behind", "late"   /ㄏㄡˋ, hou⁴/

## The Trinity – Sound(s), Semantics, and Synopses

/ㄏㄡˋ, hou⁴/

| | |
|---|---|
| behind | 落**後**, 背**後**, 敵**後**, 幕**後**; |
| appearing or falling behind in time | **後**代, **後**生, **後**輩, **後**進, **後**人, **後**半段; |
| late | 先來**後**到, **後**來居上; |
| back, rear | **後**排, **後**院, **後**門; |
| after | 前因**後**果; |
| still to come | **後**天, **後**來; |
| offspring | 名人之**後**; |
| post- | 戰**後**; |

*in classical Chinese,*

    to fall behind 　　　　　　　　「非敢**後**也，馬不進也。」;

    to put on low priority 　　　　「事君敬其事，而**後**其食。」;

    to expel 　　　　　　　　　　「願大王察玉人、李斯之意，
　　　　　　　　　　　　　　　　　　而**後**楚王、胡亥之聽。」;

    *surname* 　　　　　　　　　　姓氏

**Radical:** 彳.

# 56. 多

## Script Evolution

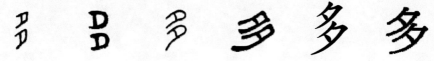

## The Story

/ㄉㄨㄛ, duo/    "more than enough", "plenty"

**Associative Compound** (會意) of

夕 (/ㄖㄡˋ, rou⁴/ "meat") and

夕 (/ㄖㄡˋ, rou⁴/ "meat")

to imply *two pieces of meat being more than enough*,

hence *"more than enough"*, *"plenty"*.

The story of *two pieces of meat being more than enough* as told through

time by the character 多 is shown below.

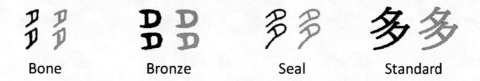

| Bone | Bronze | Seal | Standard |

## The Stroke Sequence

## The Anatomy

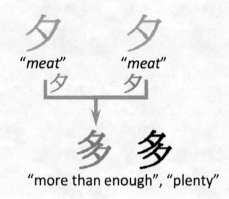

"more than enough", "plenty"

## The Trinity – Sound(s), Semantics, and Synopses

/ㄉㄨㄛ, duo/

| | |
|---|---|
| plenty, abundant | 多樣款式, 菜多得吃不完; |
| multiple, many | 多事之秋, 多才多藝, 多方人馬; |
| multi- | 多功能, 多方位; |
| plus | 一年多, 一百多人; |
| more | 多讀多寫, 多聽少說, 多多益善, 多吃點(兒), 多放點(兒)鹽; |
| often | 多來看您, 多來坐坐; |
| very, much | 多謝, 好多了, 快得多; |
| most, majority | 多是沒用的資料; |

206

| | |
|---|---|
| exceedingly | 多情; |
| extra as unnecessary | 多疑, 多慮, 多心, 多餘, 多管閒事; |
| extra | 不遑多讓, 放多點(兒)糖; |
| *in classical Chinese*, | |
| many, multiple | 「多才豐藝，強記洽聞。」; |
| often | 「若衡等輩，不可多得。」; |
| majority of a large number | 「諸侯多謀伐寡人者。」; |
| only | 「多見其不知量也。」; |
| *surname* | 姓氏 |
| /ㄉㄨㄛˊ, duo$^2$/ | |
| so, such | 多好的安排, 多美的音樂; |
| *adv.* how | 多大歲數[年紀]？ |

**Radical:** 夕.

# 57. 定

## Script Evolution

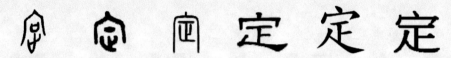

## The Story

/ㄉㄧㄥˋ, ding⁴/   "stable"

**Associative Compound** (會意) of

宀 (/ㄇㄧㄢˊ, main²/ "large house", "roof") and

正 (/ㄓㄥˋ, zheng⁴/ "orthogonal", "proper", *also providing sound*)

to imply *house for proper shelter and providing stability,*

hence "*stable*".

宀 + 正 ≡ 定 定

For obvious aesthetic reasons, Standard Form changed 2 (last) of the 5 orthogonal Strokes in 正 to the more artistic slanted Strokes as in 疋. Hence, the Standard Form of this character is the aesthetic and artistically well balanced 定 in lieu of the all too serious 宑 with almost all orthogonal Strokes.

定 宑 → 定 定

The story of *house for proper shelter and providing stability* as told through time by the character 定 (定) is shown below.

Bone      Bronze      Seal      Standard

## The Stroke Sequence

定 定 定 定 定 定 定 定

定 定 定 定 定 定 定 定

## The Anatomy

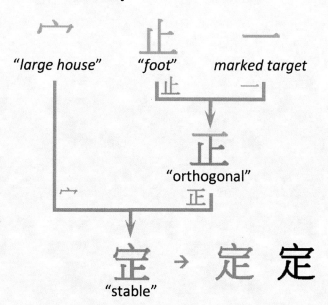

宀      止      一

"large house"      "foot"      marked target

正

"orthogonal"

定 → 定 定

"stable"

# The Trinity – Sound(s), Semantics, and Synopses

/ㄉㄧㄥˋ, ding⁴/

| | |
|---|---|
| stable | 安定, 穩定; |
| confirmed, not to be challenged | 定理, 定義, 定律, 定局, 定論, 一定, 肯定; |
| fixed | 定產, 定業; |
| regulated, controlled | 定時, 定量, 定期; |
| to fix, to stabilize | 定形, 定裝, 定案; |
| to set, to decide, to determine | 決定, 否定, 裁定, 定奪; |
| to regulate | 約定, 制定, 訂定; |
| definitely, surely, absolutely | 定能成功, 定死無疑; |
| *in classical Chinese*, | |
| exactly | 「卿云艾艾，定是幾艾？」; |
| definitely | 「定知相見日， 爛漫倒芳樽。」; |
| *surname* | 姓氏 |

**Radical:** 宀.

# 58. 學

## Script Evolution

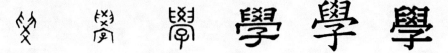

## The Story

/ㄒㄩㄝˊ, xue$^2$/     "to learn", "school"

**Associative Compound** (會意) of

臼 (/ㄐㄩˊ, ju$^2$/ "to use both hands" referring to *crafts*),

爻 (/ㄧㄠˊ, yao$^2$/ "signs", "symbols" referring to *writing symbols*,

*also providing sound*),

子 (/ㄗˇ, zi$^3$/ "child"), and

宀 (/ㄇㄧˋ, mi$^4$/ "roof" referring to *building*)

to imply *a building for children to learn crafts and writing symbols*,
hence *"to learn"*, *"school"*.

臼 + 爻 + 子 + 宀 ≡ 學 學

**Note**: ㄧㄠ and ㄩㄝ are variant sounds to each other. They are found
in many characters' multiple pronunciations.

It is interesting to note that at time of the Bone Script the character told a
simpler story of *crafts* ( 𣥺 ) *and writing symbols* ( 爻) *to learn*, hence *"to*

211

*learn*". The story of *learning crafts and writing symbols* as told through time by the character 學 is shown below.

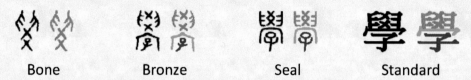

| Bone | Bronze | Seal | Standard |

Throughout history, the character 斅 (斆 /ㄒㄧㄠˋ, xiao⁴/) and 學 (/ㄒㄩㄝˊ, xue²/) were used almost interchangeably to mean "*to be aware*" or "*to become enlightened*". However, with the Radical 攵 (攴 /ㄆㄨ, pu/ "to hit lightly"), the awareness in 斅 (斆 /ㄒㄧㄠˋ, xiao⁴/) should be made by other person or people, hence "*to make aware*" or "*to enlighten*". On the other hand, the absence of 攵 (攴 /ㄆㄨ, pu/) or simply 學 (/ㄒㄩㄝˊ, xue²/) clearly indicates self-made awareness, thus "*to learn*".

Most dictionaries list 學 (/ㄒㄩㄝˊ, xue²/) as

**Associative Compound** (會意) of

爻 (/ㄐㄧㄠˋ, jiao⁴/ "to imitate") and

冖 (/ㄇㄧˋ, mi⁴/ "covered" alluding to *ignorant, not knowing*) with

臼 (/ㄐㄩˊ, ju²/ "to use both hands") *providing the sound*

to imply *learning by imitation*,

hence "*to learn*".

**Note**: ㄩ and ㄩㄝ are the same sound.

## The Stroke Sequence

**Note**: Calligraphists write the first 8 Strokes of 學 in a different sequence as shown below.

## The Anatomy

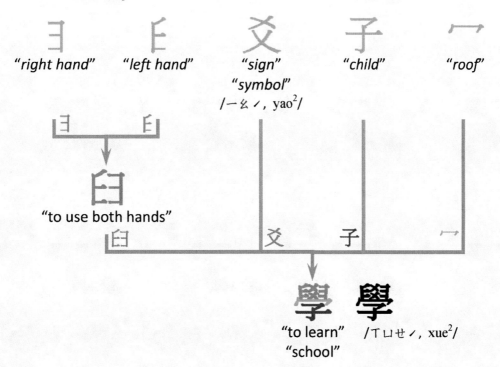

彐 "right hand"

彐 "left hand"

爻 "sign" "symbol" /一ㄠˊ, yao$^2$/

子 "child"

冖 "roof"

臼 "to use both hands"

學 學 "to learn" "school" /ㄒㄩㄝˊ, xue$^2$/

# The Trinity – Sound(s), Semantics, and Synopses

/ㄒㄩㄝˊ, xue$^2$/

| | |
|---|---|
| to learn | 學習, 學中文, 學做飯; |
| to comprehend | 不學; |
| to imitate | 學狗叫; |
| school, place where things are<br>    taught or can be learnt | 學校, 小學, 中學, 大學, 入學; |
| discipline of study or research | 科學, 文學, 語言學, 天文學; |
| educational | 學界; |
| academic | 學術; |
| theoretical | 學理; |
| scholarly | 學者; |

*in classical Chinese,*

| | |
|---|---|
| to learn | 「學於古訓乃有獲。」; |
| to study | 「仕而優則學,<br>        學而優則仕。」,<br><br>「玉不琢,不成器;<br>        人不學,不知道。」; |
| to imitate | 「劉公把他言語學了一遍。」; |
| school | 「國子先生晨入太學。」; |
| *surname* | 姓氏 |

//ㄒㄧㄠˊ, xiao$^2$//    Alternative Pronunciation only to mean the following

to imitate, to follow        學一學

**Radical:** 子 (/ㄗˇ, zi$^3$/ "youngster"); originally 臼.

214

# 59. 法

**Script Evolution**

**The Story**

/ㄈㄚˇ, fa³/    "law"

**Associative Compound** (會意) of

水 (氵/ㄕㄨㄟˇ, shui³/ "water" referring to *level* and *equality*),

廌 (/ㄓˋ, zhi⁴/ "legendary unicorn with ability to deliberate merits"),

and

去 (/ㄑㄩˋ, qu⁴/ "to remove")

to imply *an equal system to find merits and punish the wrong side*,
hence the "*law*".

It is important to note that at time of the Bronze Script the component 去
was placed at the far left corner of the Compound to emphasize *removing* as
shown below.

      Bronze      Seal      Standard

Later, the Customary Alternate 法 with 廌 removed from 灋 was created and used so extensively that 法 became the Standard Form with 灋 stepping back as Original (本字).

## The Stroke Sequence

## The Anatomy

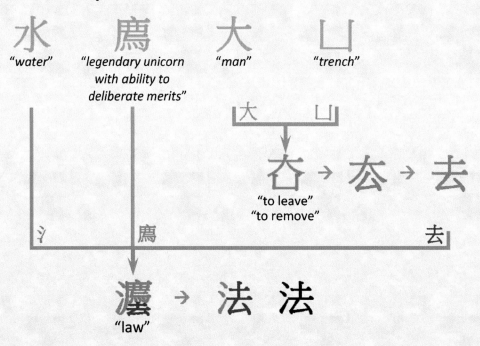

水　　　廌　　　大　　　凵
"water"　"legendary unicorn　"man"　"trench"
　　　　with ability to
　　　　deliberate merits"

奋 → 厺 → 去
"to leave"
"to remove"

氵　　廌　　　　　　　去

灋 → 法 法
"law"

## The Trinity – Sound(s), Semantics, and Synopses

/ㄈㄚˇ, fa³/

law, decree　　　　　　　　　　憲法, 民法, 守法, 違法, 法辦;

216

| | |
|---|---|
| of law, legal | 法令, 法律, 法典, 法條, 法規, 法源, 法理, 法人, 法院, 法官; |
| rule, regulation, principle | 文法, 法則, 法統; |
| technique | 書法, 畫法; |
| method | 方法, 辦法; |
| approach, style | 穿法, 吃法, 做法, 語法; |
| as role model | 效法, 師法; |
| mysterious or supernatural practice | 作法, 魔法, 法術, 法師; |
| of Buddhism | 佛法, 法會, 法衣, 法號; |
| a Chinese philosophy focusing on the importance of laws | 法家; |

*in classical Chinese*,

| | |
|---|---|
| law, decree | 「法者，憲令著於官府。」; |
| system, regulation | 「祭祀之禮，居喪之服，哭泣之位，皆如其國之故，謹修其法而審行之。」; |
| mechanism | 大水法*; |
| advisory | 法語; |
| to follow as role model | 「養天地正氣，法古今完人。」; |
| Buddhism philosophy | 「法尙[尚]應捨，何況非法？」; |
| *surname* | 姓氏 |

*:『大水法』 *The magnificent water fountains* was one of the many architectures to behold in the Chinese royal garden (圓明園, 1707) looted then devastated by the Eight-Power Allied Force in 1860.

/ㄈㄚˊ, fa$^2$/

idea, solution 想個**法**子

/ㄈㄚ, fa/ only when used as 法兒

idea, solution 沒**法**兒, 想個**法**兒

/ㄈㄚˋ, fa$^4$/

France, of France, French 法國, 法文, 法人, 法語

**Note**: Although many pronounce this character in the 3$^{rd}$ tone to mean "France, of France, French", the 4$^{th}$ tone is much more polished, proper, and preferred to avoid confusions with words like 法人 (/ㄖㄣˊ, ren$^2$/), 法王 (/ㄨㄤˊ, wang$^2$/), 法文 (/ㄨㄣˊ, wen$^2$/), 法語 (/ㄩˇ, yu$^3$/), 法幣 (/ㄅㄧˋ, bi$^4$/), and 法規 (/ㄍㄨㄟ/, gui/) or 法制 (/ㄓˋ, zhi$^4$/). Hence,

法 in 3$^{rd}$ tone (上聲),

法人 means "*legal entity*",

法王 means "(*of Buddhism*) *the supreme monk*",

法文 means "*Buddhism scripture*",

法語 means "(*of Buddhism*) *advice*",

法幣 means "*official currency*", esp. referring to *the Chinese currency from 1935 to 1948*, and

法規[制] means "*laws and regulations*", "*legal system*", whilst

法 in 4$^{th}$ tone (去聲),

法人 means "*Frenchman*",

法王 means "*King of France*",

法文 means "*French language*",

法語 means "*spoken French language*",

法幣 means "*French currency*", and

法規[制] means "*French system*".

**Radical**: 水 ( 氵).

# 60. 所

**Script Evolution**

所 所 所 所 所

**The Story**

所 所 所 所

[ㄙㄨˇ]              "chopping wood to build house",

                                 "wood chopping sound"

/ㄙㄨㄛˇ, suo$^3$/      "location"

**Associative Compound** (會意) of

斤 (/ㄐㄧㄣ, jin/ "axe for chopping wood") and

戶 (/ㄏㄨˋ, hu$^4$/ "door", "house", "household", *also providing sound*)

to imply *chopping wood to build house*,

hence *"chopping wood to build house"*, *"wood chopping sound"*.

斤 + 戶 ≡ 所 所

**Note**: ㄨ and ㄩ are variations of each other.

Later, referring to the *location* and *small area* to build the house, 所 started to carry the semantics of *"location"*, *"small area"*. This process of character creation, or re-creation rather, is called Semantic Bifurcation (假借).

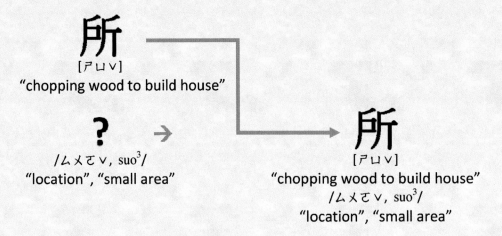

所
[ㄕㄨˇ]
"chopping wood to build house"

? → 所
/ㄙㄨㄛˇ, suo³/              [ㄕㄨˇ]
"location", "small area"       "chopping wood to build house"
/ㄙㄨㄛˇ, suo³/
"location", "small area"

The story of *chopping wood to build house* as told through time by the character 所 is shown below.

Bronze          Seal          Standard

## The Stroke Sequence

所 所 所 所 所 所 所 所
所 所 所 所 所 所 所 所

## The Anatomy

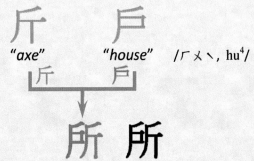

斤          戶
"axe"        "house"    /ㄏㄨˋ, hu⁴/

斤          戶
          ↓
所 所

"chopping wood to build house", "wood chopping sound"  [ㄕㄨˇ]
"location"    /ㄙㄨㄛˇ, suo³/

220

# The Trinity – Sound(s), Semantics, and Synopses

/ㄙㄨㄛˇ, suo³/

| | |
|---|---|
| location, place | 處所, 住所, 所在; |
| position, circumstance | 死得其所, 各得其所, 在所不惜; |
| organization, institution, agency | 收容所, 研究所, 鄉[鄉]公所; |
| every, all | 所向無敵, 所向披靡; |
| that which, what | 所愛, 所得, 前所未聞; |
| for | 所爲[為]何來; |
| used with 以 to mean henceforth | 所以; |
| used as in (爲[為] + noun + 所 + verb) | |
|     to indicate passive tense | 爲[為]情所苦, 爲[為]民所愛戴; |
| quantity word, for buildings | 一所學校; |

*in classical Chinese,*

| | |
|---|---|
|    place | 「厥之諫我也, 必於無人之所。」; |
|    appropriate position | 「必能使行陣和睦, 優劣得所也。」; |
|    that which, what | 「己所不欲，勿施於人。」; |
|    this | 「所來爲[為]宗族, 亦不爲[為]盤飧。」; |
|    supposedly | 「中冓之言，不可道也； 所可道也，言之醜也。」; |
|    for what | 「長勺之役, 曹劌問所以戰於莊公。」; |

still

「江陵去揚州，
　三千三百里。
　已行一千三，
**所**有二千在。」;

*surname*　　　　　　　　姓氏

**Radical:** 戶; originally 斤.

# 61. 民

## Script Evolution

甲 甲 民 民 民 民

## The Story

民 民 民 民

[ㄇㄤˊ, mang²]　　"blinded slave"

/ㄇㄧㄣˊ, min²/　　"common people"

**Associative Compound** (會意) of

目 (罒 /ㄇㄨˋ, mu⁴/ "eye") and

十 (Pictograph of *an awl-like implement*)

to imply *eye blinded by sharp awl-like implement* or

　　*person whose one eye was blinded on purpose to mark as slave,*

hence "*blinded slave to follow instructions to work*".

罒 ＋ 十 ＝ 民 民

Later, for the same sound (/ㄇㄧㄣˊ, min²/) 民 started to be used for *common people*, surrendering its original semantics of "*blinded slave*" to the Associative Compound 氓 (/ㄇㄤˊ, mang²/ "blinded slave", "aimless people", "people not local to a place") with Radical 民 ([ㄇㄤˊ, mang²] "blinded slave") and Semantic-Phonetic Component 亡 (/ㄨㄤˊ, wang²/ "in hiding").

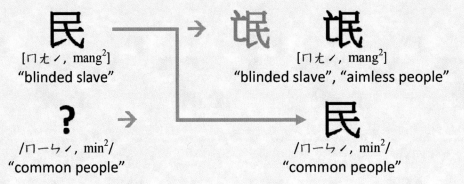

民
[ㄇㄤˊ, mang$^2$]
"blinded slave"

→ 氓 岷
[ㄇㄤˊ, mang$^2$]
"blinded slave", "aimless people"

? →
/ㄇㄧㄣˊ, min$^2$/
"common people"

民
/ㄇㄧㄣˊ, min$^2$/
"common people"

This process of character creation, or re-creation rather, is called Semantic Bifurcation (假借).

The pictures of *eye blinded by sharp awl-like implement* as rendered through time by the character 民 are shown below.

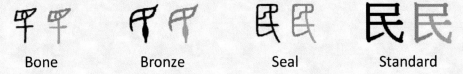

Bone      Bronze      Seal      Standard

## The Stroke Sequence

## The Anatomy

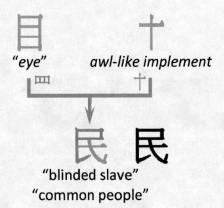

目      十
*"eye"*    *awl-like implement*

民 民
"blinded slave"
"common people"

# The Trinity – Sound(s), Semantics, and Synopses

/ㄇㄧㄣˊ, min$^2$/

| | |
|---|---|
| people (*as opposed to* government) | 人民, 平民, 公民, 民眾; |
| civilian | 民房, 民意, 民情, 民氣; |
| civil | 民政, 民法; |
| folk | 民謠, 民俗; |

*in classical Chinese,*

| | |
|---|---|
| people (of a nation) | 「民惟邦本，本固邦寧。」， |
| | 「民爲[為]貴，社稷次之，<br>　君爲[為]輕。」， |
| | 「民可使由之，<br>　不可使知之。」; |
| mankind | 「食者，民之本也。」， |
| | 「民受無地之中以生。」; |
| people's | 「輕徭薄賦，以寬民力。」 |

**Radical:** 氏 (/ㄕˋ, shi$^4$/ "family clan"), resembling the last 4 Strokes;
originally 目.

# 62. 得

**Script Evolution**

微 徬 得 得 得 得

**The Story**

得 得 得 得 得

/ㄉㄜˊ, de$^2$/    "to obtain"

**Associative Compound** (會意) of

寸 (/ㄘㄨㄣˋ, cun$^4$/ "to pass to hand"),

見 (/ㄐㄧㄢˋ, jian$^4$/ "to see"), and

彳 (/ㄔˋ, chi$^4$/ "left step" referring to *small path*")

to imply *finding something on small path and passing it to hand*,

hence "*to obtain*".

寸 + 見 + 彳 = 得 得

Standard Form has 尋 written as 寻, hence 得 in lieu of 得.

得 得 → 得 得

得 得 → 得 得

**Note:** The MPS 『彳』 is based on the form and sound of 『彳』.

226

It is important to note that 尋 is a Variant form of 得. They were often used interchangeably for a long time before the Seal Script. And 尋 is an Associative Compound of

寸 (/ㄘㄨㄣˋ, cun⁴/ "to pass to hand") and

見 (/ㄐㄧㄢˋ, jian⁴/ "to see")

to imply *finding something and passing it to hand*,

hence *"to obtain"*.

寸 ＋ 見 ＝ 尋　尋

More importantly, at time of the Bone Script and Bronze Script both characters (尋 and 得) actually had

又 (/ㄧㄡˋ, you⁴/ "hand *holding something*") and

貝 (/ㄅㄟˋ, bei⁴/ "seashell", "money" referring to *valuable object*)

not 寸 and 見, thus telling a slightly different story of *hand holding* ( 又 ) ( 𠂇 ) *a valuable object* ( 貝 ) ( 貝 ), hence *"to obtain"*. The stories of *obtaining something* as told through time by the character 尋 and 得 (得) are shown below.

Bone　　　　Bronze　　　　Seal　　　　　Standard

Most dictionaries list the character 得 (得 /ㄉㄜˊ, de²/) as **Semantic-Phonetic Compound** (形聲) of

彳 (/ㄔˋ, chi⁴/ "left step; walking") and

尋 (/ㄉㄜˊ, de²/ "to see and pass to hand")

to mean *"to obtain"*.

彳 + 尋 ≡ 得　得

"left step"　　/ㄉㄜˊ, de²/　　/ㄉㄜˊ, de²/　"to obtain"

## The Stroke Sequence

得 得 得 得 得 得 得 得 得

得 得 得 得 得 得 得 得 得

得

得

## The Anatomy

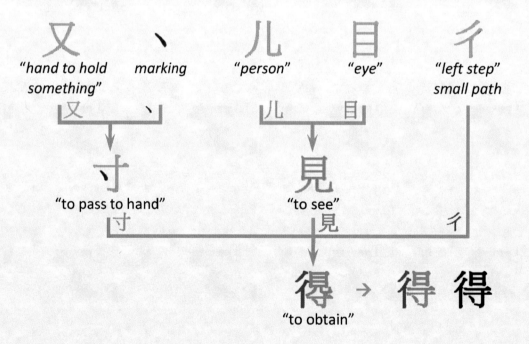

又 "hand to hold something"　、 marking　　儿 "person"　目 "eye"　彳 "left step" small path

寸 "to pass to hand"

見 "to see"

得 "to obtain" → 得 得

# The Trinity – Sound(s), Semantics, and Synopses

/ㄉㄜˊ, de$^2$/

| | |
|---|---|
| to obtain, to gain, to receive | 得獎, 得利, 得手, 得勝, 得知, 失而復得, 深得人心, 得天獨厚; |
| gain, what is gained | 得不償失; |
| to have comprehended | 得道; |
| to have lived (so many years) | 得年八十, 得壽九十; |
| to come across | 得便, 得空; |
| to content | 得意, 自得, 志得意滿; |
| to give result | 二三得六; |
| to fit, to suit | 得體, 得法, 得宜, 相得益章; |
| possessing | 得力*, 他辦事得力, 他有幾個得力的幫手; |
| subsequently thus | 得以[=才可以], 得以實現; |
| result | 不得已**, 萬不得已, 迫不得已, 逼不得已, 勢不得已, 非不得已, 情不[非]得已; |
| can, to be able to | 得過且過, 不得抽菸, 得饒人處且饒人; |
| *adv.* might as well | 得，我們就聽你的。; |
| *adv. indicating objection* | 得了，別再出餿主意了！; |
| *adv. attempting to interrupt* | 得了，別再說了！; |

*: 『得力』 means "*possessing ability (capable)*" or "*effectively*".

**: 『不得已』 means "*after all attempts failing to give results*".

| | |
|---|---|
| *adv. indicating frustration* | 得，這下可完了！； |
| *in classical Chinese,* | |
|     to obtain, to gain | 「鷸蚌相爭，漁翁**得**利。」； |
|     to fit, to suit | 「聚精會神，相**得**益章。」； |
|     to content | 「意氣揚揚，甚自**得**也。」； |
|     satisfied, content | 「面有**得**色。」； |
|     how | 「巴東之峽生凌澌，<br>   彼蒼回軒人**得**知。」； |
|     *void character* (*after verb*) | 「恰似春風相欺**得**，<br>   夜來吹折數枝花。」 |

/ㄉㄟˇ, dei³/

| | |
|---|---|
| must, have to | 你總**得**讓我把話說完； |
| need to | 天沒亮，就**得**出門(兒)； |
| *in classical Chinese,* | |
|     should be, must be | 「出了月就起身，<br>   **得**半個工夫纔回來。」 |

/ㄉㄞˇ, dai³/

| | |
|---|---|
| *colloquial* (*rare*), to suffer | 這回他可**得**了苦頭了 |

/·ㄉㄜ, de⁵/

| | |
|---|---|
| *after v. to indicate result that follows* | 吃**得**飽, 穿**得**暖, 睡**得**好, 坐**得**穩,<br>看**得**見, 覺**得**很好； |
| *after v. to indicate completion* | 進**得**門來,<br>吃**得**苦中苦，方爲[為]人上人； |
| *after v. to indicate consequence* | 蓬頭垢面見不**得**人,<br>他心胸狹隘見不**得**別人比他強； |

*after v. to indicate conclusion*        以此進度不見**得**能如期完工;

/ㄉㄜˋ, de⁴/

*as in* 得瑟, *northern colloquial* [=**得**色], *together to mean*

    to squander        一個月的工資,

                            三兩天就給他**得**瑟光了。;

    to flaunt, to show off little things        那身新衣讓她**得**瑟了好幾天,

                            不就是頂帽子,別窮**得**瑟了。

/ㄉㄜ, de/

*as in* 得瑟 [=哆嗦], *together to mean*

    to tremble        討債的又上門兒了,

                            你說他能不**得**瑟。

**Radical:** 彳; originally 寸.

231

# 63. 經

## Script Evolution

經　經　經　經　經

## The Story

經　經　經　經

/ㄐㄧㄥ, jing/　　"vertical yarn on a weaving machine"

**Associative Compound** (會意) of

糸 (糸 /ㄇㄧˋ, mi[4]/ "fine strand of silk") and

巠 (/ㄐㄧㄥ, jing/ "vertical yarn on weaving machine",

*also providing sound*)

to imply *fine strand of silk used as vertical yarn on a weaving machine*,

hence *"vertical yarn on weaving machine"*.

糸 + 巠 ≡ 經　經

It is important to note that the Semantic-Phonetic Component 巠 is the Original (本字) of 經. In other words, 經 is the re-created character from its Original 巠, a Pictograph (象形) of *vertical yarn on weaving machine*. Bearing the conception of *continuous, long and narrow*, and *light weight*, 巠 serves as the Semantic-Phonetic Component of Associative Compounds like 勁 勁 (/ㄐㄧㄥˋ, jing[4]/ "strong and powerful", /ㄐㄧㄣˋ, jin[4]/ "strength"),

脛 脛 (/ㄐ一ㄥˋ, jing[4]/ "lower leg (leg below knee)", "shin"),

徑 徑 (/ㄐ一ㄥˋ, jing[4]/ "narrow passageway"),

莖 莖 (/ㄐ一ㄥ, jing/ "stem or stalk of plant"),

頸 頸 (/ㄐ一ㄥˇ, jing[3]/ "neck"),　　氫 氫 (/ㄑ一ㄥ, qing/ "hydrogen"),

輕 輕 (/ㄑ一ㄥ, qing/ "light in load or weight"), and

婞 婞 (/ㄒ一ㄥˊ, xing[2]/ "long and slender figure of female", "svelte").

The story of *fine strand of silk used as vertical yarn on a weaving machine* as told through time by the character 經 is shown below.

| Bronze | Seal | Standard |

## The Stroke Sequence

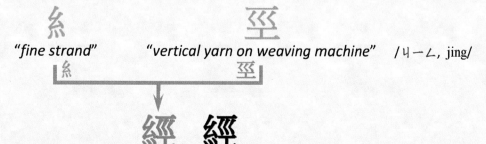

經 經 經

## The Anatomy

糸
*"fine strand"*　　　　　　巠
*"vertical yarn on weaving machine"*　　/ㄐ一ㄥ, jing/

糸　　　　　　巠

經 經
"vertical yarn on a weaving machine"　/ㄐ一ㄥ, jing/

# The Trinity – Sound(s), Semantics, and Synopses

/ㄐㄧㄥ, jing/

| | |
|---|---|
| longitude | 經緯度, 東經, 西經; |
| usual and accepted standard | 天經地義, 離經叛道; |
| common | 荒誕不經; |
| meridian pathway of human body | 經脈, 經絡; |
| religious scriptures | 佛經, 聖經, 可蘭經; |
| to operate (*business*) | 經商, 經營; |
| to govern, to manage | 經管, 經世濟民; |
| economy | 經濟; |
| to go through, to experience | 經手, 經驗, 身經百戰, 飽經患亂, 經年累月; |
| via (*a place en route to destination*) | 經上海去西安; |
| menstruation | 經期, 停經; |
| to sustain | 經得起考驗; |
| often, frequently | 經常, 經費; |

*in classical Chinese*,

| | |
|---|---|
| vertical yarn on weaving machine | 「經正而後緯成。」; |
| to survey and measure (*land*) | 「體國經野。」; |

*used with* 自 *to mean*

to hang oneself

| with a long piece of cloth | 「自經於溝瀆而莫之知也。」; |
|---|---|

elaborate extensive topic-specific

| essay or dissertation | 水經, 茶經, 馬經, 山海經; |
|---|---|

| | |
|---|---|
| five classic Confucianism books | 四書五**經**; |
| one of the 4 categories in Chinese classics | **經**、史、子、集; |
| *surname* | 姓氏 |

**Radical:** 糸 (糸).

# 64. 十

## Script Evolution

## The Story

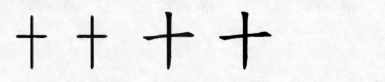

/ㄕˊ, shi² /   "ten"

**Ideograph** (指事) of *one vertical line and a horizontal line at centre*
   to denote *the number ten,*
hence *"ten"*.

It is important to note that at time of the Bone Script the character was *a simple vertical line*, the 90-degree-turned version of the iconic symbol for *the number one* (一, *a horizontal line*) to denote this being the number after which repetition starts, a decimal system. At time of the Bronze Script, *a dot* (◆) at centre of the *vertical line* (│) was added. At time of the Seal Script, the *dot* (◆) was changed to *a horizontal line* ( — ), leading to the Standard Script. The iconic symbols for *the number ten* as represented through time by the character 十 are shown below.

Bone          Bronze          Seal          Standard

## The Stroke Sequence

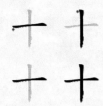

## The Trinity – Sound(s), Semantics, and Synopses

/ㄕ ˊ, shi²/

| | |
|---|---|
| ten * | 十項運動, 一班十人; |
| tenth | 第十次, 十月; |
| all | 十面埋伏; |
| utmost | 十萬火急, 十惡不赦; |
| full, complete, perfect | 十足, 十全十美 |

*:『拾』(Usage Rank #2,091) is often used in
writing financial numbers to avoid alteration.

**Radical:** 十 (itself).

# 65. 三

## Script Evolution

## The Story

/ㄙㄢ, san/    "three"

**Ideograph** (指事) with *three distinct horizontal lines*

    to denote *the number three*,

hence "*three*".

The iconic symbols denoting *the number three* as represented through time by the character 三 are shown below.

| Bone | Bronze | Seal | Standard |
|------|--------|------|----------|

## The Stroke Sequence

238

# The Trinity – Sound(s), Semantics, and Synopses

/ㄙㄢ, san/

| | |
|---|---|
| three * | 三餐, 三角, 三腳架, 三輪車; |
| third | 三月, 第三次; |
| multiple, many | 舉一反三, 三番兩次, |
| | 一問三不知; |
| repeatedly, over and over ** | 三思; |
| *often used with 兩 to mean a few* | 三兩下, 三三兩兩, 三言兩語; |
| *surname* | 姓氏 |

*: 『叁』 (參, Usage Rank #478) is often used in
writing financial numbers to avoid alteration.
A Variant form of 參, 叁 is especially for this purpose.

**: See [ㄙㄢˋ, san⁴] below.

/ㄙㄚ, sa/      northern colloquial [=仨];

| | |
|---|---|
| three people | 哥兒三[仨] |

[ㄙㄢˋ, san⁴]      Recital Pronunciation

| | |
|---|---|
| repeatedly, over and over | 三思 |

**Radical:** 一 (/一, yi/ "one"); originally 三 (itself).

# 66. 之

## Script Evolution

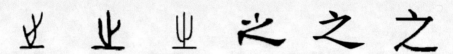

## The Story

/ㄓ, zhi/   "ready to leave for"

**Associative Compound** (會意) of

止 (ㄓ /ㄓˇ, zhi³/ "foot") and

一 (Pictograph of *ground*)

to imply *foot on ground ready to leave for some place*,

hence *"ready to leave for"*.

屮 + 一 ≡ 㞢 㞢

**Note**: The MPS 『ㄓ』 is based on this character's original form 『㞢』

and sound.

Standard Form has 㞢 written as 之, hence 之 in lieu of 㞢.

㞢 㞢 → 之 之
㞢 㞢 → 之 之

It is important to note that in Standard Script, 之 (屮) as a component is often written as 屮 then 士 as in 寺 and 志, or 亠 as in 往 and 市.

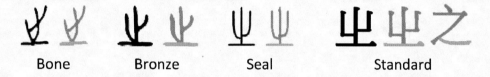

The story of *foot on ground ready to leave for some place* as told through time by the character 之 (屮) is shown below.

| Bone | Bronze | Seal | Standard |

## The Stroke Sequence

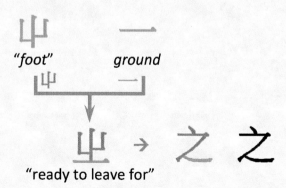

**Common Fallacy:** Combining the 2nd & 3rd Stroke as a single Stroke.

## The Anatomy

屮            一

"foot"        ground

屮            一

屮 → 之  之

"ready to leave for"

# The Trinity – Sound(s), Semantics, and Synopses

/ㄓ, zhi/

| | |
|---|---|
| ready to leave for | 之往, 之官, 之國; |
| *possessive particle* (*same as* 的),<br>    of, for | 人之初, 人民之福, 幸運之神; |
| *struc. particle* (*same as* 的) | 永遠之痛; |
| reason why | 他之能成功，在於努力不懈; |
| till, since (*with reference to time*) | 之前, 之後; |
| *void character* (*after verb*) | 總之, 總而言之; |
| *aux. word*, *for emphasis* | 久而久之; |
| *in classical Chinese*, | |
|     to go to | 「吾欲之南海，何如?」, |
| | 「百爾所思，不如我所之。」; |
|     to come out | 「如語焉而未之然。」; |
|     to take and use | 「故物舍其所長，<br>    之其所短，<br>    堯亦有所不及矣。」; |
|     *possessive particle* (of) | 「余弟死，而子來，<br>    是而子殺余之弟也。」; |
|     to | 「此自少之多，<br>    自微至著也。」; |
|     him, her, it | 「愛之深，責之切。」,<br>「愛之欲其生，<br>    恨之欲其死。」; |

| | |
|---|---|
| this | 「知以之言也，問乎狂屈。」; |
| is (*verb* to be) | 「吾見子之君子也， |
| | 是以告情于子也。」; |
| till | 「之死不悟。」; |
| as | 「比之匪人，不亦傷乎？」; |
| if | 「我之大賢與， |
| | 於人何所不容？ |
| | 我之不賢與，人將拒我， |
| | 如之何其拒人也？」; |
| *aux. word, for emphasis* | 「悵恨久之。」; |
| *surname* | 姓氏 |

**Radical:** 丿 (/ㄆㄧㄝˇ, pie³/ "the right-to-left slanted Stroke"), the 3<sup>rd</sup> Stroke; originally 止.

# 67. 進

## Script Evolution

禺　偈　雔　進　進　進

## The Story

雔　雔　雔　進　進

/ㄐㄧㄣˋ, jin⁴/　　"to move forward"

**Associative Compound** (會意) of

止 (/ㄓˇ, zhi³/ "foot" referring to *walking*),

隹 (/ㄓㄨㄟ, zhui/ "short-tailed bird"), and

彳 (/彳ㄨㄛˋ, chuo⁴/ "narrow path")

to imply *bird walking on narrow path to move forward*,

hence "*to move forward*".

止 ＋ 隹 ＋ 彳 ＝ 雔　雔

Standard Form has 辵 written as 辶, hence 進 in lieu of 雔.

雔　雔　→　進　進

**Note:** The MPS 『彳』is based on the form and sound of 『彳』.

It is important to note that *birds can walk only to move forward (cannot walk backward)*. And at time of the Bone Script the character told the story

244

with *foot* (  ) *and short-tailed bird* ( 刕 ) for *bird walking*.  At time of the Bronse Script, *a narrow path* ( 彳 ) was added to the story to emphasize *bird walking on narrow path not circling round to move backward*, thus leading to the Seal Script and Standard Script.  The stories of *bird walking to move forward* as told through time by the character 進 are shown below.

Bone        Bronze       Seal        Standard

Most dictionaries list 進 as

**Semantic-Phonetic Compound** (形聲) of

辵 (辶 / ㄔㄨㄛˋ, chuo⁴/ "to walk and stop") *for semantics* and

闐 (/ㄌㄧㄣˋ, lin⁴/ "yellow starling") in Reduced Form 閵 *for sound*

to mean *"to move forward"*.

$$ 辶 + 閵 = 進 \quad 進 $$

"to walk and stop"   /ㄌㄧㄣˋ, lin⁴/         /ㄐㄧㄣˋ, jin⁴/ "to ascend"

**The Stroke Sequence**

進 進 進 進 進 進 進 進 進 進

進 進 進 隹 隹 隹 進 進 進 進

進 進

進 進

245

## The Anatomy

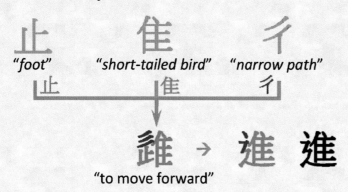

| 止 | 隹 | 彳 |
|---|---|---|
| *"foot"* | *"short-tailed bird"* | *"narrow path"* |

進 → 進 進

"to move forward"

## The Trinity – Sound(s), Semantics, and Synopses

/ㄐㄧㄣˋ, jin⁴/

| | |
|---|---|
| to move forward | 前**進**, 不**進**則退, **進**退兩難; |
| to advance | **進**攻, **進**退失據; |
| to ascend | **進**步; |
| to enter | **進**門, **進**屋, **進**入, **進**來, **進**去; |
| to start | **進**公司; |
| to present as tribute | **進**香, **進**貢; |
| to bring in | **進**貨, **進**帳[賬], 日**進**斗金; |
| to recommend | 引**進**; |
| enthusiastically, eagerly | **進**取; |
| *adv.* inside | 引**進**, 走**進**, 放**進**; |
| section of courtyard | 兩**進**院子; |
| *in classical Chinese*, | |
| to enter | 「今大開城門，必有埋伏。 |
| | 我兵若**進**，中其計也。」; |

246

| | |
|---|---|
| to take commission in office | 「治則**進**，亂則退，<br>　伯夷也。」； |
| to recommend | 「**進**賢興功，以作邦國。」； |
| to present | 「侍飲於長者，酒**進**則起。」，<br>「岑夫子，丹丘生，<br>　將**進**酒，君莫停。<br>　與君歌一曲，<br>　請君爲[為]我傾耳聽。<br>　鐘鼓饌玉不足貴，<br>　但願長醉不復醒。」； |
| section of courtyard | 「右邊一路，<br>　一間一間的房子，<br>　都有**兩進**。」； |
| *surname* | 姓氏 |

**Radical:** 辵 (辶); originally 止.

247

# 68. 等

## Script Evolution

篡 等 等 等

## The Story

篡 篡 等 等

/ㄉㄥˇ, deng³/    "type", "class"

**Associative Compound** (會意) of

竹 (⺮ /ㄓㄨˊ, zhu² "bamboo" referring to *books*) and

寺 ([ㄔˊ, shi²] "to handle appropriately", /ㄙˋ, si⁴/ "court")

to imply *organizing books by type and class*,

hence "*type*", "*class*".

⺮ + 寺 ≡ 等 等

It is important to note that the Semantic-Phonetic Component 寺 is the Original (本字) of 持 (/ㄔˊ, shi²/ "to handle appropriately" Usage Rank #384). In other words, 持 is the re-created character from its Original 寺 ([ㄔˊ, chi²]). Later, for the same sound (/ㄙˋ, si⁴/) 寺 started to carry the semantics of "*court*" surrendering its original semantics of "*to handle appropriately*" to the Associative Compound 持 (/ㄔˊ, shi²/) of

手 (扌 /ㄕㄡˇ, shou³/ "hand") and

寺 ([ㄔˊ, chi²] originally "to handle appropriately", *also providing sound*)
to imply *handling appropriately*,
hence *"to handle appropriately"*.

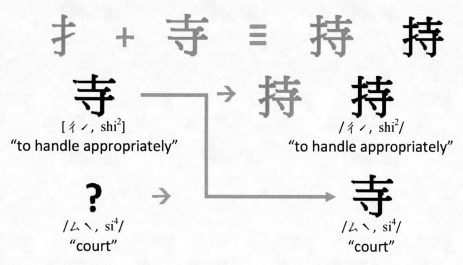

This process of character creation, or re-creation rather, is called Semantic
Bifurcation (假借).

## The Stroke Sequence

## The Anatomy

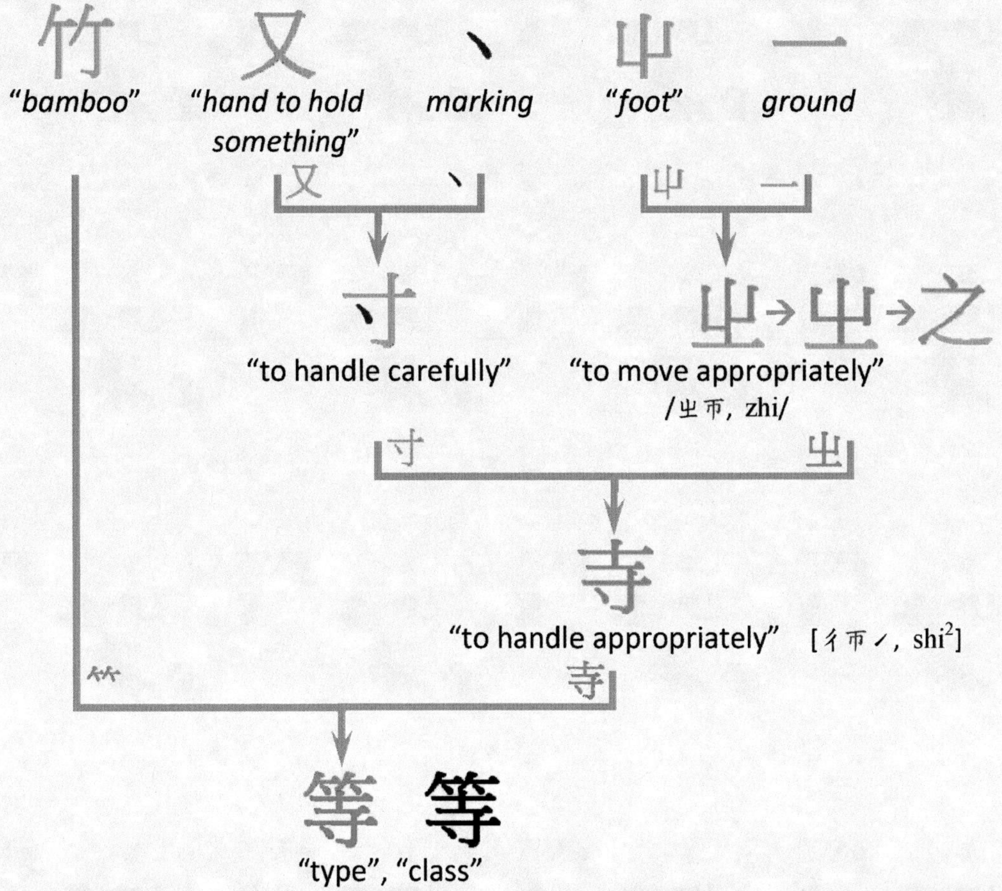
竹 又 丶 屮 一
"bamboo"
"hand to hold something"
marking
"foot"
ground
又 丶
屮 一
寸
"to handle carefully"
屮→屮→之
"to move appropriately"
/ㄓ ㄭ, zhi/
寸
屮
寺
"to handle appropriately"
[ㄔ ㄭ ˊ, shi2]
⺮
寺
等 等
"type", "class"

## The Trinity – Sound(s), Semantics, and Synopses

/ㄉㄥˇ, deng3/

| | |
|---|---|
| type, kind | 何等情況, 這等工程; |
| class, grade, level | 上等, 甲等, 劣等, 低等; |
| degree | 何等嚴重; |
| equal, equivalent | 相等, 等於, 均等, 平等, 等量; |
| same | 高低不等, 等高; |
| et al. | 一干人等; |

| | |
|---|---|
| etc. | 北京，上海**等**大城市; |
| so on and so forth | 早餐有牛奶雞蛋水果**等等**; |
| to wait (for) | **等**車, **等**待, (請)**等等**, **等**不及, |
| | **等**一下, **等**(一)會(兒), **等**你回來; |

in classical Chinese,

    type of small scale for gold, silver,

    or herbal medicine ingredient     **等**子,

    「大**等**秤進，小**等**秤出。」

**Radical:** 竹 (⺮).

# 69. 部

**Script Evolution**

襚 鄁 部 部 部

**The Story**

鄁 鄁 部 部

/ㄅㄨㄟ, bu⁴/     "large military compound", "military unit"

"ministry"

**Semantic-Phonetic Compound** (形聲) of

邑 (阝 /ㄧㄟ, yi⁴/ "city", "community") *for semantics* and

音 (/ㄆㄡˇ, pou³/ "to denounce") *for sound*

to mean *"large military compound"*, *"military unit"*, *"ministry"*.

阝 + 音 = 部 部

"city"     /ㄆㄡˇ, pou³/     /ㄅㄨㄟ, bu⁴/   "ministry"

**Note**: ㄡ and ㄨ are alternate sounds to each other.

The character 部 for *large military compound* as written through time is shown below.

Bronze          Seal          Standard

## The Stroke Sequence

部 部 部 部 部 部 部 部 部 部

部 部 部 部 部 部 部 部 部 部

部

部

## The Anatomy

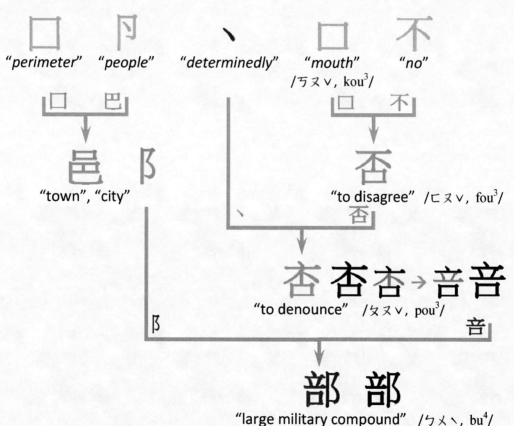

口 卩
*"perimeter"* *"people"*

丶
*"determinedly"*

口 不
*"mouth"* *"no"*
/ㄎㄡˇ, kou³/

口 巴
→
邑 阝
*"town"*, *"city"*

口 不
→
否
*"to disagree"* /ㄈㄡˇ, fou³/

丶
否
→
咅 咅咅→音音
*"to denounce"* /ㄆㄡˇ, pou³/

阝
音
→
部 部
*"large military compound"* /ㄅㄨˋ, bu⁴/
*"military unit"*
*"ministry"*

# The Trinity – Sound(s), Semantics, and Synopses

/ㄅㄨˋ, bu⁴/

| | |
|---|---|
| military unit under command | 部隊, 率部投敵; |
| headquarter of military unit | 營部, 師部, 總部, 司令部; |
| to command | 所部者眾; |
| to deploy | 部署, 部陣, 部防, 部了眼線[綫], 部下*天羅地網; |
| subordinate | 舊部, 部下**; |
| ministry, government department | 外交部, 教[教]育部; |
| department | 出版部, 編輯部; |
| category | 部首, 部件, 按部就班; |
| section, part | 局部, 全部, 胸部, 頭部, 尾部, 部分, 上(半)部, 下(半)部; |

*quantity word*, *for*

| | |
|---|---|
| publications | 一部辭典; |
| plays | 兩部單元劇; |
| films | 三部電影; |
| vehicles | 一部車; |
| machines | 兩部電腦, 三部起重機; |

*: 『部下 (/ㄒㄧㄚˋ, xia⁴/』 means *"to deploy securely"*.

**: 『部下 (/‧ㄒㄧㄚ, xia⁵/』 means *"subordinate"*.

*in classical Chinese*,

| | |
|---|---|
| military unit | 「昆陽即破, 一日之閒, 諸部亦滅矣。」; |

| | |
|---|---|
| to organize and arrange orderly | 「分別**部**居，不相雜廁也。」; |
| to command | 「春，漢王**部**五諸侯兵， |
| | 　　凡五十六萬人，東伐楚。」, |
| | 「世忠獨**部**敢死士殊死鬥， |
| | 　　敵稍卻。」; |

*used with 署 to mean*

| | |
|---|---|
| to deploy | 「漢王大說，遂聽信策， |
| | 　　**部**署諸將。」; |
| subordinate | |
| 　in military command | 「依舊收了書， |
| | 　　空手徑來衙門前招人牌下， |
| | 　　等著**部**署李霸遇來投見他。」; |
| martial art intructor | 「看了這**部**署每打拳耍棍， |
| | 　　眞[真]個高強。」 |

**Radical:** 邑 ( 阝 ).

# 70. 度

**Script Evolution**

度 度 度 度

**The Story**

庹 庹 度 度

/ㄉㄨㄟ, du⁴/   "standard"

**Associative Compound** (會意) of

又 (/ㄧㄡˋ, you⁴/ "hand holding something", *also providing sound*),

廿 (Pictograph of *a stone stove*), and

广 (/ㄧㄢˇ, yan³/ "house")

to imply *installing stone stove in the house following careful*

*measurements and constraints* or *standard procedures*,

hence "*standard (procedure)*".

又 + 廿 + 广 ≡ 度 度

**Note**: 又 and ㄨ are the same sound.

Most dictionaries list the characters 度 (/ㄉㄨˋ, du⁴/) as

**Semantic-Phonetic Compound** (形聲) of

又 (/ㄧㄡˋ, you⁴/ "hand *holding something*") *for semantics* and

庶 (/ㄕㄨˋ, shu⁴/ "multitude") in Reduced Form 庶 *for sound*

to mean "*system*".

$$又 + 庶 \equiv 度$$

度

"hand" /ㄕㄨˋ, shu⁴/ /ㄉㄨˋ, du⁴/ "system"

## The Stroke Sequence

度度度度度度度度度
度度度度度度度度度

## The Anatomy

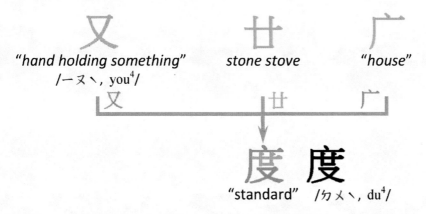

又

"*hand holding something*"    廿    广
/一ㄡˋ, you⁴/    *stone stove*    "*house*"

又    廿    广

度 度

"standard"    /ㄉㄨˋ, du⁴/

## The Trinity – Sound(s), Semantics, and Synopses

/ㄉㄨˋ, du⁴/

| | |
|---|---|
| standard, normality, limit | 尺度, 限度, 過度, 須索無度; |
| system | 制度, 法度; |
| measurable level or degree | 長度, 程度, 進度, 硬度, 溼度, 精度, 密度, 酸度, 鹹度, 配合度; |
| length | 度量衡*; |

*: 『度量衡』 means "*length, capacity, and weight measuring system*".

| | |
|---|---|
| deportment, disposition | 器**度**, 大**度**, 風**度**, 態**度**; |
| dimension | 三**度**空間; |
| to spend time, to live through | **度**過, **度**日如年, 光陰虛**度**; |
| *quantity word*, *for* | |
|     repeated occurrences | 三**度**光臨, 再**度**奪冠; |
|     units | 耗電兩百**度**; |
|     degrees (*angle, temperature, etc.*) | 六十**度**三十分, 攝氏三十六**度**; |
| *in classical Chinese*, | |
|     standard | 「夭行失其**度**,<br>　　陰氣來干陽。」; |
|     system | 「亦所以奉太尊之烈,<br>　　遵文武之**度**。」; |
|     deportment, disposition | 「常有大**度**,<br>　　不事家人生產作業。」; |
|     appearance | 「生因竊往。扣其關,<br>　　果有女道士三四人,<br>　　謙喜承迎,儀**度**皆潔。」; |
|     repeated occurrences | 「青山依舊在,<br>　　幾**度**夕陽紅。」; |
|     to pass through | 「黃河遠上白雲間,<br>　　一片孤城萬仞山。<br>　　羌笛何須怨楊柳,<br>　　春風不**度**玉門關。」; |
|     to move across waterway [=渡] | 「若夫經制不定,<br>　　是猶**度**江河亡維楫。」; |

surname 姓氏

/ㄉㄨㄛˋ, duo⁴/　Alternative Pronunciation //ㄉㄨㄛˊ, duo²//

　　to consider, to ponder　　　　　　審**度**, 揣**度**, 審時**度**勢;

　　to speculate　　　　　　　　　　量**度**, 忖**度**,
　　　　　　　　　　　　　　　　　　以小人之心，**度**君子之腹;

　　*in classical Chinese*,

　　　　to consider, to ponder　　　　「**度**，揆也。」,

　　　　　　　　　　　　　　　　　「神之格思，不可**度**思，
　　　　　　　　　　　　　　　　　　　矧可射思。」,

　　　　　　　　　　　　　　　　　「受其脈書上下經、
　　　　　　　　　　　　　　　　　　　五色診、奇咳術、
　　　　　　　　　　　　　　　　　　　揆**度**陰陽外變。」,

　　　　　　　　　　　　　　　　　「賢家試自心量**度**！」,

　　　　　　　　　　　　　　　　　「只見他搖頭側腦費量**度**。」;

　　　　to speculate　　　　　　　　「庾曰：『可謂以小人之慮，
　　　　　　　　　　　　　　　　　　　度君子之心。』」;

　　　　to measure　　　　　　　　「夫**度**田非益寡，
　　　　　　　　　　　　　　　　　　　而計民未加益。」,

　　　　　　　　　　　　　　　　　「試使山東之國，
　　　　　　　　　　　　　　　　　　　與陳涉**度**長絜大，
　　　　　　　　　　　　　　　　　　　比權量力，
　　　　　　　　　　　　　　　　　　　則不可同年而語矣！」

**Radical:** 广 (/一ㄢˇ, yan³/ "house (under sheltering cliff)"); originally 又.

# 71. 家

**Script Evolution**

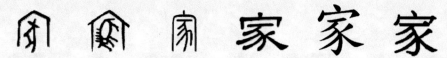

**The Story**

/ㄐㄧㄚ, jia/　　"home"

**Associative Compound** (會意) of

　　宀 (/ㄇㄧㄢˊ, mian²/ "large house", "roof") and

　　豕 (/ㄕˇ, shi³/ "pig")

to imply *a living place where pigs are raised as livestock*,

hence "*home*".

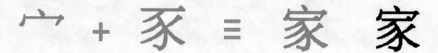

The story of *a living place where pigs are raised as livestock* as told through time by the character 家 is shown below.

| Bone | Bronze | Seal | Standard |

Most dictionaries list the character 家 (/ㄐㄧㄚ, jia/) as

**Semantic-Phonetic Compound** (形聲) of

宀 (/ㄇㄧㄢˊ, mian[2]/ "large house", "roof") *for semantics* and
豭 (/ㄐㄧㄚ, jia/ "male boar") in Reduced Form 豭 *for sound*
to mean *"home"*.

| 宀 | + | 豭 | = | 家 | 家 |
|---|---|---|---|---|---|
| "roof" | | /ㄐㄧㄚ, jia/ | | /ㄐㄧㄚ, jia/ | "home" |

## The Stroke Sequence

家 家 家 家 家 家 家 家 家 家
家 家 家 家 家 家 家 家 家 家

## The Anatomy

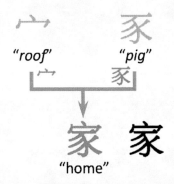

"roof"      "pig"

家 家
"home"

## The Trinity – Sound(s), Semantics, and Synopses

/ㄐㄧㄚ, jia/

| | |
|---|---|
| home | 回家, 離家, 家園, 家鄉[鄉]; |
| household | 家庭, 家用, 家事; |
| family | 家人, 家屬, 家小, 家眷, 成家; |
| *used with* 國 *to mean* nation | 國家; |
| domesticated | 家畜, 家禽; |

261

| | |
|---|---|
| *humble way to refer to* | |
| one's own family member | 家父, 家母, 家兄, 家弟; |
| *placed after noun to refer to* | |
| oneself | 自家, 咱家, 哀家; |
| other people | 姑娘家, 小孩子家, 婦道人家; |
| discipline, school | 儒家, 法家, 道家, 百家爭鳴; |
| person in specific business entity | 農家, 商家, 店家, 東家; |
| person with special training or knowledge | 專家, 文學家, 科學家; |
| to practise nepotism | 家天下; |
| *quantity word, for* | |
| families | 共十家住戶; |
| shops, enterprises | 兩家店, 三家報社, 五家公司; |
| *in classical Chinese,* | |
| home (home town) | 「少小離家老大回, 鄉[鄉]音無改鬢毛衰。」; |
| family | 「修身，齊家，治國， 平天下。」; |
| ruling district of a bureaucrat | 「丘也聞有國有家者, 不患寡而患不均, 不患貧而患不安。」; |
| private property | 「夫賣庸而播耕者, 主人費家而美食。」; |
| to reside | 「又若君居淄右, 妾家河陽。」; |

      *struc. particle* [=的, 地]        「大碗家寬懷暢飲。」;

   *surname*                      姓氏

/《ㄨ, gu/

  *in classical Chinese,*

   *respectful title for women*      曹大家 [=姑, aunt]

**Radical:** 宀.

# 72. 電

## Script Evolution

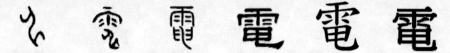

## The Story

/ㄉㄧㄢˋ, dian⁴/    "lightning"

"electricity"

**Associative Compound** (會意) of

雨 (/ㄩˇ, yu³/ "rain") and

申 (/ㄉㄧㄢˋ, dian⁴/ originally "lightning", *also providing sound*)

to imply *lightening from the rain source* (*cloud*),

hence "*lightning*", "*electricity*".

It is important to note that the Semantic-Phonetic Component 申 (㐭) is the Original (本字) of 電. In other words, 電 is the re-created character from its Original 申, a Pictograph (象形) of *lightning*. Later, for the same sound (/ㄕㄣ, shen/) and referring to the extending characteristics of lightning 申 started to carry the semantics of "*to extend*", "*to express*" surrendering its original semantics of "*lightening*" to the Associative Compound 電. And of course, it was only natural for the character (電) for *"lightning"* to also carry the semantics of *"electricity"*.

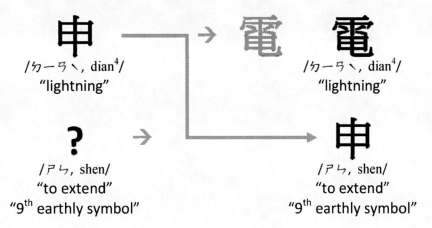

This process of character creation, or re-creation rather, is called Semantic Bifurcation (假借).

Thanks to the popularization of electricity and all the electrically powered appliances, tools, devices, utensils, machines, and even toys that have become the inevitable part of our lives since dawn of the last century, the character 電 has continuously escalated in the frequently used characters list in the past 100 years. Currently, standing at #72, there is however not much advancement to expect of it.

The pictures of *lightning* as rendered through time by the character 申 and the story of *lightening from the rain source* (*cloud*) as told through time by the character 電 are shown below.

| Bone | Bronze | Seal | Standard |

## The Stroke Sequence

電 電 電

## The Anatomy

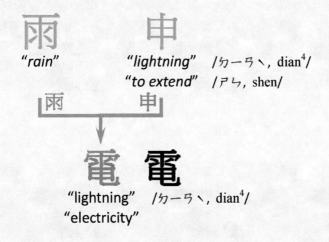

雨

"rain"

申

"lightning" /ㄉㄧㄢˋ, dian⁴/
"to extend" /ㄕㄣ, shen/

電 電

"lightning" /ㄉㄧㄢˋ, dian⁴/
"electricity"

## The Trinity – Sound(s), Semantics, and Synopses

/ㄉㄧㄢˋ, dian⁴/

| | |
|---|---|
| lightning | 打雷閃**電**, 雷**電**交加; |
| electricity | 發**電**, 用**電**, **電**力, **電**能, 交流**電**; |
| electrical | **電**梯, **電**燈, **電**池, **電**車, **電**氣; |
| electron(ic) | **電**子, **電**郵; |
| telephone, telegram | 回**電**, 急**電**, 賀**電**, **電**文; |

266

| | |
|---|---|
| electrical shock | 觸**電**; |
| to get electrical shock | 被**電**了一下; |
| *adj.* lightning | 風馳**電**掣; |
| *in classical Chinese*, | |
|     *adj.* lightning | 「今躬率所統， |
| |     爲[為]士卒先， |
| |     催進諸軍，一時**電**擊。」; |
|     decisively | 「秀骨嶽立，英謀**電**斷。」 |

**Radical:** 雨.

# 73. 力

**Script Evolution**

ㄨ  ㄥ  𠠲  力  力  力

**The Story**

𠠲  𠠲  力  力

/ㄌㄧˋ, li⁴/    "strength", "force", "effort"

**Pictograph** (象形) of *a plough used in farming requiring one's*
   *strength, force, and effort,*
hence *"strength", "force", "effort"*.

<u>**Note**</u>: The MPS『ㄌ』is based on this character's original form『ㄌ』
      and sound.

It is important to note that 力 originally carried the semantics of *"to plough"*, *"to remove with force"* with the sound /ㄌㄧˊ, li²/. Later, 力 started to carry rhe semantics of *"strength"*, *"force"*, *"effort"* surrendering its original semantics of *"to plough"*, *"to remove with force"* to the Associative Compound 犁 (/ㄌㄧˊ, li²/ Usage Rank #2,115) with Radical 牛 (/ㄋㄧㄡˊ, niu²/ "ox") and Semantic-Phonetic Component 利 (/ㄌㄧˋ, li⁴/ "sharp-edged" referring to *sharp-edged tool, also providing sound*).

牛 + 利 ≡ 犁  犁

268

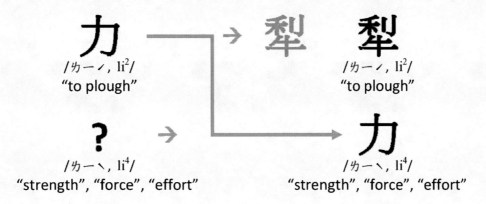

/ㄌㄧˊ, li²/
"to plough"

/ㄌㄧˊ, li²/
"to plough"

?

/ㄌㄧˋ, li⁴/
"strength", "force", "effort"

/ㄌㄧˋ, li⁴/
"strength", "force", "effort"

This process of character creation, or re-creation rather, is called Semantic Bifurcation (假借).

The pictures of *a plough used in farming* as rendered through time by the character 力 are shown below.

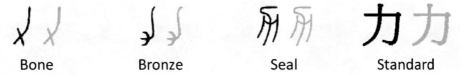

| Bone | Bronze | Seal | Standard |

## The Stroke Sequence

力 力
力 力

## The Trinity – Sound(s), Semantics, and Synopses

/ㄌㄧˋ, li⁴/

| | |
|---|---|
| strength | 臂力, 肌力, 體力, 力大無窮; |
| force | 蠻力, 重力, 動力, 力距, 力臂, 向心力, 離心力; |
| effort | 全力, 用力, 賣力, 出力, 使力, 盡心盡力, 全心全力, 一心一力; |

| | |
|---|---|
| giving all efforts to | 力爭上游, 力排眾議; |
| ability | 能力, 智力, 實力, 得力, 理解力, 自制力, 量力而爲[為]; |
| labour | 勞力; |
| labourer | 苦力; |
| energy | 心力, 力不從心; |
| power | 權力, 電力, 水力, 風力, 馬力; |

*in classical Chinese*,

| | |
|---|---|
| physical strength | 「有力如虎，執轡如組。」, |
| | 「力拔山兮氣蓋世。<br>　時不利兮騅不逝。<br>　騅不逝兮可奈何！<br>　虞兮虞兮奈若何！」; |
| force, power | 「以力服人者，非心服也。」; |
| exerting every ounce of effort to | 「樓船力攻燒敵。」; |
| *surname* | 姓氏 |

**Radical:** 力 (itself).

# 74. 如

## Script Evolution

如 如 如 如 如 如

## The Story

如 如 如 如

/ㄖㄨˊ, ru² /   "to be as"

**Associative Compound** (會意) of

女 (/ㄋㄩˇ, nü³/ "girl", "woman", "female", *also providing sound*) and

口 (/ㄎㄡˇ, kou³/ "mouth")

to imply *a girl to follow father's teaching* and

        *a woman to listen to husband's words*,

hence *"to be as"*.

女 + 口 ≡ 如 如

<u>**Note**</u>: ㄩ and ㄨ are the same sound.

The story of *a girl to follow father's teaching* and *a woman to listen to husband's words* as told through time by the character 如 is shown below.

如 如    如 如    如 如    如 如

Bone        Bronze       Seal        Standard

## The Stroke Sequence

## The Anatomy

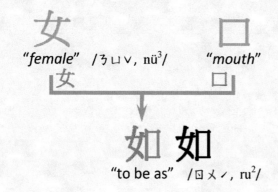

女
*"female"* /ㄋㄩˇ, nü³/

口
*"mouth"*

女　口

如 如
*"to be as"* /ㄖㄨˊ, ru²/

## The Trinity – Sound(s), Semantics, and Synopses

/ㄖㄨˊ, ru²/

| | |
|---|---|
| to be as | 如意, 如願; |
| according to | 如約, 如期, 如願, 如意, 如數奉還; |
| as (*conj. for comparison*) | 如常, 完好如初, 一切如故, 愛人如己; |
| like (*prep.*) | 如同, 如魚得水, 如花似玉, 正如他說, 如臨大敵, 如臨深淵, 如履薄冰, 如沐春風, 往事如煙; |
| as such | 例如, 譬如, 如此, 如是; |
| as good as | 生不如死, 遠親不如近鄰; |

| | |
|---|---|
| if, supposedly | 如果, 如蒙賞光; |
| to go to | 如廁; |
| used with 不 *at beginning of sentence to mean* better yet | 不如我們搭火車去; |
| used with 何 *to mean* how, what | 如何, 如何是好; |
| used after adj. *to mean* as *adj.* as | 快如閃電; |
| used after adj. *to emphasize adj.* | 突如其來; |
| in classical Chinese, | |
| to follow | 「有律以如己也。」; |
| as (*conj. for comparison*) | 「大絃嘈嘈如急雨，<br>　小絃切切如私語。」; |
| to go to | 「公將如棠觀魚者。」; |
| as good as | 「夫被堅執銳，義不如公；<br>　坐而運策，公不如義。」; |
| than | 「人之困窮，甚如饑寒。」; |
| assuming, if | 「如不可求，從吾所好。」; |
| or | 「安見方六七十，<br>　如五六十，<br>　而非邦也者。」; |
| used after adj. *to emphasize adj.* | 「子之燕居，申申如也，<br>　夭夭如也。」; |
| surname | 姓氏 |

**Radical:** 女.

# 75. 水

## Script Evolution

水 水 水 水 水 水

## The Story

水 水 水 水

/ㄕㄨㄟˇ, shui³/   "water"

**Pictograph** (象形) of *flowing water*,

hence "*water*".

<u>Note</u>: Also in the form 『 氵 』as Radical or component.

The pictures of *flowing water* as rendered through time by the character 水 are shown below.

水   水   水   水水

Bone        Bronze        Seal        Standard

## The Stroke Sequence

水 水 水 水

水 水 水 水

**Common Fallacy:** Combining the 3rd & 4th Stroke as a single Stroke.

# The Trinity – Sound(s), Semantics, and Synopses

/ㄕㄨㄟˇ, shui³/

| | |
|---|---|
| water | 喝水, 水份, 水蒸氣; |
| in *or* by water | 水產, 水生物; |
| large body of water (*vs land*) | 潛水, 游水, 不諳水性, 水陸兩棲, 江水東流, 涉水而過; |
| flood, deluge | 淹水, 水災, 發大水; |
| liquid | 淚水, 汗水, 雨水, 墨水, 藥水; |
| juice | 橘子水; |
| drink | 茶水; |
| extra income or expense | 油水; |
| watery | 這梨太水了，一點也不脆; |
| like water, ever changing | 水性楊花; |
| *in classical Chinese*, | |
|     large body of water | 「今殷其淪喪，若涉大水，其無津涯。」; |
|     *one of five elements of the Universe in ancient Chinese philosophy* | 水、火、木、金、土; |
| *name for Mercury* (*the planet*) | 水星; |
| *surname* | 姓氏 |

**Radical:** 水 (itself).

275

# 76. 化

## Script Evolution

彡 北 化 化 化 化

## The Story

化 化 化 化

/ㄏㄨㄚˋ, hua⁴/     "to give new life or new meaning"

**Associative Compound** (會意) of

匕 (/ㄏㄨㄚˋ, hua⁴/ Pictograph of a *person flipped L-R*

       *then upside down* to imply *altering*) and

人 (亻 /ㄖㄣˊ, ren²/ "person")

to imply *altering a person* or *giving a person new life*,

hence *"to give new life or meaning"*.

匕 + 亻 ≡ 化 化

It is worthwhile to note and examine how this Pictograph 人 (尺) in 化

gets flipped and turned in the Bone, Bronze, and Seal Script to imply *altering*.

<u>Bone Script:</u>

𠤎    turned U-D    𠤎      𠤎    flipped L-R    𠤎    to give    彡

It is clear that the left *person* was turned upside down and the right *person*

was flipped L-R in Bone Script.

<u>Bronze Script:</u>

ㄱ  flipped L-R  ㅏ  then turned U-D  ㄴ  to give  北

<u>Seal Script:</u>

ㅈ  flipped L-R  ㄷ  then turned U-D  ㅂ  to give  ㅄ

It is clear from time of the Bronze Script that the left *person* was left alone, whilst the right *person* was flipped L-R first then turned upside down. Some font designs have 匕 shaped as 匕 (L-R flipped 人), hence 化, 化, etc. The story of *giving a person new life* as told through time by the character 化 is shown below.

| 𠤎𠤎 | 北北 | ㅄㅄ | 化化 |
|---|---|---|---|
| Bone | Bronze | Seal | Standard |

## The Stroke Sequence

化 化 化 化

化 化 化 化

**Common Fallacy:**

Exchanging the 3rd & 4th Stroke.

## The Anatomy

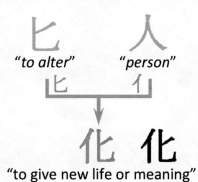

匕        人
*"to alter"*   *"person"*

匕        亻

化 化

"to give new life or meaning"

# The Trinity – Sound(s), Semantics, and Synopses

/ㄏㄨㄚˋ, hua⁴/

| | |
|---|---|
| to give new life or new meaning | 造化, 化育; |
| to alter | 感化, 教[教]化; |
| civilization | 化外之地; |
| to change | 變化, 千變萬化, 潛移默化; |
| utmost beyond words or imagination | 化境; |
| to treat as | 物化; |
| -fy (*after noun or adj.*) | 美化, 電氣化; |
| -ize (*after noun or adj.*) | 現代化; |
| chemistry, chemical | 化學, 化工, 理化; |
| to dissolve, to change matter's state | 溶化, 消化; |
| to destroy | 火化, 焚化; |
| to exit life | 羽化; |
| to ask for donation | 化緣, 募化; |

*in classical Chinese*,

| | |
|---|---|
| to change | 「故聖人法與時變，<br>禮與俗化。」; |
| to civilize | 「夫君子所過者化，<br>所存者神。」; |
| to cultivate | 「逮奉聖朝，沐浴清化。」; |
| to ask for donation | 「也有坐在地上就化錢的。」; |
| to exit life | 「惟君平昔，聰明絕人，<br>今雖化去，夫豈無物！」; |

to dissolve 「有聖人作，鑽燧取火，
以**化**腥臊，而民說之。」；

to incinerate 「獻過了種種香火，
**化**了眾神紙馬，
燒了薦亡文疏，
佛事已畢，又各安寢。」

/ㄏㄨㄚ, hua/

beggar, pauper **化**子 [=叫**花**子]

**Radical:** 匕 (/ㄅㄧˇ, bi[3]/ "person *in L-R flipped image*", "scoop").

**Note**: 匕 is listed under 匕 with no additional Strokes.

# 77. 高

## Script Evolution

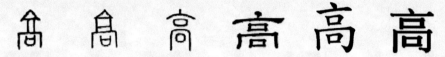

## The Story

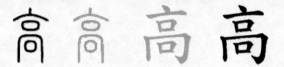

/ㄍㄠ, gao/     "tall", "high"

**Pictograph** (象形) of *a tall structure for observing faraway places*

to refer to *tall* and *high* objects,

hence *"tall"*, *"high"*.

The pictures of *a tall structure for observing faraway places* as rendered through time by the character 高 are shown below.

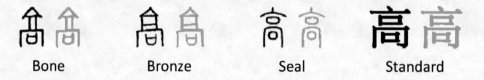

Bone       Bronze       Seal       Standard

## The Stroke Sequence

# The Trinity – Sound(s), Semantics, and Synopses

/ㄍㄠ, gao/

| | |
|---|---|
| tall | 高樓, 高臺, 高大, 高壯; |
| high | 高等, 高級, 高中*, 高價, 高速, 高位, 高價, 高山, 高地, 高原, 高度**, 高纖, 高蛋白, 高解析, 高能量, 高海拔, 山高水遠, 高處不勝寒; |
| Highly | 高爆彈; |
| High-level | 高深, 高科技; |
| height | 標高, 增高, 身高[長], 高度***; |
| high place | 居高臨下, 登高望遠, 高瞻遠矚, |
| high position | 好高騖遠, 高不成低不就; |
| at high place, position, or level | 高掛, 高聳, 高中****, 高架橋; |
| towards high place, position, or level | 高昇, 高就, 高攀*****, 提高, 升高, 跳高, 債臺高築; |
| high-minded, highly skilled | 高人******, 高手; |

*:  『高中 (/ㄓㄨㄥ, zhong/)』 means *"high school"*.

**:  as *adj.* or *adv.*

***:  as *noun*.

****:  『高中 (/ㄓㄨㄥˋ, zhong⁴/)』 means *"achieved high position in selection process"*.

*****:  『高攀』 often suggests *"exceeding one's expectation or what is expected of a person"*.

******: 『高人』 does not mean *"a tall person"*; 『長人』 does.

| high and away | 高抬貴手; |
|---|---|
| lofty, superior | 高貴, 高尚[尚], 高傲; |
| loud and high volume (*of sound*) | 高聲, 高歌; |
| elevated (*of spirit*) | 高興, 高亢, 興高彩烈; |
| in elevated spirit or high-flown style | 高談闊論; |
| in a carefree or elated spirit | 高枕無憂; |
| exceptional, outstanding | 高論, 高見, 高徒, 高材生; |
| over | 高估; |
| old (*for age*) | 高齡, 高壽, 年事已高; |

*in classical Chinese,*

| high | 「我欲乘風歸去，<br>又恐瓊樓玉宇，<br>高處不勝寒。」; |
|---|---|
| | 「不登高山， |
| height | 不知天之高也。」; |
| high place | 「吾嘗跂而望矣，<br>不如登高之博見也。 |
| high position | 「居廟堂之高，則憂其民。」; |
| towards high level | 「高築牆，廣積糧，<br>緩稱王。」; |
| in a carefree spirit | 「無楚、韓之患，<br>則大王高枕而臥，<br>國必無憂矣。」; |
| superior | 「輕辭天子，非高也，<br>勢薄也。」; |

| | |
|---|---|
| your (*respectful way of address*) | 「**高**台未傾，愛妾尚[尚]在，<br>悠悠爾心，亦何可言。」; |
| to respect, to revere | 「以其不收也外之，<br>而**高**其輕世也。」, |
| | 「愈窮愈榮，雖死，<br>天下愈**高**之。」; |
| old (*for age*) | 「且陛下春秋**高**，法令亡常，<br>大臣亡罪夷滅者數十家。」; |
| suburb | 「仲春之月，玄鳥至。<br>至之日，以太牢祠於**高**禖，<br>天子親往。」; |
| to seclude | 「賦詩歸來，**高**蹈獨善。」; |
| *medicine*, vital [=膏] | 「爰從寢疾，遽致**高**肓。」; |
| *name for golf* | **高**(爾夫)球; |
| *surname* | 姓氏 |

**Radical:** 高 (itself).

# 78. 都

## Script Evolution

## The Story

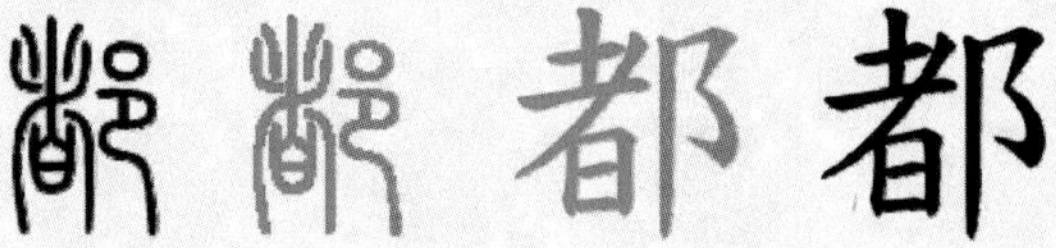

/ㄉㄨ, du/ "city where the deceased emperor's temple is located"
"capital city"

**Associative Compound** (會意) of

邑 (阝 /ㄧˋ, $yi^4$/ "city") and

者 ([ㄓㄨˇ, $zhu^3$] originally "to cook" referring to *setting fire to mourn, also providing sound*)

to imply *city to have mourning ceremonies for the deceased emperor*, hence "*city where the deceased emperor's temple is located*".

阝 + 者 = 都 都

The story of *city to have mourning ceremonies for the deceased emperor* as told through time by the character 都 is shown below.

Bronze Seal Standard

## The Stroke Sequence

都 都 都 都 都 都 都 都 都 都

都 都 都 都 都 都 都 都 都 都

都

都

## The Anatomy

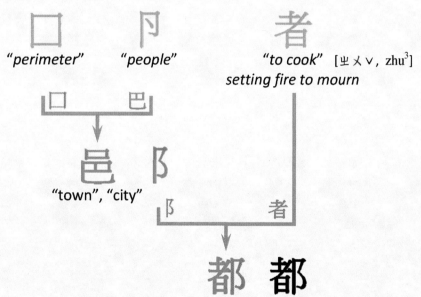

口 "perimeter"  卩 "people"  者 "to cook" [ㄓㄨˇ, zhu³]
*setting fire to mourn*

口 巴 → 邑 阝
"town", "city"

阝 者 → 都 都
"city where deceased emperor's temple is located"  /ㄉㄨ, du/
"capital city"

## The Trinity – Sound(s), Semantics, and Synopses

/ㄉㄨ, du/

capital city                    首都;

| | |
|---|---|
| city, metropolitan area | 都市, 花都, 港都; |
| *in classical Chinese,* | |
| to set capital city at | 「項王自立爲[為]西楚霸王，<br>王九郡，**都**彭城。」; |
| to hold high position | 「蘇秦、張儀一當萬乘之主，<br>而**都**卿相之位。」; |
| to combine all | 「頃撰其遺文，<br>**都**爲[為]一集。」; |
| elegant | 「一少年出，丰采甚**都**。」; |
| *surname* | 姓氏 |
| /ㄉㄡ, dou/ | |
| all | **都**好, **都**是, **都**來了; |
| even | 一動**都**不動, 連小孩(兒)**都**知道; |
| *in classical Chinese,* | |
| void character | |
| (*at beginning of sentence*) | 「驩兜曰：<br>『**都**！共工鳩僝功。』」 |

**Radical:** 邑 ( 阝 ).

# 79. 自

## Script Evolution

## The Story

[ㄅㄧˊ, bi²]    "nose"

/ㄗˋ, zi⁴/    "self", "oneself"

**Pictograph** (象形) of *a person's nose*,

hence "*nose*".

Later, 自 started to carry the semantics of "*self*", "*oneself*" as the Chinese would often point to their own noses to refer to *themselves*, and the Semantic-Phonetic Compound 鼻 (/ㄅㄧˊ, bi²/) with Radical 自 ([ㄅㄧˊ, bi²] "nose") and Phonetic Component 畀 (/ㄅㄧˋ, bi⁴/ "to bestow") was then created for *nose*.

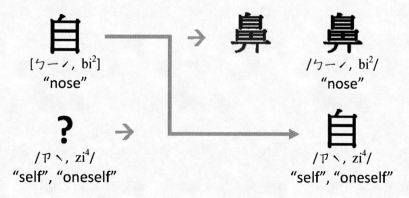

This process of character creation, or re-creation rather, is called Semantic Bifurcation (假借).

It is important to note that in the Seal Script, 自 (/ㄗˋ, zi⁴/ "self") as a component was often written with only one horizontal Stroke in the centre as shown below and should not be confused with the Pictograph of *a husked white rice grain* 白 (/ㄅㄞˊ, bai²/ "white", *surname* Usage Rank #311).

      "self"                             "white", *surname*

This single horizontal Stroke version is often found in Standard characters like 習 (/ㄒㄧˊ, xi²/ Usage Rank #413), **Associative Compound** (會意) of

> 羽 (/ㄩˇ, yu³/ "wings of bird") and
> 自 (/ㄗˋ, zi⁴/ "self")

to imply *a fledging young chick fluttering two wings on its own*
                  *to practise flying*,

hence *"to practise"*, *"frequently"*, *"habit"*.

The Semantic Component 自, though with only one horizontal Stroke in the centre, should not be thought as the character 白 (/ㄅㄞˊ, bai²/ "white"). The pictures of *a person's nose* as rendered through time by the character 自 are shown below.

   Bone               Bronze            Seal            Standard

## The Stroke Sequence

自 自 自 自 自 自

自 自 自 自 自 自

## The Trinity – Sound(s), Semantics, and Synopses

/ㄗ丶, $zi^4$/

| | |
|---|---|
| self, oneself | 自己, 自言自語, 自給自足, 自以爲[為]是; |
| self motivated | 自覺, 自願, 自主, 自轉; |
| by oneself | 自傳; |
| automatic | 自動化, 自來水; |
| naturally | 自然, 自不待言, 公道自在人心; |
| origin | 其來有自; |
| from | 自從, 自古以來; |

*in classical Chinese*,

| | |
|---|---|
| where thing starts | 「知風之自, 知微之顯, 可以入德也。」; |
| originally | 「開元遺曲自淒涼, 況近秋天調是商。」; |
| naturally | 「我無爲[為]而民自化, 我好靜而民自正。」, 「姊姊們暮年相見, 自不必說悲喜交集, 泣笑敍闊一番。」; |

289

| | |
|---|---|
| still, as usual | 「閣中帝子今何在？<br>　檻外長江空**自**流。」; |
| from | 「有朋**自**遠方來，<br>　不亦樂乎？」; |
| if | 「**自**非聖人，<br>　外寧必有內憂。」; |
| although | 「**自**吾母而不得吾情，<br>　吾惡乎用吾情？」，<br>「**自**天子不能具鈞駟，<br>　而將相或乘牛車。」; |
| *surname* | 姓氏 |

**Radical:** 自 (itself).

# 80. 二

## Script Evolution

## The Story

/ㄦ丶, er⁴/     "two"

**Ideograph** (指事) with *two distinct horizontal lines*

　　to denote *the number two,*

hence *"two".*

The iconic symbols denoting *the number two* as represented through time by the character 二 are shown below.

| Bone | Bronze | Seal | Standard |
|------|--------|------|----------|

## The Stroke Sequence

## The Trinity – Sound(s), Semantics, and Synopses

/儿ㄟ, er⁴/

| | |
|---|---|
| two * | 二十, 接二連三; |
| second | 第二位, 二月; |
| different | 心無二意; |

*in classical Chinese,*

| | |
|---|---|
| different | 「其子有二心，故廢之。」, |
| | 「卓然高行，口無二言。」; |
| to change | 「必報德，有死無二。」, |
| | 「爲[為]人臣者死有餘罪，<br>　況敢逃其死而二其心乎？」; |
| second to none | 「此所謂功無二於天下，<br>　而略不世出者也。」 |

*:『貳』(Usage Rank #5,095) is often used in
　　　writing financial numbers to avoid alteration.

**Radical:** 二 (itself).

# 81. 理

## Script Evolution

理　理　理　理

## The Story

理　理　理　理

/ㄌㄧˇ, li³/ 　 "to treat and carve jade"

　　　　　　　"to process carefully and properly"

**Associative Compound** (會意) of

玉 (王 王 /ㄩˋ, yu⁴/ "jade") and

里 (/ㄌㄧˇ, li³/ "place to reside" referring to *workshop*,

　　　　　　*also providing sound*)

to imply *workshop to treat and carve jade*,

hence *"to treat and carve jade"*, *"to process carefully and properly"*.

王 ＋ 里 ＝ 理　理

Most dictionaries list the character 理 (/ㄌㄧˇ, li³/) as

**Semantic-Phonetic Compound** (形聲) of

玉 (王 王 /ㄩˋ, yu⁴/ "jade") *for semantics* and

里 (/ㄌㄧˇ, li³/ "place to reside") *for sound*

to mean *"to treat and carve jade"*, *"to process carefully and properly"*.

王 + 里 ≡ 理 理
"jade"    /ㄌㄧˇ, li³/    /ㄌㄧˇ, li³/    "to treat and carve jade"

**The Stroke Sequence**

理 理 理 理 理 理 理 理 理 理
理 理 理 理 理 理 理 理 理 理
理
理

**The Anatomy**

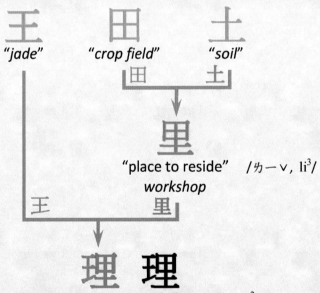

王　　　田　　　土
"jade"    "crop field"    "soil"

田　土

里

"place to reside"    /ㄌㄧˇ, li³/
*workshop*

王　　里

理 理

"to treat and carve jade"    /ㄌㄧˇ, li³/
"to process carefully and properly"

# The Trinity – Sound(s), Semantics, and Synopses

/ㄌㄧˇ, li$^3$/

| | |
|---|---|
| to process carefully and properly | 辦理, 處理; |
| to arrange in order | 整理, 治理, 管理, 理家, 把文件理一理; |
| (*of hair*) to cut or trim | 理髮, 理頭; |
| to give attention to | 搭理, 別理他, 不理不睬; |
| grain, marbling | 紋理, 肌理; |
| laws of things | 天理, 公理, 定理, 眞[真]理; |
| reason | 道理, 理由; |
| order | 有條有理; |
| physics | 物理, 理化, 理工; |

*in classical Chinese,*

| | |
|---|---|
| to treat and carve jade | 「鄭人謂玉，未理者璞。」; |
| marbling | 「建城縣出燃石，色黃理疏，以水灌之則熱，安鼎其上，可以炊也。」; |
| order, layering | 「井井兮其有理也。」; |
| to be familiar with | 「英雄貫滿東京府，曾理兵書習六韜。」; |
| *surname* | 姓氏 |

**Radical:** 玉 (王).

# 82. 起

## Script Evolution

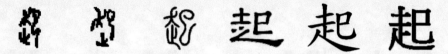

## The Story

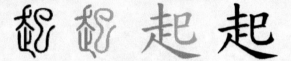

/ㄑ一ˇ, qi³/ "to arise"

**Associative Compound** (會意) of

走 (/ㄗㄡˇ, zou³/ "to walk briskly") and

巳 (Pictograph of *a sitting (kneeling) person*)

to imply *a sitting (kneeling) person arising to walk*,

hence "*to arise*".

$$走 \;+\; 巳 \;\equiv\; 起 \quad 起$$

It is important to note that ancient Chinese sat on their heels. Therefore, the depiction of *a properly sitting person* is very much like *a kneeling person*. And the *sitting (kneeling) person* () is only obvious in the rather rare Pottery Script (古陶文). The story of *a sitting (kneeling) person arising to walk* as told through time by the character 起 is shown below.

| Pottery | Bronze | Seal | Standard |
|---------|--------|------|----------|

## The Stroke Sequence

起 起 起 起 起 起 起 起 起 起

起 起 起 起 起 起 起 起 起 起

**Common Fallacy:** Starting the last Stroke lower as to leave a gap between the starting points of the 8th and 10th (last) Stroke such that the component 『巳』is turned to 『巳』(/ㄧˇ, yi³/ "already", "to cease" Usage Rank #180).

## The Anatomy

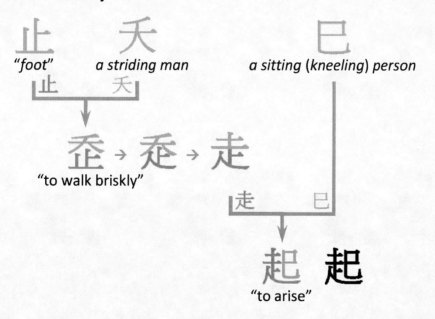

止 "foot"    夭 *a striding man*    巳 *a sitting (kneeling) person*

止    夭

歨 → 赱 → 走

"to walk briskly"

走    巳

起 **起**

"to arise"

## The Trinity – Sound(s), Semantics, and Synopses

/ㄑㄧˇ, qi³/

to arise (from), to get up                起立, 起來, 起身, 起牀[床], 坐而言不如起而行, 東山再起;

to launch                                起義;

297

| | |
|---|---|
| to start, to begin | 起筆, 起程, 起風, 起草, 起碼*, 起用, 起動, 起(個)頭, 從今起, 起個大綱; |
| to gather, to attract | 起疑, 不起眼, 肅然起敬; |
| to regain, to recover (from) | 起色, 起死回生, 一病不起; |
| to withdraw, to take out | 起貨, 起出, 起子**; |
| to build, to establish | 白手起家, 平地起高樓; |
| to raise, to lift | 起重機; |
| *used with* 來 *after verb to mean* *** | |
| as is [=上來] | 吃起來, 喝起來, 聞起來, 看起來; |
| as is | 說起來簡單, 聽起來還不錯, 做起來就不知道了; |
| to start | 話還沒說兩句, 就吵起來了, 這兩隻狗一見面就打起來了, 這孩子一鬧起來就沒完沒了; |
| in a continuous manner (state) | 買賣雖小, 維持起來也不容易, 躲起來, 關起來, 藏起來, 想起來, 走起路來, 說起話來, 做起事來; |
| up | 站起來, 坐起來, 扶起來, 撐起來; |
| *after verb, to mean* of, about | 想起, 談起; |

*: 『起碼』 *minimal wager to start a gambling game* to mean "at least", "minimally".

**: 『起子 (/ ˙ ㄗ, zi⁵/)』 means "screwdriver" with focus on its purpose of *taking out the screw*.

***: 『起來』 by itself means "*to get up*".

*after verb with* 得 *or* 不 *to mean*

    -able                            經得**起**考驗, 經不**起**打擊,

                                      承受不**起**壓力;

*quantity word, for*

    events                        多**起**車禍;

    waves of people           兩**起**客人;

*in classical Chinese,*

    to arise                   「雞鳴而**起**，孳孳爲[為]善者，

                              舜之徒也。」;

    to start, to begin       「次日**起**馬*，

                              范進獨自送在三十里之外，

                              轎前打恭。」,

                              「但他在宦途中，

                              是個鑽營的能手，

                              由縣丞**起**馬**，

                              不數年連升總督。」;

    to start career as     「蕭何、曹參皆**起**秦刀筆吏，

                              當時錄錄未有奇節。」;

    to gather motion       「大風**起**兮雲飛揚，

                              威加海內兮歸故鄉[鄉]。」;

    to recover (from)       「玄乃發墨守，鍼膏肓，

                              **起**癈疾。」;

    to build                   「治城郭，**起**譙樓。」;

\*: 『**起**馬』means *"to start a journey"*, *"to set out to leave"*.

\*\*: 『**起**馬』means *"to begin a political career"*.

to take commission 「甚東山何事，當時也道，

                                            為[為]蒼生**起**。」；

to originate 「以述漢書，**起**元高祖。」；

one of four structures in
  Chinese literary style       **起**、承、轉、合

**Radical:** 走.

# 83. 小

## Script Evolution

小  八  川  小  小  小

## The Story

川  川  小  小

/ㄒㄧㄠˇ, xiao³/    "small"

**Pictograph** (象形) of *three small sand grains*,
hence "*small*".

It is important to note that at time of the Bone Script, the Pictograph of *four small sand grains* was simply the Variant form of another Pictograph of *three small sand grains* which carried the semantics of both "*sand*" and "*small*". At time of the Bronze Script, the Pictograph of *three small sand grains or dots* was only used to carry the semantics of "*small*", whereas the semantics of "*sand*" was given to a new Associative Compound 沙 沙 of

水 (氵/ㄕㄨㄟˇ, shui³/ "water") and

少 (Pictograph of *four small sand grains*, originally a Variant form of 小)

to imply *small sand grains by the water*,

hence "*sand*".

Meanwhile, the Pictograph of *four small sand grains* was used as a separate character carrying the semantics of "few" with a Variation Sound (/ㄕㄠˇ,

shao³/) of 小 (/ㄒㄧㄠˇ, xiao³/ "small").  At time of the Seal Script, the Pictograph of *four small sand grains* was written as ⺌ with the dots turned to lines just as the Pictograph of *three small sand grains* was written as ⼮. Such is the story of how a single Pictograph in two forms (*four dots* and *three dots*) became three distinct characters.

The pictures of *three small sand grains* and *four small sand grains* as rendered through time by the character 小 (/ㄒㄧㄠˇ, xiao³/ "small") and 少 (/ㄕㄠˇ, shao³/ "few") are shown below.

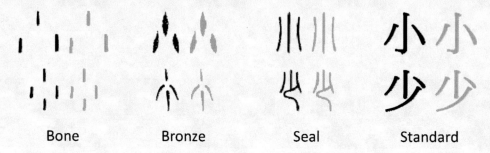

| Bone | Bronze | Seal | Standard |

The story of *small sand grains by the water* as told through time by the character 沙 (/ㄕㄚ, sha/ "sand") is shown below.

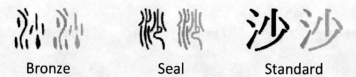

| Bronze | Seal | Standard |

Most dictionaries list this character as **Associative Compound** (會意) of

八 (/ㄅㄚ, ba/ "eight", "to divide") and

丨 (/ㄍㄨㄣˇ, gun³/ "through")

to imply *dividing through to give small results*,
hence "*small*".

$$八 \; + \; 丨 \; \equiv \; 小 \quad 小$$

## The Stroke Sequence

## The Trinity – Sound(s), Semantics, and Synopses

/ㄒㄧㄠˇ, xiao³/

| | |
|---|---|
| small | 小動物, 小人物, 小鎮[鎮]; |
| little | 小狗崽; |
| young | 小弟, 小妹, 小生, 小姐, 年紀小; |
| young people, minor | 家小; |
| little bit | 小試身手, 不無小補; |
| to belittle | 小看; |
| narrow | 小心眼(兒); |
| *used with* 心 *alone to mean* caution | 小心, 小心點(兒); |
| humble way to call oneself or<br>    refer to one's own | 小店, 小兒; |
| cunning, devious | 小人; |
| (*before name*) intimate way to<br>    call someone | 小李, 小老弟; |
| concubine | 嫁給人家當小的; |
| short (*for time*) | 小住, 小睡; |
| *in classical Chinese*,<br>    young child | 「既醉既飽，小大稽首。」; |

303

to despise                       「將自用也，必小羅。」；

the cunning, the devious     「今大王親近羣[群]小，

                                           漸漬邪惡所習。」；

to ignore, to overlook       「莫小二千石，

                                           當安遠俗人。」

**Radical:** 小 (itself).

# 84. 長

## Script Evolution

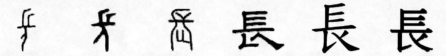

## The Story

/ㄓㄤˇ, zhang³/      "senior"

/ㄔㄤˊ, chang²/      "long"

**Pictograph** (象形) of *a person* ( 丿 ) *with long hair* ( 匚 )

     rendering *an old or senior person*

       to imply *senior* and *long*,

hence "*senior*", "*long*".

It is important to note that at time of the Seal Script the *senior person* was rendered as a Variant form ( 凵 ) of 人 (/ㄖㄣˊ, ren²/ "person") with *long hair falling all the way down* ( 兂 ), thus leading to the Standard Script. The pictures of *senior person with long hair* as rendered through time by the character 長 are shown below.

Bone        Bronze        Seal        Standard

## The Stroke Sequence

長 長 長 長 長 長 長 長
長 長 長 長 長 長 長 長

## The Trinity – Sound(s), Semantics, and Synopses

/ㄓㅊˇ, zhang³/

| | |
|---|---|
| people senior or with higher status | 兄長, 尊長, 師長, 長幼有序; |
| senior (older) | 他長我三歲; |
| eldest in siblings | 長男, 長女, 長子, 長孫, 長兄; |
| to develop (*of human or animal*) | 長瘤, 長痣, 長瘡, 他長得很高; |
| to grow up | 長大, 生長的地方; |
| to grow (*crop, plant, etc.*) | 土壤貧瘠什麼都長不出來,<br>樹木長得很茂盛; |
| to increase, to enhance, to advance | 長進, 長見識, 此消彼長; |
| to promote (to give favour to) | 長他人志氣，滅自己威風; |
| to progress | 日有所長; |
| leader, person in charge | 部長, 首長, 家長; |

*in classical Chinese,*

| | |
|---|---|
| old | 「子之年長矣,<br>而色若孺子，何也？」; |
| elderly | 「君先而臣從,<br>父先而子從,<br>兄先而弟從,<br>長先而少從。」; |

| | |
|---|---|
| to grow up | 「生於斯，**長**於斯。」; |
| to be born | 「我雖不是樹上生，<br>　　卻是石裏[裡]**長**的。」; |
| to grow, to develop | 「苟得其養，無物不**長**。」; |
| to rear | 「**長**孤幼，養老疾。」; |
| to advance | 「君子道**長**，小人道消也。」; |
| to lead, to command | 「**長**十萬大軍。」; |
| to be in charge of | 「使一郡皆寒，賢者**長**一縣，<br>　　一縣之界能獨溫乎？」; |
| to respect | 「乃惟四方之多罪逋逃，<br>　　是崇是**長**，是信是使。」 |

/ㄔㄤˊ, chang²/

| | |
|---|---|
| long (*time*) | **長**夜漫漫, 夜**長**夢多; |
| extended (time) | **長**工, **長**期, **長**久; |
| always, for ever | 天**長**地久, 松柏**長**青; |
| far (*distance, space*) | 萬里**長**征, **長**途拔涉; |
| long | **長**髮, **長**衫, **長**短不一; |
| length, distance | **長**度, **長**跑, 全**長**一千一百多公里; |
| tall (*premodifier for person's height*) | **長**人*; |
| height (*of person*) | 身**長**[高]; |
| advantage, strength | **長**處, 各有所**長**, 截**長**補短; |
| expertise, specialty | 專**長**, 特**長**; |

*: Do not use 『高』 as a premodifier, *i.e.* 『高人』, for "*a tall person*", because 『高人』 means "*a high-minded or highly skilled person*".

| | |
|---|---|
| to be specialized in | 長於工藝; |
| *in classical Chinese,* | |
|     strength, specialty | 「請掩足下之短者， |
| | 誦足下之**長**。」; |
|     long (*for object length*) | 「帶**長**劍兮挾秦弓， |
| | 首身離兮心不懲。」; |
|     long (*for time*) | 「披褐守**長**夜， |
| | 晨雞不肯鳴。」; |
|     far | 「秦時明月漢時關， |
| | 萬里**長**征人未還。」; |
|     for ever | 「夫文猶可**長**用， |
| | 而武難久行也。」; |
|   *surname* | 姓氏 |
| /ㄓㄤˋ, zhang[4]/ | |
| *in classical Chinese,* | |
|     redundant, extra | 「平身無**長**物。」; |
|     powerful, prosperous | 「此神農之所以**長**， |
| | 而堯舜之所以章也。」 |

**Radical:** 長 (itself).

# 85. 物

## Script Evolution

₩ 岁 物 物 物 物

## The Story

物 物 物 物

/ㄨˋ, wu⁴/    "ox to butcher", "butchered ox"

"large creature or thing", "everything outside of oneself"

**Associative Compound** (會意) of

牛 (牛 /ㄋㄧㄡˊ, niu² "ox") and

勿 ([ㄨㄣˇ, wen³] originally "to kill", *also providing sound*)

to imply *ox to butcher*,

hence *"ox to butcher"*, *"butchered ox"*.

牛 + 勿 ≡ 物 物

Later, for the same sound (/ㄨˋ, wu⁴/) 物 started to carry the semantics of *"large creature or thing"*, *"everything outside of oneself"*. It is important to note that the Semantic-Phonetic Component 勿 (/ㄨˋ, wu⁴/ Usage Rank #2,092) is an Associative Compound (會意) of

刀 (/ㄉㄠ, dao/ "knife") and

ノ (／ Pictograph of *dripping blood*)

309

to imply *knife with dripping blood,*

hence *"to kill (with knife)"* with original pronunciation [ㄨㄣˇ, wen³].

It is worth noting that the *dripping blood* (*blood drops*) was obvious in the stories told by the Bone Script and Bronze Script, whilst the killing implement used was sometimes a *bow* (弓) as shown below.

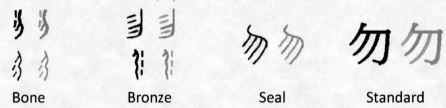

| Bone | Bronze | Seal | Standard |

Thus, 勿 (/ㄨˋ, wu⁴/) is not a Pictograph of *hanging cloth sign* as most dictionaries list it. Later, for the same sound (/ㄨˋ, wu⁴/) 勿 started to carry the semantics of *"do not"*, *"never"* surrendering its original semantics of *"to kill"* to the Associative Compound 刎 (/ㄨㄣˇ, wen³/ Usage Rank #5,543) with Radical 刀 (刂 /ㄉㄠ, dao/ "knife") and Semantic-Phonetic Component 勿 ([ㄨㄣˇ, wen³] "to kill"). This process of character creation, or re-creation rather, is called Semantic Bifurcation (假借).

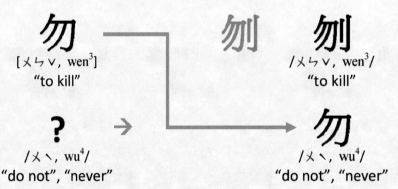

The story of *ox to butcher* as told through time by the character 物 is shown below.

| Bone | Bronze | Seal | Standard |

310

Most dictionaries list the character 物 (/ㄨˋ, wu⁴/) as
**Semantic-Phonetic Compound** (形聲) of

牛 (牛 /ㄋㄧㄡˊ, niu²/ "ox") *for semantics* and

勿 (/ㄨˋ, wu⁴/ "hanging cloth sign") *for sound*

to mean *"large creature or thing"*, *"everything outside of oneself"*.

牛 + 勿 ≡ 物 物

"ox"　　　/ㄨˋ, wu⁴/　　　/ㄨˋ, wu⁴/　　"everything
　　　　　　　　　　　　　　　　　　　　　　outside of oneself"

## The Stroke Sequence

物 物 物 物 物 物 物 物

物 物 物 物 物 物 物 物

## The Anatomy

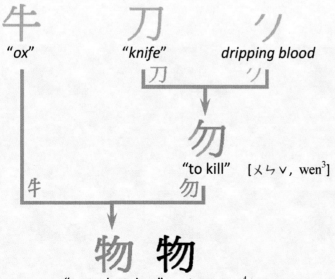

牛　　　　刀　　　　ノ
"ox"　　　"knife"　　dripping blood

　　　　　刀　　ノ
　　　　　　↓

　　　　　勿
　　　　"to kill"　[ㄨㄣˇ, wen³]

牛　　　　勿
　　　↓

物 物

"ox to butcher"　　/ㄨˋ, wu⁴/
"large creature or thing", "everything outside of oneself"

# The Trinity – Sound(s), Semantics, and Synopses

/ㄨˋ, wu⁴/

thing, object 萬**物**, 人事**物**, **物**以類聚;

other people **物**議;

substance 言之有**物**;

to look for **物**色;

*in classical Chinese,*

ox (livestock) to butcher 「三十維**物**，爾牲則具。」;

all things in the universe 「方以類聚，**物**以羣[群]分，
吉凶生矣。」;

thing, object (outside oneself) 「不以**物**喜，不以己悲。」，

「**物物**而不物於**物**，
則胡可得而累邪！」;

to control 「**物**物而不**物**於物，
則胡可得而累邪！」;

other people 「直以慵疏招**物**議，
休將文字占時名。」;

substance 「體有萬殊，**物**無一量。」;

system 「復禹之績，祀夏配天，
不失舊**物**。」;

to select 「欲知天道察其數，
欲知地道**物**其樹，
欲知人道從其欲。」;

**Radical:** 牛 (牜).

# 86. 現

## Script Evolution

現 現 現 現

## The Story

現 現 現 現

/ㄒㄧㄢˋ, xian⁴/　"to show", "to reveal"

**Associative Compound** (會意) of

玉 (王王 /ㄩˋ, yu⁴/ "jade" referring to *precious valuable items*) and

見 (/ㄐㄧㄢˋ, jian⁴/ "to see", *also providing sound*)

to imply *allowing precious valuable items to be seen*,

hence *"to show"*, *"to reveal"*.

王 + 見 ≡ 現 現

Most dictionaries list the character 現 (/ㄒㄧㄢˋ, xian⁴/) as

**Semantic-Phonetic Compound** (形聲) of

玉 (王王 /ㄩˋ, yu⁴/ "jade") *for semantics* and

見 (/ㄐㄧㄢˋ, jian⁴/ "to see") *for sound*

to mean *"to become or make noticeable"*, *"to show"*.

王 + 見 ≡ 現 現
"jade"　　/ㄐㄧㄢˋ, jian⁴/　　/ㄒㄧㄢˋ, xian⁴/ "to show"

It is important to note that 現 is a relatively new character and did not exist at time of the Seal Script (thus in grey colour as shown above). Before its creation, the character 見 was used.

## The Stroke Sequence

現 現 現 現 現 現 現 現 現 現
現 現 現 現 現 現 現 現 現 現
現
現

## The Anatomy

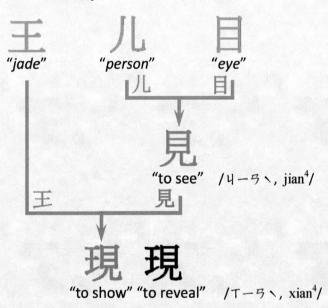

王 儿 目
"jade" "person" "eye"

見
"to see" /ㄐㄧㄢˋ, jian⁴/

現 現
"to show" "to reveal" /ㄒㄧㄢˋ, xian⁴/

314

# The Trinity – Sound(s), Semantics, and Synopses

/ㄒㄧㄢˋ, xian⁴/

| | |
|---|---|
| to show, to reveal | 顯**現**, 呈**現**, 湧**現**, **現**身; |
| revealing | **現**象; |
| immediately, without delay | **現**世報, **現**買**現**賣, **現**做**現**吃; |
| now, current, contemporary | **現**在, **現**役, **現**代; |
| real | **現**實, **現**金; |
| cash | 兌**現**, 付**現**, 貼**現**; |

*in classical Chinese,*

| | |
|---|---|
| to appear | 「我道是南海水月觀音**現**。」; |
| presently | 「卓問三人**現**居何職。」; |
| current | 「生滅遷變，酬於往因；<br>　善惡交謝，生乎**現**境。」; |
| real | 「要我這個爐，<br>　須是三百兩**現**銀子。」 |

**Radical:** 玉 (王).

# 87. 實

## Script Evolution

## The Story

/ㄕㄟ, shi²/   "wealth"

**Associative Compound** (會意) of

宀 (/ㄇㄧㄢˊ, mian²/ "large house", "roof") and

貫 (/ㄍㄨㄢˋ, guan⁴/ "valuable merchandise")

to imply *house full of valuable merchandise*,

hence *"wealth"*.

The story of *house full of valuable merchandise* as told through time by
the character 實 is shown below.

| Bronze | Seal | Standard |

## The Stroke Sequence

## The Anatomy

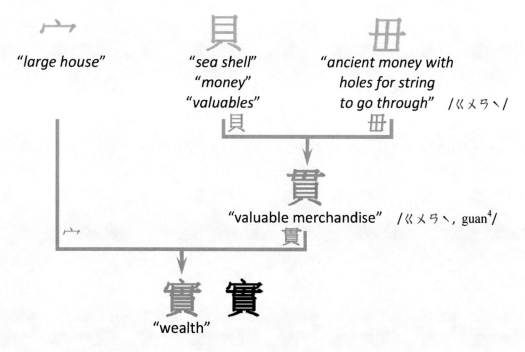

宀
*"large house"*

貝
*"sea shell"*
*"money"*
*"valuables"*

冊
*"ancient money with holes for string to go through"* /ㄍㄨㄢˋ/

貫
"valuable merchandise" /ㄍㄨㄢˋ, guan⁴/

實 實
"wealth"

## The Trinity – Sound(s), Semantics, and Synopses

/ㄕˊ, shi²/

wealth, ampleness

殷實;

| actual happening | 做**實**, 事**實**, 史**實**, 寫**實**; |
| fact | 有名無**實**, 名**實**相符, 名符其**實**; |
| fruit, produce, result | 果**實**, 開花結**實**, 春華秋**實***; |
| solid | **實**心, 結**實**, 踏**實**, 紮**實**; |
| true, real | **實**話, **實**情, **實**力, **實**踐**, |
| | 確**實**, 眞[真]**實**, 腳踏**實**地, |
| | 眞[真]才**實**學, 眞[真]材**實**料; |
| being real, having real value | **實**在, **實**用, **實**際; |
| actual | **實**體, **實**驗***; |
| honest | 誠**實**, 忠**實**; |

*:　『春華秋**實**』means *"flower in spring and produce in autumn"*.

**:　『**實**踐』 *making real* or *making reality* to mean *"to realize"*.

***:『**實**驗』 *examining actual procedural results* to mean
　　　　　　　*"to experiment"*.

*in classical Chinese,*

| ampleness | 「君之倉廩**實**, 府庫充。」; |
| solid | 「察子之事, 田野蕪, |
| | 　倉廩虛, 囹圄**實**。」; |
| honest | 「此皆良**實**, 志慮忠純, |
| | 　是以先帝簡拔以遺陛下。」; |
| fruit, produce | 「魏王貽我大瓠之種, |
| | 　我樹之成, 而**實**五石。」; |
| to strengthen, to fortify | 「損四鎮[鎮], 肥中國, |
| | 　罷安東, **實**遼西。」 |

**Radical:** 宀.

318

# 88. 加

**Script Evolution**

**The Story**

/ㄐㄧㄚ, jia/     "to commend"

"to add (to)"

**Associative Compound** (會意) of

    口 (/ㄎㄡˇ, kou³/ "mouth" referring to *spoken words*) and

    力 (/ㄌㄧˋ, li⁴/ "effort")

to imply *spoken words commending efforts dedicated*,

hence *"to commend"*.

It is important to note that 加 is the synonym to 嘉 (/ㄐㄧㄚ, jia/ "to commend"), **Associative Compound** (會意) of

    壴 (/ㄓㄨˋ, zhu⁴/ "ceremonial drum" referring to *ceremony*),

    力 (/ㄌㄧˋ, li⁴/ "effort"), and

    口 (/ㄎㄡˇ, kou³/ "mouth" referring to *spoken words*)

to imply *spoken words given at ceremony for efforts dedicated*,

hence *"to commend"*.

# 壴 + 力 + 口 ≡ 嘉 嘉

It is quite easy to see that 加 is actually the simple version of 嘉. Later, for the same sound (/ㄐㄧㄚ, jia/) and referring to *commending words adding to the efforts* the character 加 started to carry the semantics of *"to add (to)"* giving its original semantics of *"to commend"* back to 嘉. At time of the Bone Script, the character 嘉 told the story of *ceremony* (  ) *for the efforts dedicated* ( ). The stories of *celebrating and commending efforts dedicated* as told through time by the character 嘉 and 加 are shown below.

| Bone | Bronze | Seal | Standard |
|------|--------|------|----------|

## The Stroke Sequence

## The Anatomy

口     力

*"mouth"*     *"effort"*

口    力

↓

加 加

"to commend"
"to add (to)"

# The Trinity – Sound(s), Semantics, and Synopses

/ㄐ一ㄚ, jia/

| | |
|---|---|
| to add (to) | 加水, 加油, 添油加醋, 在茶裏[裡]加些牛奶; |
| to increase | 增加, 加碼, 加工, 加把勁(兒), 加油 (for cheering); |
| *with* 冕 *to mean* to crown | 加冕; |
| *math*, addition, to add | 加法, 加減乘除, 一加二等於三; |

*in classical Chinese*,

| | |
|---|---|
| to commend [=嘉] | 「王孔加子白義。」; |
| to add to | 「夫加之以衡軛。」; |
| to apply to | 「車服不維，刀鋸不加，理亂不知，黜陟不聞。」; |
| to enhance | 「既富矣，又何加焉？」; |
| to exceed | 「無以加之。」; |
| further (*in comparison*) | 「鄰國之民不加少，寡人之民不加多。」; |
| in addition | 「今海內爲[為]一，土地人民之眾不避湯、禹，加以亡天災數年之水旱，而畜積未及者，何也？」; |
| *name for Canada* | 加拿大, 到加國旅遊; |
| *surname* | 姓氏 |

**Radical:** 力; originally 口.

# 89. 量

**Script Evolution**

**The Story**

/ㄌㄧㄤˋ, liang⁴/ "to assess"

**Associative Compound** (會意) of

日 (/ㄖˋ, ri⁴/ "Sun"),

東 (/ㄉㄨㄥ, dong/ originally "large item wrapped and tied"

referring to *heavy luggage, also providing soun*d)

in Reduced Form 東, and

土 (/ㄊㄨˇ, tu³/ "land", "ground")

to imply *using the Sun's presence and position*

*to assess when to lay heavy luggage on ground*,

hence *"to assess"*.

日 + 東 + 土 = 量 量

**Note**: ㄥ and ㄤ are the same sound.

It is important to note that the Semantic-Phonetic Component 東 was not in Reduced Form in the Seal Script as shown above. At time of the Clerical

Script, 東 was trimmed with the centre Stroke shortened and bottom two Strokes removed, thus 東, to give the character an overall cleaner presence.

It is interesting to note that at time of the Bone Script the character told a simpler story of *the Sun* (日) *over a heavy luggage* (東) to imply *using the Sun's presence and position to assess when to go or stop when travelling with heavy luggage*, hence *"to assess"*. The stories of *using the Sun's presence and position to assess when to lay heavy luggage on ground* as told through time by the character 量 are shown below.

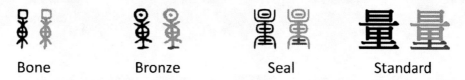

| Bone | Bronze | Seal | Standard |

Most dictionaries list the character 量 (/ㄌㄧㄤˊ, liang$^2$/) as **Semantic-Phonetic Compound** (形聲) of

重 (/ㄓㄨㄥˋ, zhong$^4$/ "weight") in Reduced Form 重 *for semantics* and

鄉 (/ㄒㄧㄤˋ, xiang$^4$/ "short while") in Reduced Form 鄉 *for sound*

to mean *"to measure (weight)"*.

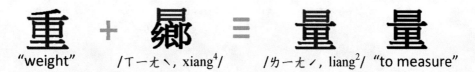

"weight"     /ㄒㄧㄤˋ, xiang$^4$/     /ㄌㄧㄤˊ, liang$^2$/ "to measure"

## The Stroke Sequence

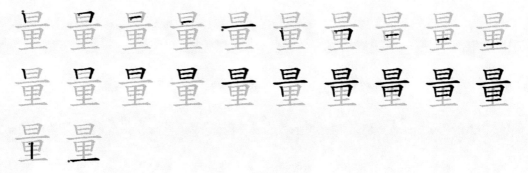

# 量 量

## The Anatomy

日     東     土

*"Sun"*    *"large item wrapped and tied"*    *"ground"*

/ㄉㄨㄥ, dong/

量 量   *"to assess"*   /ㄌㄧㄤˋ, liang⁴/

## The Trinity – Sound(s), Semantics, and Synopses

/ㄌㄧㄤˋ, liang⁴/

| | |
|---|---|
| to assess, to reckon | 忖量, 思量, 打量, 考量, 量入爲[為]出, 量力而爲[為], 不自量力, 量他沒這個膽; |
| capacity | 容量, 器量, 膽量, 肚量, 酒量, 海量, 度量衡*; |
| magnanimity | 雅量, 寬宏大量, 寬容大量, 大人大量; |
| amount | 含量, 力量, 重量, 能量, 熱量, 雨量, 劑量, 產量, 銷量, 存量, 用量, 多量, 少量, 大量, 小量, 酌量, 適量; |
| number, quantity | 數量, 大量, 車流量; |

*:『度量衡』means *"length, capacity, and weight measuring system"*.

*physics*,

| | |
|---|---|
| quantum | 量子, 量子力學; |
| *used with* 向 *to mean* vector | 力是向量; |

*in classical Chinese*,

| | |
|---|---|
| to assess | 「量敵而後進， |
| | 　慮勝而後會。」; |
| talent, ability | 「時左將軍劉備以亮有殊量， |
| | 　乃三顧亮於草廬之中。」; |
| capacity, tolerance | 「沈沈玉卮酒， |
| | 　量淺難負荷。」; |
| magnanimity | 「敏而好學，雅量豁然。」; |
| standard container for capacity measurement | 「量者，龠、合、升、斛也。」; |
| limit | 「以日星爲[為]紀， |
| | 　故事可列也； |
| | 　月以爲[為]量， |
| | 　故功有藝也。」 |

/ㄌㄧㄤˊ, liang$^2$/

| | |
|---|---|
| to measure, to take measurement | 丈量, 測量, 量體溫, 量身訂製; |
| to weigh all alternatives | 衡量, 商量, 量度 (/ㄌㄨㄛˋ/ //ˊ//); |

*in classical Chinese*,

| | |
|---|---|
| to consider, to deliberate | 「其多所裁量若此。」, |
| | 「惟應微密處， |
| | 　猶欲細商量。」 |

**Radical:** 里 (/ㄌㄧˇ, li$^3$/ "place to reside"); originally 日.

# 90. 兩

## Script Evolution

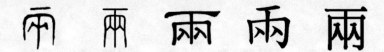

## The Story

[ㄌㄧㄤˋ, liang[4]]  *quantity word for* wagons

/ㄌㄧㄤˇ, liang[3]/  "pair", "two"

**Pictograph** (象形) of *yoke of a wagon* to imply *unit of wagon*,

hence *quantity word for* wagons.

Later, for the same sound (/ㄌㄧㄤˇ, liang[3]/) the character started to carry
the semantics of *"pair"*, *"two"* since the yoke is harness for two animals.  The
original use as *quantity word for* wagons was then given to the Associative
Compound 輛 with Radical 車 (/ㄔㄜ, che/ "wagon") and Semantic-Phonetic
Component 兩 ([ㄌㄧㄤˋ, liang[4]] *quantity word for wagons*).

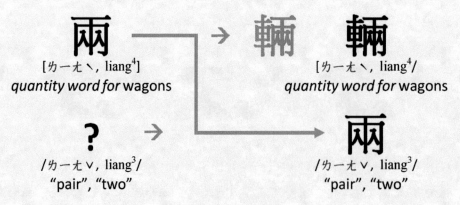

This process of character creation, or re-creation rather, is called Semantic Bifurcation (假借).

The pictures of *yoke of a wagon* as rendered through time by the character 兩 are shown below.

Bronze        Seal        Standard

## The Stroke Sequence

**Common Fallacy:** Writing the two 『入』 as 『人』.

## The Trinity – Sound(s), Semantics, and Synopses

/ㄌㄧㄤˇ, liang³/

| | |
|---|---|
| pair, two | 兩夫妻, 兩姊妹, 兩兄弟, 兩本書, 兩小無猜, 銀貨兩訖; |
| both | 兩敗俱傷, 勢不兩立, 模棱兩可, 兩全其美; |
| a few | 兩下子, 過兩天就好了; |
| *often used with* 三 *to mean* a few | 三兩下, 三三兩兩, 三言兩語; |
| *weight unit* (1 兩 = 31.25 grammes) | 夠足斤兩; |
| *in classical Chinese,* | |
|     *quantity word, for* | |
|         wagons [=輛] | 「百兩御之。」; |

pair                                   「同居長干里，

　　　　　　　　　　　　　　　兩小無嫌猜。」；

both                                   「今兄弟遘惡，

　　　　　　　　　　　　　　　此勢不兩全。」

**Radical:** 入 (/ㄖㄨˋ, ru⁴/ "to enter"); originally 兩 [网] (itself).

# 91. 體

## Script Evolution

䖝豐 體 體 體 體

## The Story

體 體 體 體

/ㄊㄧˇ, ti³/  "human body"

**Associative Compound** (會意) of

骨 (/ㄍㄨˇ, gu³/ "bone with muscle") and

豐 (/ㄌㄧˇ, li³/ "ceremonial vessel for precious oblations" referring to

*precious organs in human body, also providing sound*)

to imply *skeletal bone with muscle and precious organs in human body*,

hence "*human body*".

骨 + 豐 = 體 體

It is important to note that at time of the Bronze Script the character told the story of *body* (䖝身 /ㄕㄣ, shen/) *with precious organs* (豐豐) that is 體. At time of the Seal Script, the story used the *skeletal bone with muscle* (骨骨) to emphasize the overall body anatomy, thus leading to the Standard Script. The stories of *skeletal bone with muscle and precious organs in human body* as told through time by the character 體 (體) are shown below.

|                     |                     |                     |
|:-------------------:|:-------------------:|:-------------------:|
| Bronze | Seal | Standard |

It is important to point out that every native Chinese language user knows that a character much simpler in form than 體 is often used in hand writing or even as a substitute altogether. And that character is 体, a Standard character in its own right and a Semantic-Phonetic Compound of

人 (亻 /ㄖㄣˊ, ren$^2$/ "person") *for semantics* and
本 (/ㄅㄣˇ, ben$^3$/ "root", "basics") *for sound*

to mean "*coarse*", "*dumb*".

    "person"        /ㄅㄣˇ, ben$^3$/     /ㄅㄣˋ, ben$^4$/   "coarse", "dumb"

The fallacy of using 体 (/ㄅㄣˋ, ben$^4$/ "coarse", "dumb") for 體 (/ㄊㄧˇ, ti$^3$/ "human body") that is condemned in the benchmark 康熙 (/ㄎㄤ ㄒㄧ, kang xi/) Dictionary arose from the convenient but careless and incorrect belief that 体 is an Associative Compound of

人 (亻 /ㄖㄣˊ, ren$^2$/ "person") and
本 (/ㄅㄣˇ, ben$^3$/ "root", "basics")

to imply *the basics of a person*,
hence "*human body*".

**The Stroke Sequence**

體 體 體 體 體 體 體 骨 骨 骨

體 體 體 體 體 體 體 體 體 體

骨 體 體 體 體 體 體 體 體 體

體 體 體

**體 體 體**

## The Anatomy

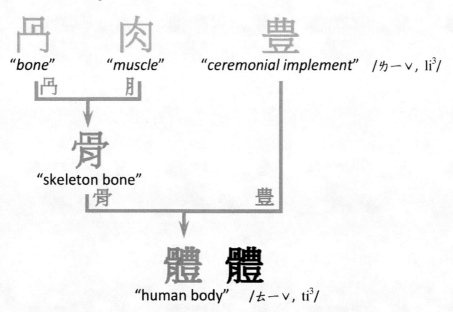

冎     肉     豊

*"bone"*     *"muscle"*     *"ceremonial implement"* /ㄌㄧˇ, li³/

冎     月

骨

"skeleton bone"

骨        豊

體 **體**

"human body" /ㄊㄧˇ, ti³/

## The Trinity – Sound(s), Semantics, and Synopses

/ㄊㄧˇ, ti³/

human body          身**體**, 肉**體**, 軀**體**, **體**形, **體**育,

**體**態輕盈, **體**無完膚, 貴**體**安康;

| | |
|---|---|
| of physical body | 體能, 體力, 體格, 體重, 體溫; |
| major body part | 肢體, 上體, 下體, 五體投地; |
| main structure | 車體, 主體, 物體, 形體, 總體, 整體結構; |
| entity | 集體, 體制, 體統; |
| in person, personally | 體驗, 體會, 體認; |
| to be empathetic | 體諒, 體恤; |
| to practise | 身體力行; |
| appropriateness | 得體; |
| *used with* 面 *to mean* | |
|    presentable | 這孩子長得體面*; |
|    appropriacy | 倉促之舉有失體面; |
|    honourable | 年輕時做了些不體面的事; |
| style (*of handwriting or literary*) | 字體, 文體; |
| state of substance | 固體, 液體, 氣體; |
| *philosophy*, fundamentals | 中學爲[為]體，西學爲[為]用; |
| *geometry*, solid geometrical figure | 點、線[綫]、面、體, 正方體, 長方體, 球體, 圓柱體; |
| *in classical Chinese*, | |
|    limbs | 「四體不勤。」; |
|    to practise | 「故聖人以身體之。」; |
|    to be empathetic | 「汝體吾此心。」 |

**Radical:** 骨.

# 92. 機

## Script Evolution

檓 機 機 機

## The Story

檓 檓 機 機

/ㄐㄧ, ji/　　"weaving machine", "machine"

**Associative Compound** (會意) of

木 (/ㄇㄨˋ, mu⁴/ "wood") and

幾 (/ㄐㄧ, ji/ originally "weaving machine", *also providing sound*)

to imply *wood framed weaving machine*,

hence *"weaving machine"*, *"machine"*.

木 + 幾 ≡ 機 機

It is important to note that the Semantic-Phonetic Component 幾 is the Original (本字) of 機. In other words, 機 is the re-created character from its Original 幾, Associative Compound (會意) of

幺幺 (/ㄧㄡ, you/ "silk strands"),

戈 (Pictograph of *a machine*), and

人 (/ㄖㄣˊ, ren²/ "person")

to imply *silk strands on a machine operated by a person*,

hence *"weaving machine"*.

$$\text{絲} + \text{戈} + \text{人} \equiv \text{幾} \quad \text{幾}$$

Later, 幾 started to carry the semantics of *"small chance"*, *"extremely small"* for the same sound (/ㄐㄧ, ji/) surrendering its original semantics of *"weaving machine"* to the Associative Compound 機 (/ㄐㄧ, ji/) with Radical 木 (/ㄇㄨˋ, mu[4]/ *"wood"*) and Semantic-Phonetic Component 幾 (/ㄐㄧ, ji/ *"weaving machine"*).

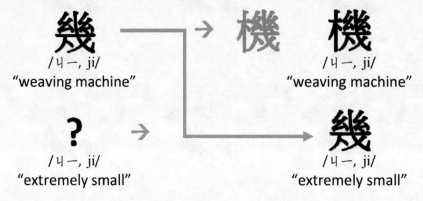

幾
/ㄐㄧ, ji/
"weaving machine"

→ 機 機
/ㄐㄧ, ji/
"weaving machine"

？
/ㄐㄧ, ji/
"extremely small"

→ 幾
/ㄐㄧ, ji/
"extremely small"

This process of character creation, or re-creation rather, is called Semantic Bifurcation (假借).

## The Stroke Sequence

機機機機機機機機機機
機機機機機機機機機機
機機機機機機
機機機機機機

## The Anatomy

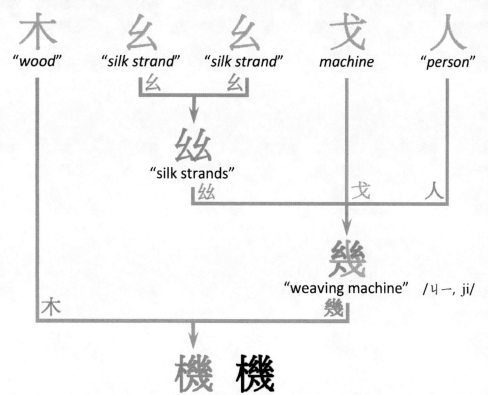

"weaving machine" /ㄐㄧ, ji/

機 機
"weaving machine" /ㄐㄧ, ji/
"machine"

## The Trinity – Sound(s), Semantics, and Synopses

/ㄐㄧ, ji/

| | |
|---|---|
| machine | 打字機, 發電機, 洗衣機, 果汁機, 縫紉機; |
| machinery | 機械, 機牀[床], 電機; |
| mechanism | 有機, 無機, 機能; |
| engine, motor | 輪機, 機車, 發動機, 機動部隊; |
| aeroplane | 機場, 戰機, 客機, 貨機; |
| well organized and operated | 機關; |

| | |
|---|---|
| clever, ingenious | 機智, 機巧, 機靈[伶]; |
| cleverness, genius | 神機妙算, 靈機一動; |
| flexible, adaptive | 機動調節; |
| important, of high priority | 機密, 機要; |
| occasion | 機緣, 隨機應變; |
| opportunity | 機會, 機遇, 時機, 錯失良機; |
| cause | 動機; |
| desire, plot within one's mind | 心機; |

*in classical Chinese,*

| | |
|---|---|
| weaving machine | 「寒衣一匹素，<br>　夜借鄰人機。」; |
| occasion | 「候時而來，順陰陽之數；<br>　應節爲[為]變，<br>　審藏用之機。」; |
| motive | 「一家仁，一國興仁；<br>　一家讓，一國興讓；<br>　一人貪戾，一國作亂，<br>　其機如此。」; |
| scheme or plan in one's mind | 「我醉君復樂，<br>　陶然共忘機。」 |

**Radical:** 木.

# 93. 還

## Script Evolution

懈 愚 還 還 還 還

## The Story

還 還 還 還 還

/ㄏㄨㄢˊ, huan[2]/    "to return"

**Associative Compound** (會意) of

目 (罒 /ㄇㄨˋ, mu[4]/ "eye" referring to *eye showing hope*) and

遠 (/ㄩㄢˇ, yuan[3]/ "far away", *also providing sound*)

to imply *eye of person travelling far away showing hope to return*,

hence *"to return"*.

罒 **+** 遠 **≡** 還 還

**Note**: ㄩㄢ and ㄨㄢ are the same sound.

To make it less crowded vertically, Standard Form has 睘 written as 睘,
hence 還 in lieu of 還.

還 還 → 還 還

還 還 → 還 還

337

It is important to note that at time of the Bone Script the character told a different story of *en route* ( 彳亍 行) *to banishment* ( 方 [ㄈㄤˋ, fang⁴], *also providing sound*) *with eye showing hope* ( 目) *to return one day*, because the character 還 was not created until time of the Bronze Script. 遠 (/ㄩㄢˇ, yuan³/ "far away" Usage Rank #546), **Associative Compound** (會意) of

辵 (辶 /ㄔㄨㄛˋ, chuo⁴/ "to walk and stop" referring to *travelling*),

衣 (/一, yi/ "garment", "clothing"),

囗 (Pictograph of *packed personal items)*, and

止 (屮 中 /ㄓˇ, zhi³/ "foot" referring to *porter*)

to imply *travelling afar with clothing and personal items carried by porter*, hence *"far away"*.

辵 + 衣 + 囗 + 屮 ≡ 遠 遠

The stories of *a person going far away hoping to return* and *travelling afar* as told through time by the characters 還 (還) and 遠 are shown below.

| Bone | Bronze | Seal | Standard |
|---|---|---|---|
| | | | 還還還 |
| | | | 遠遠 |

Most dictionaries list the character 還 (還 /ㄏㄨㄢˊ, huan²/) as **Semantic-Phonetic Compound** (形聲) of

辵 (辶 /ㄔㄨㄛˋ, chuo⁴/ "to walk and stop") *for semantics* and

睘 (/ㄑㄩㄥˊ, qiong²/ "to gawp in surprise") *for sound*

to mean *"to return"*.

辵 + 睘 ≡ 還 還

"to walk and stop"    /ㄑㄩㄥˊ, qiong²/    /ㄏㄨㄢˊ, huan²/    "to return"

338

**Note:** ㄩㄥ and ㄨㄢ are the same sound.

## The Stroke Sequence

## The Anatomy

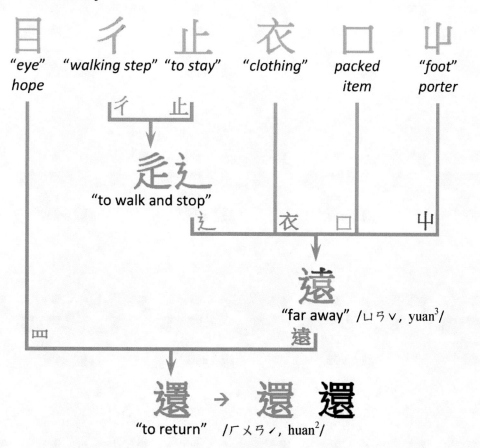

目
*"eye"*
hope

彳
*"walking step"*

止
*"to stay"*

衣
*"clothing"*

口
packed
item

屮
*"foot"*
porter

彳 止

辵辶
*"to walk and stop"*

遠
*"far away"* /ㄩㄢˇ, yuan³/

還 → 還 還
*"to return"*  /ㄏㄨㄢˊ, huan²/

339

# The Trinity – Sound(s), Semantics, and Synopses

/ㄏㄨㄢˊ, huan$^2$/

| | |
|---|---|
| to turn back, to go back | 往**還**, 生**還**, **還**鄉[鄉]; |
| to return | 交**還**, 退**還**, **還**書, **還**政於民; |
| to recover, to return to original | **還**原, **還**俗; |
| to reciprocate | **還**禮, **還**願, **還**擊, **還**手, **還**口, 以牙**還**牙，以眼**還**眼; |
| to pay back, to return favour | **還**債, **還**人情; |
| to negotiate (to go back and forth) | 討價**還**價, **還**個價; |
| to circle | **還**[環]繞; |
| yet | 欲語**還**休; |

*in classical Chinese*,

| | |
|---|---|
| to turn back | 「乍暖**還**寒猶未定。」; |
| to go back | 「黃沙百戰穿金甲，<br>　　不破樓蘭終不**還**。」; |
| to pay back | 「況聞處處鬻男女，<br>　　割慈忍愛**還**租庸。」; |
| since (such time) | 「秦漢而**還**，多事四夷。」; |
| to circle [=環] | 「**還**廬樹桑，菜茹有畦。」; |
| *surname* | 姓氏 |

/ㄏㄞˊ, hai$^2$/

| | |
|---|---|
| even more | 他比我**還**高, 今天比昨天**還**熱; |
| moreover | 自己不看也就算了，<br>　　**還**叫別人也不要看; |

| | |
|---|---|
| still | **還**沒有到, **還**不算晚, **還**來得及, **還**是老樣子, **還**有別的嗎？; |
| actually | 他**還**眞[真]不怕冷, **還**眞[真]被我給說中了; |
| without interruption (exception) | 下了課**還**要工作; |
| or | 這是字**還**是畫; |
| or would rather | 您是想聽音樂，**還**是想看電影; |

*in classical Chinese,*

| | |
|---|---|
| instead | 「不得人間壽，<br>　　**還**留身後名。」; |
| already | 「上國獻詩**還**不遇，<br>　　故園經亂又空歸。」; |
| also | 「半羞**還**半喜，<br>　　欲去又依依。」 |

/ㄒㄩㄢˊ, xuan$^2$/

*in classical Chinese,*

| | |
|---|---|
| to twist | 「羅衣何飄颻，<br>　　輕裾隨風**還**。」; |
| promptly thereafter | 「忽過新豐市，<br>　　**還**歸細柳營。」; |
| light and agile | 「子之**還**兮，<br>　　遭我乎峱之間兮。」 |

**Radical:** 辵 (辶); originally 目 (罒).

# 94. 當

## Script Evolution

## The Story

[ㄉㄤ∨, dang³]     "to block off"

/ㄉㄤ, dang/     "to match"

**Associative Compound** (會意) of

田 (/ㄊㄧㄢˊ, tian² / "crop field" referring to *sizeable piece of land*) and

尚 (尚 /ㄕㄤˋ, shang⁴/ originally "shelter making a difference"

referring to *shelter to block off elements*,

*also providing sound*)

to imply *land and shelter to block off harm and elements*,

hence *"to block off"*.

$$田 + 尚 = 當 \quad 當$$

It is important to note that at time of the Bronze Script the character told the story of *dirt mound* (⬭) *and shelter* (⬭) *blocking off* (—) *harm and elements*. The stories of *using natural and man-made objects to block off harm and elements* as told through time by the character are shown below.

| Bronze | Seal | Standard |

Later, for the same sound (/ㄉㄤ, dang/) and referring to the *matching* nature for blocking, 當 started to carry the semantics of *"to match"* surrendering its original semantics to the Associative Compound 擋 (/ㄉㄤˇ, dang[3]/ Usage Rank #1,955) with Radical 手 (扌 /ㄕㄡˇ, shou[3]/ "hand") and Semantic-Phonetic Component 當 ([ㄉㄤˇ, dang[3]] "to block off"). This process of character creation, or re-creation rather, is called Semantic Bifurcation (假借).

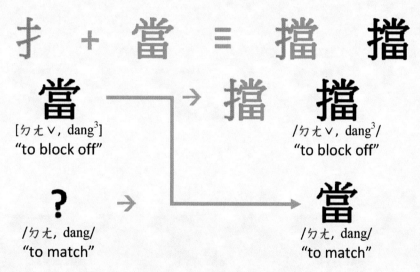

Most dictionaries list the character 當 (/ㄉㄤ, dang/) as

**Semantic-Phonetic Compound** (形聲) of

田 (/ㄊㄧㄢˊ, tian[2]/ "crop field") *for semantics* and

尚 (尚 /ㄕㄤˋ, shang[4]/ "to desire *for better*", "to elevate") *for sound*

to mean *"to match"*.

| 田 | + | 尚 | = | 當 | 當 |

"crop field"　　　/ㄕㄤˋ, shang[4]/　　　/ㄉㄤ, dang/　　"to match"

## The Stroke Sequence

## The Anatomy

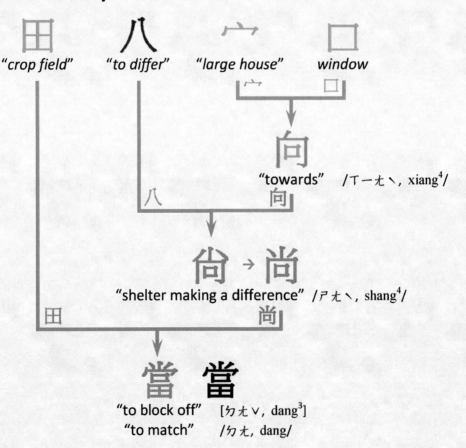

田 "crop field"  八 "to differ"  宀 "large house"  口 window

宀 口 → 向 "towards" /ㄒㄧㄤˋ, xiang⁴/

八 向 → 尚 → 尚 "shelter making a difference" /ㄕㄤˋ, shang⁴/

田 尚 → 當 當 "to block off" [ㄉㄤˇ, dang³] "to match" /ㄉㄤ, dang/

344

# The Trinity – Sound(s), Semantics, and Synopses

/ㄉㄤ, dang/

| | |
|---|---|
| to match, to be compatible | 門**當**戶對, 旗鼓相**當**; |
| to be | **當**選, **當**兵, **當**老師, **當**學生; |
| (to be) on | **當**班, **當**差; |
| to be in charge of | **當**家, **當**位, **當**事, **當**權, **當**政; |
| to be responsible for | 擔**當**, 不敢**當**, 敢做敢**當**; |
| to face towards | **當**面, **當**機立斷, **當**頭棒喝, 首**當**其衝, **當**眾把話說清楚; |
| to properly deserve | 罪不**當**斬; |
| *used with* 心 *to mean* | |
|     to be watchful, cautious | **當**心; |
| to treat as (*also* /ㄉㄤ丶, dang[4]/) | 安步**當**車, 以茶**當**酒; |
| right at (*place*) | **當**街搶劫, **當**場決定; |
| at (*time*) | 正**當**頭, 適**當**其時; |
| when | **當**我們同在一起; |
| that particular (*time period*) | |
|     (*also* /ㄉㄤ丶, dang[4]/) | **當**年, **當**時, **當**天; |
| this particular (*time period*) | **當**下, **當**今; |
| as appropriate | **當**仁不讓, **當**省則省，**當**用則用; |
| tip end of an object | 瓜**當**, 瓦**當**; |
| *in classical Chinese,* | |
|     during | 「**當**堯之時，天下猶未平。」; |

| as appropriate | 「安得亡國之言！ |
| | 此非人臣所**當**議也！」 |

**/ㄉㄤ∨, dang³/**

| to regard as | 你**當**我是誰; |
| *in classical Chinese,* | |
| to block off [=擋] | 「昔大禹治水， |
| | 山陵**當**路者毀之。」; |
| to resist [=擋] | 螳臂**當**車, 銳不可**當**, |
| | 「一身轉戰三千里， |
| | 一劍曾**當**百萬師。」 |

**/ㄉㄤ丶, dang⁴/**

| appropriate, proper | 恰**當**, 適**當**, 妥**當**, |
| | 不**當**之處，請多指敎[教]; |
| trickery, cunning plot | 勾**當**, 上**當**; |
| to pawn | 典**當**, 質**當**, **當**鋪; |
| to consider as | **當**眞[真], 不**當**回事(兒); |
| to treat as (*also* /ㄉㄤ, dang/) | 安步**當**車, 以茶**當**酒; |
| that particular (*time period*) | |
| (*also* /ㄉㄤ, dang/) | **當**年, **當**時, **當**天; |
| *colloquial*, to fail (a college course) | 電磁學被**當**了; |
| *in classical Chinese,* | |
| appropriate | 「夫古天地順而四時**當**， |
| | 民有德而五穀昌。」 |

**Radical:** 田.

346

# 95. 使

## Script Evolution

## The Story

/ㄕˇ, shi³/  [ㄕ一ˇ]          "to command"

**Associative Compound** (會意) of

人 (亻/ㄖㄣˊ, ren² "person" referring to *carrying the duty of*) and

吏 (/ㄌㄧˋ, li⁴ "bureaucrat", "people manager", *also* providing *sound*)

to imply *carrying the duty of a bureaucrat*,

hence "*to command*".

It is important to note that at time of the Bone Script the character 使 shared the same form with its Semantic-Phonetic Component 吏 ( ), Associative Compound of

又 (/一ㄡˋ, you⁴ "hand holding something") and

(Pictograph of *a hunting spear* with a catch )

to imply *a hunting event worth talking about*,

hence "*event*" (事), "*bureaucrat (responsible for major events)*" (吏).

347

Thus, 事 (/ㄕㄟ, shi⁴/ "event" Usage Rank #124),

　　吏 (/ㄌㄧㄟ, li⁴/ "bureaucrat" Usage Rank #1,735), and

　　使 (/ㄕ∨, shi³/ "to command")

all shared the same character form at time of the Bone Script, whereas 事 and 吏 continued to share the same form until time of the Seal Script when the character form bifurcated to two separate ones thus two distinct characters for *"event"* and *"bureaucrat"* as shown below.

Bone　　　　Bronze　　　　Seal　　　　Standard

Most dictionaries list the character 使 (/ㄕ∨, shi³/ [ㄕㄧ∨]) as

**Semantic-Phonetic Compound** (形聲) of

　　人 (亻 /ㄖㄣˊ, ren²/ "person") *for semantics* and

　　吏 (/ㄌㄧㄟ, li⁴/ "bureaucrat", "people manager") *for sound*

to mean *"to command"* with ancient pronunciation of [ㄕㄧ∨].

亻 ＋ 吏 ≡ 使　使

　"person"　　/ㄌㄧㄟ, li⁴/　　[ㄕㄧ∨]　"to command"

**The Stroke Sequence**

使 使 使 使 使 使 使 使

使 使 使 使 使 使 使 使

348

## The Anatomy

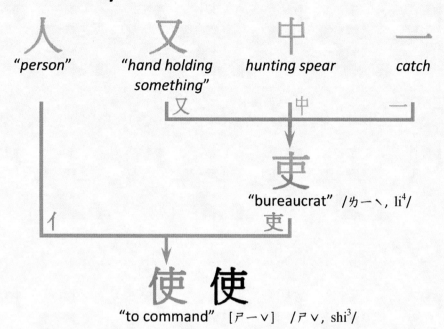

人
*"person"*

又
*"hand holding something"*

中
*hunting spear*

一
*catch*

吏
"bureaucrat" /ㄌㄧˋ, li⁴/

使 使
"to command"  [ㄕㄧˇ]  /ㄕˇ, shi³/

## The Trinity – Sound(s), Semantics, and Synopses

/ㄕˇ, shi³/

| | |
|---|---|
| to command, to summon | 使喚; |
| to use, to operate | 使用, 不好使; |
| to apply | 使得, 使不得, 使勁(兒), 使點(兒)力, 藉力使力; |
| to use person's labour | 役使; |
| to make, to have | 使人擔憂, 命運使然; |
| to indulge (to summon irrationally) | 使性子; |
| to scheme and practise | 使壞; |
| to be true | 假使; |
| envoy | 使者; |

ambassador, embassy          大**使**, **使**節, 出**使**, **使**館;

*in classical Chinese,*

    to send, to dispatch

「若得如此，宋江星夜
**使**人回家搬取老父，
以絕根本。」；

    to make, to have

「維子之故，
**使**我不能餐兮。」，

「出師未捷身先死，
長**使**英雄淚滿襟。」；

    to use person's labour

「節用而愛人，**使**民以時。」，

「古之**使**人，歲不過三日；
今之勞擾，
殆無二日休停。」；

    to carry out duty as envoy

「行己有恥，**使**于四方，
不辱君命，可謂士矣。」；

    if, assuming

「如有周公之才之美，
**使**驕且吝，
其餘不足觀也已。」，

「**使**天地有口能食，
祭食宜食盡。」

**Radical:** 人 (亻).

# 96. 點

## Script Evolution

點　黜　點　點　點

## The Story

黜　黜　點　點

/ㄉㄧㄢˇ, dian³/    "dark spot"

**Associative Compound** (會意) of

黑 (/ㄏㄟ, hei/ "black" referring to *dark colour*) and

占 (/ㄓㄢˋ, zhan⁴/ "to occupy" referring to *area*, *spot*,

*also* providing *sound*)

to imply *area or spot of dark colour*,

hence "*dark spot*".

黑 ＋ 占 ≡ 點　點

The story of *area or spot of dark colour* as told through time by the character 點 is shown below.

Bronze　　　Seal　　　Standard

## The Stroke Sequence

點 點 點 點 點 點 點 點 點 點
點 點 點 點 點 點 點 點 點 點
點 點 點 點 點 點 點
點 點 點 點 點 點 點

## The Anatomy

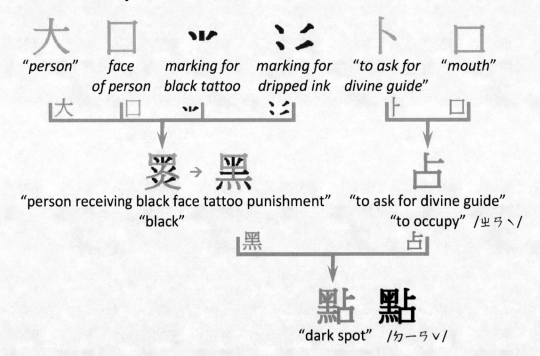

大 "person"　口 face of person　⺌ marking for black tattoo　氵 marking for dripped ink　卜 "to ask for divine guide"　口 "mouth"

炗 → 黑
"person receiving black face tattoo punishment"
"black"

占
"to ask for divine guide"
"to occupy" /ㄓㄢˋ/

黑　占

點 點
"dark spot" /ㄉㄧㄢˇ/

## The Trinity – Sound(s), Semantics, and Synopses

/ㄉㄧㄢˇ, dian³/

dark spot　　　　　　　　　斑點, 污[汙]點;

drop, droplet　　　　　　　雨點, 點點滴滴;

| | |
|---|---|
| essential area, aspect, point | 優**點**, 缺**點**, 重**點**, 弱**點**; |
| bullet, key | 下列三**點**來說明; |
| punctuation | 標**點**, 逗**點**; |
| appointed time, measured time | 準**點**, 誤**點**, 鐘**點**; |
| hour, o'clock | 整**點**, 下午三**點**半, 五**點**一刻; |
| fixed place or standard | 終**點**, 起**點**, 冰**點**, 沸**點**, 燃**點**; |
| snack, food in small quantity | 西**點**, 茶**點**, 糕**點**, **點**心, 早**點**, 餐**點**, 麵[麵]**點**; |
| a little bit | 快**點**(兒), 慢**點**(兒), 輕**點**(兒), 早**點**(兒), 晚**點**(兒), 多**點**(兒), 一**點**(兒)小事, 吃**點**(兒)東西吧; |
| *one of the 8 basic Strokes in* *Chinese characters* (*calligraphy*) | **點**、橫、豎、撇、捺、折、提、鈎, 三**點**水; |
| to mark with a dot | 可圈可**點**; |
| to start (*for small beginning*) | **點**火, **點**燃, **點**燈; |
| to pick, to select (*by pointing*) | **點**菜, **點**歌, **點**播節目; |
| to check, to match | **點**貨, **點**名, 清**點**, 盤**點**; |
| to hint, to point out | **點**醒, **點**化, **點**出主題, 一**點**就懂; |
| to lightly touch | 蜻蜓**點**水, 以腳**點**地, **點**石成金, **點**到爲[為]止; |
| to dispense (*for small amount*) | **點**眼藥; |
| to place (*small pieces*) decoratively | 裝**點**, **點**綴; |

| | |
|---|---|
| *math*, radix point | 小數**點**, 三**點**一四一五九; |
| *geometry*, point | **點**、線[綫]、面、體; |
| *in classical Chinese*, | |
|    to decorate | 「**點**以銀黃，爍以琅玕。」 |

**Radical:** 黑.

# 97. 從

## Script Evolution

從　従　從　從　從　從

## The Story

從　従　從　從　從

/ㄘㄨㄥˊ, cong²/　"to follow"

**Associative Compound** (會意) of

从 (/ㄘㄨㄥˊ, cong²/ "to listen to each other" referring to *staying close,*
　　　　　*also providing sound*),

彳 (/彳ㄟˋ, chuo⁴/ "narrow path"), and

止 (/ㄓˇ, zhi³/ "foot" referring to *walking*)

to imply *staying close walking on a narrow path,*

hence "*to follow*".

从 ＋ 彳 ＋ 止 ≡ 從 従

It is important to note that at time of the Bone Script the character told
the story of *staying close* ( 从 ) *on a narrow path* ( 彳 ). The stories of *staying
close* and *following step by step* as told through time by the character 從 are
shown below.

| 術術 | 泌泌 | 訕訕 | 趴趴 從 |
|------|------|------|---------|
| Bone | Bronze | Seal | Standard |

## The Stroke Sequence

從 從 從 從 從 從 從 從 從 從
從 從 從 從 從 從 從 從 從 從
從

從

## The Anatomy

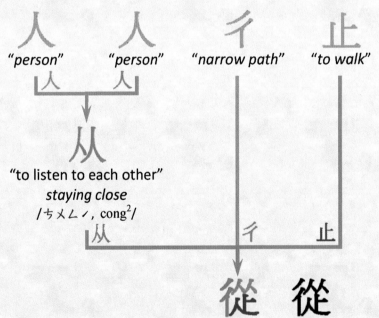

人       人       彳       止

*"person"*    *"person"*    *"narrow path"*    *"to walk"*

人    人

从

"to listen to each other"
*staying close*
/ㄘㄨㄥˊ, cong$^2$/

从      彳      止

從 從

*staying close walking on a narrow path*
"to follow"    /ㄘㄨㄥˊ, cong$^2$/

# The Trinity – Sound(s), Semantics, and Synopses

/ㄘㄨㄥˊ, cong²/

| | |
|---|---|
| to follow | 跟從, 力不從心; |
| to obey | 服從, 從命; |
| to accept suggestion or advice | 言聽計從, 從善如流; |
| to yield | 至死不從; |
| to join | 從軍, 從商, 從政; |
| to become | 從良; |
| to engage, to undertake | 從事; |
| always, ever | 他從未遲到過; |
| based on guideline or strategy | 從速解決, 從寬處理, 一切從簡, 從嚴懲罰; |
| from | 從此, 從今以後, 從頭到尾, 從那裏[裡]來？; |

*in classical Chinese*,

| | |
|---|---|
| to follow | 「道不行，乘桴浮于海，從我者其由與？」; |
| to obey | 「樂者敦和率神而從天。」; |
| from | 「露從今夜白，月是故鄉[鄉]明。」; |
| *surname* | 姓氏 |

/ㄘㄨㄥ, cong/　*used with* 容 *to mean*

| | |
|---|---|
| relaxed | 從容以待; |
| plenty, not restricted | 時間很從容; |

357

*in classical Chinese*,

| relaxed | 「與晟飲酒，**從容**訪問，<br>　　晟終不言。」； |
| to instigate, to incite | 「微知淮南、衡山有逆計，<br>　　日夜**從容**勸之。」； |
| plenty | 「東山到底不明白，<br>　　卻是驟得了千來兩銀子，<br>　　手頭**從容**。」 |

/ㄗㄨㄥˋ, zong⁴/

| attendant, servant | 侍**從**, 僕**從**; |
| playing an assisting role, deputy | **從**犯, **從**吏, 主**從**有別; |
| blood relative next to direct family | **從**父, **從**子, **從**兄弟; |

*in classical Chinese*,

| deputy | 「前世職次皆無**從**品，<br>　　魏氏始置之。」 |

/ㄗㄨㄥ, zong/

*in classical Chinese*,

| footmarks, foot tracks [=蹤] | 「今乃以妾尚[尚]在之故，<br>　　重自刑以絕**從**。」, |
| | 「上問：『變事**從**跡安起？』<br>　　湯陽驚曰：<br>　　『此殆文故人怨之。』」 |

**Radical:** 彳 (/ㄔˋ, chi⁴/ "small step", "to walk"); originally 从.

# 98. 業

**Script Evolution**

業　業　業　業　業

**The Story**

業　業　業　業　業

/ㄧㄝˋ, ye⁴/　"enterprise"

**Pictograph** (象形) of *decorated musical instrument rack*

to imply *great achievement, enterprise deserving such adornment*,

hence *"great achievement"*, *"enterprise"*.

For obvious aesthetic reasons, Standard Form changed 巾 with all orthogonal Strokes to 木 with two artistic slanted Strokes. Hence, the Standard Form of this character is the aesthetic and artistically well balanced 業 in lieu of the square bottomed 業.

It is interesting to note that at time of the Bronze Script a Variant form of the character told the story of *decorated musical instrument rack* (業) *attracting praises and discussions* ( 凵 ). The stories of *great achievement deserving the adornment of decorated rack for its ceremonial musical instruments* as told through time by the character 業 (業) are shown below.

| Bronze | Seal | Standard |
|--------|------|----------|

## The Stroke Sequence

業 業 業 業 業 業 業 業 業 業

業 業 業 業 業 業 業 業 業 業

業 業 業

業 業 業

## The Trinity – Sound(s), Semantics, and Synopses

/ㄧㄝˋ, ye$^4$/　　Alternative Pronunciation //ㄋㄧㄝˋ, nie$^4$//

　　great achievement　　　　　　功業, 豐功偉業;

　　enterprise, undertaking　　　　創業, 事業;

　　industry　　　　　　　　　　農業, 商業, 工業;

　　occupation　　　　　　　　　敬業, 業務, 各行各業;

　　property, business　　　　　　產業, 祖業, 家業, 業主;

　　work　　　　　　　　　　　就業, 業績, 業餘;

　　study　　　　　　　　　　　修業, 課業, 畢業;

　　already　　　　　　　　　　業已完工;

| | |
|---|---|
| apprehensively | 兢兢業業; |
| to engage (*as occupation*) | 業農, 業商; |
| *Buddhism*, Karma | 善業, 惡業, 業障; |
| *in classical Chinese*, | |
|     decorated plaque of ancient | |
|     musical instrument rack | 「業，大版也 |
| |     所以飾縣鐘鼓。」, |
| | 「設業設虡，崇牙樹羽。」; |
|     study | 「業精於勤，荒於嬉。」; |
|     to inherit | 「臺駘能業其官。」; |
|     in constant motion | 「赫赫業業，有嚴天子。」; |
|     imposing | 「戎車既駕，四牡業業。」; |
| *surname* | 姓氏 |

**Radical:** 木 (/ㄇㄨˋ, mu⁴/ "wood"); originally 業 (itself).

# 99. 本

**Script Evolution**

**The Story**

/ㄅㄣˇ, ben[3]/  "root"

**Ideograph** (指事) with *line* (一) at *bottom of a tree* (木) to refer to *its root*, hence "*root*".

$$木 + 一 = 本 \quad 本$$

It is important to note and thus avoid the common fallacy of writing 本 as 夲 (/ㄊㄠ, tao/ "to advance with all might"), Associative Compound (會意) of

大 (/ㄉㄚˋ, da[4]/ "grand") and

十 (/ㄕˊ, shi[2]/ "ten")

to imply *gathering the grand effort of ten people*,

hence "*to advance with all might*".

$$大 + 十 = 夲 \quad 夲$$

$$本 \; 本 \neq 夲 \quad 夲$$

It is interesting to note that at time of the Bronze Script the Ideographic *markings* ( ●●● ) were placed at all the tree's root branches. The story of *root of tree* as told through time by the character 本 is shown below.

| Bronze | Seal | Standard |

## The Stroke Sequence

## The Anatomy

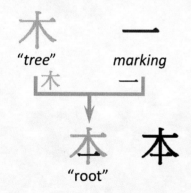

## The Trinity – Sound(s), Semantics, and Synopses

/ㄅㄣˇ, ben³/

| | |
|---|---|
| root, fundamentals, basics | 根本, 基本, 本末倒置; |
| to base on | 一本初衷, 本著良心; |
| original | 本來, 本能, 本名, 變本加厲, 江山易改，本性難移; |

363

| | |
|---|---|
| main | 本體, 本位, 校本部; |
| one's own | 本人, 本身, 本尊, 本領, 本事 (/ㆍㄕ, shi[5]/); |
| local, domestic | 本地, 本國; |
| cost, capital investment | 成本, 本金, 夠本, 賠本, 本錢, 將本圖利, 一本萬利; |
| current, this | 本月, 本年度; |
| book volume, edition, version | 書本, 版本, 影本, 精裝本; |
| script | 腳本, 話本, 劇本; |
| pamphlet | 奏本, 本事 (/ㄕㄟ, shi[4]/); |
| *quantity word, for* | |
|     books, printed matters, etc. | 三本書, 兩本筆記簿; |
| *in classical Chinese,* | |
|     root of plant | 「是以畝廣以平，<br>   則不喪本。」; |
|     fundamentals | 「君子務本，本立而道生。」; |
|     to base on | 「本之春秋以求其斷。」; |
|     initially | 「本定天下，<br>   諸將及（項）籍也。」; |
|     originally | 「本圖宦達，不矜名節。」; |
|     our | 「立之于本朝之上，<br>   倚之于三公之位。」; |
| *surname* | 姓氏 |

**Radical:** 木 (/ㄇㄨˋ, mu[4]/ "tree").

# 100. 重

## Script Evolution

倸　東　䡆　重　重　重

## The Story

䡆　䡆　㙣　重　重

/ㄓㄨㄥˋ, zhong⁴/　"heavy"

**Associative Compound** (會意) of

人 (亻 /ㄖㄣˊ, ren²/ "person"),

東 (/ㄉㄨㄥ, dong/ originally "large parcel (wrapped and tied)",

*also providing soun*d), and

土 (/ㄊㄨˇ, tu³/ "ground")

to imply *a person dragging a large parcel on ground because it is heavy*,

hence "*heavy*".

亻 + 東 + 土 ≡ 㙣　㙣

Standard Form has last 2 Strokes of 東 removed and its centre vertical
Stroke joined with that of 土, hence 重 in lieu of 㙣.

㙣　㙣　→　重　重

# 壼 壼 → 重 重

It is important to note that at time of the Bone Script the character told the story of *person* ( 𝄆 ) *carrying a large heavy parcel* ( 𝄇 ) *on his back.* At time of the Bronze Script the *person* ( 𝄈 ) was placed on top of the *large heavy parcel* ( 𝄉 ) to imply *person dragging the large heavy parcel.* At time of the Seal Script the character told the story of *person* ( 𝄊 ) *dragging the large heavy parcel* ( 𝄋 ) *on ground* ( 𝄌 ), thus leading to the Standard Script. The stories of *person moving large heavy parcel* as told through time by the character 重 (壼) are shown below.

| Bone | Bronze | Seal | Standard |
|------|--------|------|----------|

## The Stroke Sequence

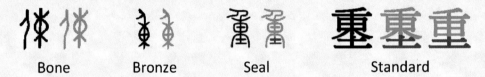

## The Anatomy

人　　　　　東　　　　　土
"person"　"large heavy parcel"　"ground"
　　　　　/ㄉㄨㄥ, dong/

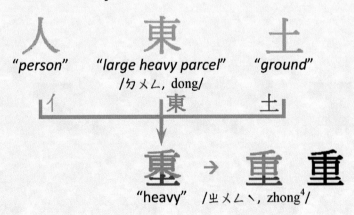

重 → 重 重
"heavy"　/ㄓㄨㄥˋ, zhong⁴/

# The Trinity – Sound(s), Semantics, and Synopses

/ㄓㄨㄥˋ, zhong$^4$/

| | |
|---|---|
| heavy | 沈**重**, 厚**重**, **重**物, **重**擔, **重**裝, **重**刑, **重**罰, **重**裝備, **重**責大任; |
| weight | 淨**重**, 體**重**, 載**重**量; |
| strong, thick, dense | **重**兵, **重**霧瀰漫, 好**重**的氣味, 顏色太**重**了; |
| critical | **重**臣, 機房**重**地, 軍事**重**鎮[鎮]; |
| key | **重**點; |
| heavy responsibility | 忍辱負**重**; |
| severe | **重**病, **重**傷, **重**聽, **重**創, **重**感冒; |
| high priced, high valued | **重**賞, **重**謝, **重**金禮聘; |
| important, carrying weight | **重**要, **重**頭戲, 輕**重**緩急; |
| stressed, accented | **重**音; |
| to value | 尊**重**, 敬**重**, 器**重**, **重**感情; |
| to have preference | **重**文輕武, **重**男輕女; |
| to place special attention | 注**重**, **重**衣著; |
| to give special emphasis | **重**情**重**義, **重**質不**重**量; |
| *physics*, gravity | **重**力, **重**心; |
| *in classical Chinese*, | |
| to carry more weight | 「人固有一死，或**重**於泰山，或輕於鴻毛。」; |
| prudent | 「**重**用兵者強，輕用兵者弱。」; |

367

to increase 「今故興事動眾以增國城，
　　　是**重**吾罪也。」；

often 「復茲夕陰起，
　　　野色**重**蕭條。」

/ㄔㄨㄥˊ, chong[2]/

to repeat 重複；

to overlap 重疊, 重婚；

to be the same 他跟我**重**名；

again, over 重來, 重生, 重新, 重遊故地,
重修舊好；

layer, level 困難**重重**, 遠渡**重**洋, **重重**森林,
重山峻嶺；

*in classical Chinese*,

to add 「**重**色而衣之，
**重**味而食之。」

**Radical:** 里 (/ㄌㄧˇ, li[3]/ "place to reside"); originally 人 (亻).

# The Statistics

## Characters Classes

Within the first 100 characters, Pictographs are at an extremely high percentage (24%) compared to their overall percentage (< 5%) in the Chinese characters. This is because these Pictographs, though having gained few or no extended semantics for thousands of years, continue to be the basics of the written and spoken Chinese language. The rankings of the characters classes in this 100 characters are a little inconsistent with those in the entire characters collection,

1. Semantic-Phonetic Compound,

2. Associative Compound,

3. Pictograph,

4. Ideograph.

Here Associative Compounds (65) are leading Semantic-Phonetic Compounds (4) that are even fewer in number than the Pictographs (24) and Ideographs (7). The table and charts of this 100 characters by their classes are presented herewith.

| | |
|---|---|
| Pictograph | 24 |
| Ideograph | 7 |
| Associative Compound | 65 |
| Semantic-Phonetic Compound | 4 |

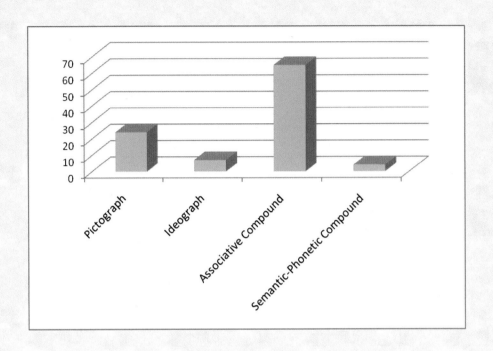

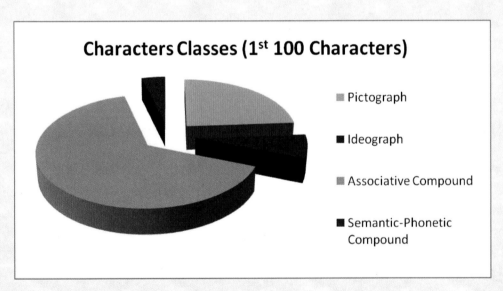

**Characters Classes (1ˢᵗ 100 Characters)**

- Pictograph
- Ideograph
- Associative Compound
- Semantic-Phonetic Compound

# Characters Anatomies

From the composition anatomy perspective, 30 of this 100 characters are Singletons and 70 are Composites (Compounds of various levels) as shown in the table and charts below.

| | |
|---|---|
| Singleton | 30 |
| Compound (1 Level) | 34 |
| Compound (2 Levels) | 28 |
| Compound (3 Levels) | 8 |

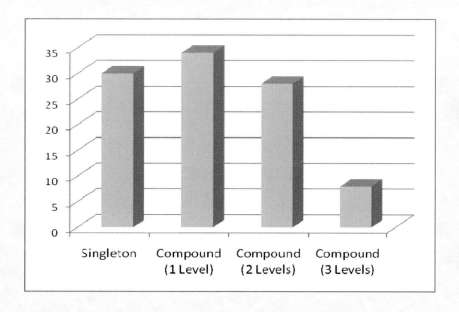

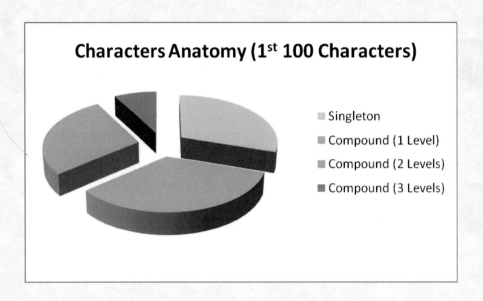

Characters Anatomy (1st 100 Characters)

- Singleton
- Compound (1 Level)
- Compound (2 Levels)
- Compound (3 Levels)

## Characters Stroke Numbers

For characters Stroke numbers, the most concerned statistics of Chinese characters, the first 100 characters are already exemplary. That is more than 85% of them have 12 Strokes or less with majority of them having 3 to 11 Strokes.

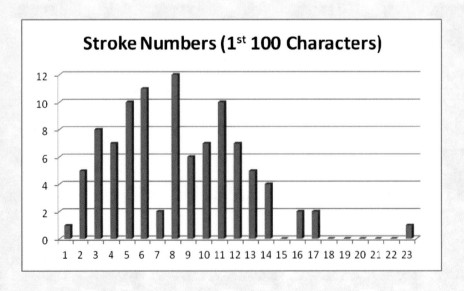

Stroke Numbers (1st 100 Characters)